THE PRECARIOUS LIVES OF SYRIANS

McGill-Queen's Refugee and Forced Migration Studies

SERIES EDITORS: MEGAN BRADLEY AND JAMES MILNER

Forced migration is a local, national, regional, and global challenge with profound political and social implications. Understanding the causes and consequences of, and possible responses to, forced migration requires careful analysis from a range of disciplinary perspectives, as well as interdisciplinary dialogue.

The purpose of the McGill-Queen's Refugee and Forced Migration Studies series is to advance in-depth examination of diverse forms, dimensions, and experiences of displacement, including in the context of conflict and violence, repression and persecution, and disasters and environmental change. The series will explore responses to refugees, internal displacement, and other forms of forced migration to illuminate the dynamics surrounding forced migration in global, national, and local contexts, including Canada, the perspectives of displaced individuals and communities, and the connections to broader patterns of human mobility. Featuring research from fields including politics, international relations, law, anthropology, sociology, geography, and history, the series highlights new and critical areas of enquiry within the field, especially conversations across disciplines and from the perspective of researchers in the global South, where the majority of forced migration unfolds. The series benefits from an international advisory board made up of leading scholars in refugee and forced migration studies.

1 *The Criminalization of Migration*
Context and Consequences
Edited by Idil Atak and James C. Simeon

2 *A National Project*
Syrian Refugee Resettlement in Canada
Edited by Leah K. Hamilton, Luisa Veronis, and Margaret Walton-Roberts

3 *Strangers to Neighbours*
Refugee Sponsorship in Context
Edited by Shauna Labman and Geoffrey Cameron

4 *Send Them Here*
Religion, Politics, and Refugee Resettlement in North America
Geoffrey Cameron

5 *The Precarious Lives of Syrians*
Migration, Citizenship, and Temporary Protection in Turkey
Feyzi Baban, Suzan Ilcan, and Kim Rygiel

THE PRECARIOUS LIVES OF SYRIANS

Migration, Citizenship, and Temporary Protection in Turkey

FEYZI BABAN, SUZAN ILCAN, AND KIM RYGIEL

McGill-Queen's University Press
Montreal & Kingston | London | Chicago

© McGill-Queen's University Press 2021

ISBN 978-0-2280-0803-3 (cloth)
ISBN 978-0-2280-0804-0 (paper)
ISBN 978-0-2280-0918-4 (ePDF)
ISBN 978-0-2280-0919-1 (ePUB)

Legal deposit third quarter 2021
Bibliothèque nationale du Québec

Printed in Canada on acid-free paper that is 100% ancient forest free (100% post-consumer recycled), processed chlorine free

We acknowledge the support of the Canada Council for the Arts.

Nous remercions le Conseil des arts du Canada de son soutien.

Library and Archives Canada Cataloguing in Publication

Title: The precarious lives of Syrians : migration, citizenship, and temporary protection in Turkey / Feyzi Baban, Suzan Ilcan, and Kim Rygiel.
Names: Baban, Feyzi, author. | Ilcan, Suzan, author. | Rygiel, Kim, author.
Description: Includes bibliographical references and index.
Identifiers: Canadiana (print) 20210215828 | Canadiana (ebook) 20210215895 | ISBN 9780228008040 | ISBN 9780228008033 (cloth) | ISBN 9780228008040 (paper) | ISBN 9780228009184 (ePDF) | ISBN 9780228009191 (ePUB)
Subjects: LCSH: Syrians—Turkey—Social conditions. | LCSH: Syrians—Turkey—Economic conditions. | LCSH: Refugees—Legal status, laws, etc.—Turkey. | LCSH: Refugees—Government policy—Turkey. | LCSH: Syria—History—Civil War, 2011- —Refugees.
Classification: LCC HV640.5.S97 B33 2021 | DDC 956.9104/231—dc23

Set in 11/14 Minion Pro with Artegra Sans Condensed
Book design & typesetting by Garet Markvoort, zijn digital

CONTENTS

Figures
vii

Acknowledgments
ix

INTRODUCTION
Living under Temporary Protection:
"Anything Can Happen
at Any Moment"
3

CHAPTER ONE
Responses to Forced Migration:
Humanitarian Emergency, Temporary Protection,
and Counter-Responses to Precarity
20

CHAPTER TWO
Precarious Mobilities: Externalization Policies
and the EU–Turkey Statement
60

CHAPTER THREE
Precarious Legal Frameworks
in Turkey
95

CONTENTS

CHAPTER FOUR

Precarity through Irregular Access
to Social Services: Implications for Living and
Working Conditions
125

CHAPTER FIVE

Resisting Precarity: Claiming Rights
to Belong and to Stay
151

CHAPTER SIX

Precarious Resistances and Claiming
the Right to Leave
Maissaa Almustafa
182

Conclusion
198

Notes
213

References
225

Index
265

FIGURES

1.1 Cabinet conclusions (top secret). 1951 UN Convention on Refugees and Protocol on Stateless Persons: Canadian participation.   30

1.2 Zaatari refugee camp, Jordan, 2013. Photo by Rene Wildangel/Heinrich-Böll-Stiftung, https://flic.kr/p/djS7U3.   34

1.3 Turkish Red Crescent, Kilis, Turkey, 2013. Photo by Felton Davis, https://flic.kr/p/SZokhs.   37

1.4 Syrian refugees cross into Hungary, 26 August 2015. Photo by AP Photo/Bela Szandelszky, https://flic.kr/p/xs3a85.   55

2.1 Evros/Meriç River, land border crossing between Turkey and Greece.   72

2.2 Dinghy washed up ashore on Lesvos, 2 August 2013.   87

2.3 "Moria refugee camp – hot spot – registration centre," Lesvos, Greece, 11 July 2018. Photo by Nicolas Economou, Shutterstock, 1133715044.   89

2.4 "Third day of fire in Moria refugee camp on Lesbos Island in Greece, displacing 13,000 asylum seekers. The largest refugee camp in Europe completely burned down." Moria, Lesvos, Greece, 10 September 2020. Photo by Nicolas Economou, Shutterstock, 1820769854.   91

FIGURES

3.1 Neither refugee nor guest poster from conference, İstanbul, Turkey, 2015. 97

3.2 Food Ration Card, İstanbul, Turkey, July 2015. 105

3.3 Broken windows of a Syrian shop in Önder, Ankara, Turkey, 16 July 2016. 116

4.1 Syrian accommodation, Gaziantep, Turkey, July 2015. 132

4.2 Food ration for a Syrian family, İstanbul, Turkey, July 2015. 136

4.3 Syrians working in a workshop in Gaziantep, Turkey, October 2019. 145

5.1 Syrian restaurant, Tarbuş, İstanbul, Turkey, July 2015. 153

5.2 Baklava shop, İstanbul, Turkey, July 2015. 157

5.3 Shop with Arabic signage, İstanbul, Turkey. 158

5.4 Pages café, İstanbul, Turkey, July 2016. 163

5.5 Store in Fatih neighbourhood, İstanbul, Turkey, August 2016. 169

5.6 Jewellery made by Syrian women working with Small Projects, İstanbul, Turkey, August 2016. 172

ACKNOWLEDGMENTS

The three authors contributed equally to the research for and writing of this book, and we thank each other for our collaborative spirit and friendship. The book is produced from a four-year study, 2015–19, extended to 2020, titled "Humanitarian Aid, Citizenship Politics, and the Governance of Syrian Refugees in Turkey," funded by the Social Sciences and Humanities Research Council of Canada (#435-2015-0802). This research has benefited enormously from, and would not be the same without, lengthy interviews, discussions, and engagements with Syrians living in Turkey and with those community and organization members who support and learn from them. We also thank everyone for their generosity, not only for sharing their time in putting us in contact with many people in communities, organizations, learning centres, and institutes, but also for participating in meaningful and informal conversations, and sharing their knowledge and rich understandings. To all the individuals who we have had the opportunity to learn from, thank you. Without you sharing your knowledge and experiences and your support for the research, this book would not be possible.

We would like to give particular mention to our friends and colleagues in Turkey for their friendship and ongoing support for the project. A special thank you to our friends in Gaziantep, and in particular Ayşegül Ateş, Hatice Gültekin, Mehmet Nuri Gültekin, and Kemal Vural Tarlan, for their kindness, generosity, and intellectual engagement with the project, and for sharing their extensive expertise and networks with us. This work would also not have been possible without the help and friendship of Nur Incetahteci, Yahya Kayali, and Murat Kaya.

We would like to thank Maissaa Almustafa for her contribution on chapter 6 and for sharing her research and networks on refugee journeys with us and this book. She also played an invaluable role as

ACKNOWLEDGMENTS

a research assistant and in providing translation during our field research trips.

We would also like thank our other research assistants: Laura Connoy, Violette Khammad, Zeynep Masri, Ali Mostolizadeh, Engy Nouhy, Yazgulu Sezgin, Derya Tarhan, and Diana Thomaz for their valuable contributions to our research, including library, media, policy, and field research.

Thank you to the many colleagues who provided direct support and insights on this research at conferences and workshops, and through informal conversations during the research and writing of this book. To name only a few of these colleagues, we thank: Maurizio Albahari, Ilker Ataç, Susan Banki, Şule Can, Christina Clark-Kazak, François Crépeau, Seçil Dağtaş, Jennifer Hyndman, Luin Goldring, Reena Kukreja, Patricia Landolt, Cetta Mainwaring, Elisa Pascucci, Katharina Scherke, Pinar Şenoğuz, Vicki Squire, Maurice Stierl, and Margaret Walton-Roberts. A book such as this takes many years to complete and we would like to thank our families and friends for their continual support and other colleagues who have provided intellectual engagement and support more broadly along the way, particularly: Tanya Basok, Engin Isin, Fuat Keyman, Sean Lockwood, Rianne Mahon, Alison Mountz, Andrew Thompson, and William Walters.

Thank you to the anonymous reviewers for their valuable and critical feedback. We also thank Jonathan Crago at McGill-Queen's University Press for his appreciated advice and insights, and for his unwavering support of this book project. Thank you to Matthew Kudelka and John Parry for their assistance with editing this book.

Finally, we are appreciative of our universities, Trent University, University of Waterloo, and Wilfrid Laurier University, and the Balsillie School of International Affairs for their ongoing institutional support throughout the project.

THE PRECARIOUS LIVES OF SYRIANS

INTRODUCTION

Living under Temporary Protection:
"Anything Can Happen at Any Moment"

> It is a special protection status, anything can happen. Anything
> can happen at any moment ... This temporary status is very
> volatile. If you use it for good, you can have positive outcomes.
> If not, you can change anything any time. You don't have a foun-
> dation. There is no international law, no Turkish law, nothing.
> It can restrict you from travelling, from accessing health care.
> Everything is at the discretion of the Turkish government at
> all times. Syrians realize this too. (Interview with NGO worker,
> 19 July 2016, Gaziantep, Turkey)

The above quotation encapsulates the concerns that have motivated the
writing of this book. The Syrian war, now entering its tenth year, has displaced more than 12 million Syrians, with some 6.6 million internally
displaced and another 5.6 million who have fled since 2011 to neighbouring countries such as Turkey, Jordan, and Lebanon, which host
the majority of Syrian refugees (UNHCR n.d., "Syria Emergency"). Indeed, regionally, according to United Nations High Commissioner for
Refugees (UNHCR) figures, the Middle East "hosts more refugees than
any other region from 2015 to 2018, more than 30 per cent" (UNHCR
n.d., "Figures at a Glance"; Şahin Mencütek 2018, 14). Yet none of these
countries grant legal refugee status to Syrians. Instead, these countries
have adopted a variety of other policy responses to refugee governance, policies that change over time and are affected by the domestic
and foreign policy concerns of the various governments and their relations with a variety of other governmental and non-governmental

actors (Şahin Mencütek 2018). Indeed, as we illustrate in this book, Syrians in Turkey are often not simply subject to shifting policy responses; they also find themselves the objects of a form of "ping-pong politics" in Turkish domestic and foreign affairs (Baban, Ilcan, and Rygiel 2017a). As Gökalp Aras (2019) reminds us, migration and asylum policies often play an important role in foreign policy as well as diplomatic relations between Turkey and neighbouring countries. As a result, Syrians live in precarious conditions throughout the region. Compared to many of its neighbouring countries, Turkey is often regarded as providing better living conditions and more rights to Syrians. Nevertheless, despite the relatively better conditions in Turkey, we believe it is important to understand just what such conditions look like in order to understand the impact of temporary protection status on Syrians' lives. As we detail in this book, temporary protection status often places Syrians in greater precarity, without more permanent pathways to permanent residency or citizenship.

Turkey initially opened its borders to Syrians as guests, later developing a framework for temporary protection status (see chapters 1 and 3). In 2011, before the Syrian crisis, the number of applications for international protection in Turkey was almost 18,000 (Government of Turkey 2019), a tiny fraction of its overall population of around 83 million (UN DESA 2019). Turkey had signed the 1951 Refugee Convention and the 1967 Protocol, but had maintained the geographical limitation to the Convention (see chapter 3; Soykan 2010). This has meant that only asylum-seekers from Europe were provided with refugee status. Thus, prior to the Syrian crisis, Turkey was more often seen as a country of transit migration, with the majority of non-European refugees travelling through Turkey en route to other European destinations (İçduygu and Yükseker 2012). In this context, more than 3.6 million Syrians was an unprecedented number of refugees to arrive in Turkey (Batalla and Tolay 2018), which suddenly found itself host to the largest refugee population in the world (Fleming 2016). The Turkish government was forced to act quickly, introducing its first ever asylum law in April 2014 (one that, unfortunately, maintained the geographical limitation as discussed in chapter 3). Given these numbers, the speed and scope of the Turkish government's response was impressive: The UNHCR praised Turkey in 2015, stating that it "has maintained an

Introduction: Living under Temporary Protection

emergency response of a consistently high standard" (Law Library of Congress 2016c).

Turkey's record was also impressive at first when compared to the relative inaction displayed by many European governments in terms of providing sufficient protection and resettlement to Syrians. According to The UNHCR (2018g), while the developing regions host some 84 per cent of the world's refugee population, Germany is the only European country to make the list of top ten refugee-hosting countries, having taken in the majority of the nearly 1 million refugees, many of them Syrians, who arrived in Europe in 2015. The arrival of refugees that year – equivalent to less than 1 per cent of Europe's total population of just over half a billion[1] – spurred reactionary xenophobia in Europe and generated a rise in far-right anti-immigrant parties in several European countries.[2] Moreover, since 2015, European countries have continued to shirk their 1951 Refugee Convention responsibilities to re-settle refugees; despite the ongoing need for resettlement, the numbers taken in have declined for the fourth straight year, to 580,800, comparable to the figure prior to 2015 (Eurostat 2019; Calamur 2019). Given this broader European context, we must acknowledge the strength of Turkey's response, which was to open its borders and take in some 3.6 million Syrians to date.

Turkey's initial response to the Syrian refugees also looks more generous when we compare it to that of its neighbours, such as Lebanon and Jordan. Together, Turkey, Lebanon, and Jordan host almost "93 per cent of all internationally displaced Syrians," with Lebanon hosting "the largest number of refugees relative to its national population – in this case, one in every six people being a refugee" (as compared with Jordan [1 in 11] and Turkey [1 in 28] as per the UNHCR 2017b figures, Şahin Mencütek 2018, 15).

Estimates of the number of refugees Jordan currently hosts range from 650,000 (based on UNHCR numbers of registered refugees) and 1.3 million (the government's own figure, which includes Syrians not officially registered with the UN) (Su 2017). Syrians, like all other refugees and asylum-seekers in Jordan, are not officially recognized as refugees and do not have any special rights or protection. Rather, they are subject to Law No. 24 of 1973 concerning Residency and Foreigners' Affairs (Law Library of Congress, "Jordan," 2016). This law does not distinguish between refugees and asylum-seekers and other types of foreigners; instead, it applies to *all* foreigners, with a foreigner being defined as "anyone who does not have Jordanian nationality" (Article 2). Most Syrian people in Jordan are urban refugees, 48 per cent of whom are children and 4 per cent the elderly, and 85 per cent of Syrian refugees in Jordan live below the poverty line (UNHCR 2018b). Other Syrian refugees live in one of four official refugee camps, the largest being the Zaatari camp. Reports document the horrific conditions in the camps; they are places of poverty, lack of schools, abuse and harassment (particularly for girls), and child labour (Summers 2017; UNHCR 2013). Moreover, while refugees could initially leave the camps, after 2014 the government only allowed refugees to move to urban areas if sponsored by a relative; however, it has since extended a limited amnesty to some refugees who left without permission (HRW 2018a). Refugees living in urban centres also experience extreme hardship and poor living conditions, including poor housing conditions lack of education, and few job opportunities (UNHCR 2013). Regarding health care, in one survey, more than three quarters of the respondents said they were unable to access medicine (UNHCR 2017c). The Jordanian government has recently taken steps to broaden refugees' rights and improve their access to services. In March 2018, for example, the government announced it would be taking steps to regularize the legal status of unregistered Syrians (UNHCR 2018g). After registering, Syrians can obtain a service card from the Ministry of the Interior that enables them to access services such as health and education (UNHCR 2018g). Yet at the same time, the government announced that Syrian refugees would no longer be entitled to pay the non-insured Jordanian rate for health services; instead, they would have to pay 80 per cent of foreigner rates, amounting to a "two-to-five-fold" increase in costs, an increase that the UNHCR expects will significantly compound health insecurity for many Syrians (UNHCR 2018e). Finally, reports by organizations such as Human Rights Watch (HRW 2017, 2018a) have noted that Jordan has started deporting Syrians back to Syria, contrary to the 1951 Convention's core principle of non-refoulement. Jordan is not a signatory to the Convention; even so, it holds a Memorandum of Understanding (MOU) with the UNHCR outlining its commitments to uphold international refugee law and the principle of non-refoulement (Su 2017; Law Library of Congress 2016a).

Like Jordan, Lebanon hosts almost 1 million registered Syrians (952,562) (UNHCR n.d., "Operation Portal refugee situations"), although the government estimates the numbers to be much higher (1.5 million) (UNHCR 2019c). Like Jordan, Lebanon is not a signatory to the 1951 Refugee Convention and has no domestic legislation pertaining specifically to the status of refugees within its borders. Instead, like Jordan, it holds a MOU with the UNHCR (signed in 2003) that provides for the "issuing of temporary residence permits to asylum seekers" and allows for the UNHCR to "adjudicate claims for asylum," with the government issuing "a temporary residence permit, normally for three months but possibly extended to six to nine months, allowing the UNHCR to find a durable solution for the refugee in question" (Law Library of Congress 2016b). In 2015, the Lebanese government restricted access to its territory for Syrians (UNHCR 2019c). According to the most recent UNHCR 2017 "Vulnerability Assessment of Syrian Refugees" (VASyR) report, over 74 per cent of Syrians surveyed had no legal residency (UNHCR 2017f). The report also notes that Syrians living in Lebanon have become worse off in recent years, with "58 per cent of households living in extreme poverty" and "76 per cent of refugee households living below the poverty line," meaning that "three quarters of Syrian refugees in Lebanon now live on less than US$4 per day" (UNHCR 2017f). More than half of Syrian children in Lebanon remain out of school, with the number significantly higher for adolescents fifteen to seventeen years of age (UNHCR 2019c).

The conditions for Syrian refugees in Turkey are certainly better than in Jordan and Lebanon, particularly because Syrians there are extended special temporary status, which brings certain limited rights. Nevertheless, it is important to know what the "best" situation means for Syrians living under temporary protection in Turkey. As indicated by the non-governmental organization (NGO) worker at the top of this chapter, temporary protection status is a far cry from the ideals of protection set out under the 1951 UN's Refugee Convention and the UN Protocol Relating to the Status of Refugees (the 1967 Protocol).

Whatever its shortcomings as detailed in this book, temporary protection has become the *de facto* preferred form of assistance undertaken by Turkey and supported by the international community. Rather than providing Syrians with refugee rights, as set out under the 1951 Charter (to name but a few of these: Article 26 stipulates freedom of movement within a territory; Articles 17 to 19 stipulate rights to employment; Article 21 stipulates rights to housing; Article 22 stipulates rights to education), temporary protection leaves Syrians at the mercy of the Turkish government's policy shifts and discretionary powers. As the NGO worker puts it, "Anything can happen at any moment."

Some Syrians in Turkey have received humanitarian assistance, and others have found support through the temporary protection status, which, as detailed in this book, provides rights (albeit restricted) to health care, education, and (limited) employment. But many more Syrians in Turkey have spent years eking out an existence, living in limbo with little or no real opportunity to regularize their presence and acquire Turkish citizenship. According to Turkey's Interior Ministry, as of 1 August 2019, of the 3.6 million Syrians in Turkey, only 92,280 had been granted Turkish citizenship (Mülteciler Derneği 2019). In a 2015 report, the *Migrant Integration Policy Index*, Huddleston and colleagues (2015, 10) noted that "Turkey's legal framework is unfavorable for integration," ranking at the bottom of a list of thirty-eight developed nations (8). The same report noted that immigrants and refugees have "restricted rights and little-to-no-state support" and that "policies are unfavourable for labour market mobility, education, and political participation." Moreover, Turkey had "the weakest protections against discrimination because a dedicated antidiscrimination law and agency are still lacking and pending approval by Parliament" (210). All of this points to why this book focuses on the precarious living conditions facing Syrians in Turkey. We refer to these conditions collectively as the "architecture of precarity" (Ilcan, Rygiel, and Baban 2018). This architecture includes the following three layers of scaffolding: precarious status, precarious space, and precarious movement (see chapter 1 for an elaboration of the architecture of precarity). These three aspects of Syrians' lives in Turkey are developed across the chapters of this book.

Precarious status refers to precarious socio-legal statuses, such as temporary protection. These statuses, which are assigned to many Syrian refugees in Turkey, contribute to still more insecure living conditions and result in less access to services and rights. This form of status can determine specific and, at times, limited rights to residence, health care, welfare, or work – rights that can, as noted by the NGO worker above, be granted or restricted at the Turkish government's discretion. As the NGO worker explains, temporary protection status is just that – *temporary* – and as such, "anything can happen." This includes halting the registration of Syrians altogether, which began in 2018 and continues to this day. That year, the Turkish government stopped registering Syrians in İstanbul and in nine provinces near or on the Syrian border (HRW 2018b; see also AIDA n.d.). According to Human Rights Watch (2018, n.p.), the failure to register Syrians so that they can stay in Turkey legally is leading to unlawful deportations and coerced returns to Syria, along with abuse and denial of access to health care.

Precarious space refers to socio-spatial domains, which, for marginal groups such as refugees, acquire meaning through the precarious experiences of daily life. These spaces are sites of struggle and negotiation and involve interplay between the personal and political. In their daily lives in Turkish cities, Syrians both negotiate and resist their precarious conditions as they interact with the larger society around them.

Finally, *precarious movement* refers to governing practices that deny migrant and refugee subjects rights in transit, detain them, or compel them to relocate. As noted by the NGO worker above, living under temporary protection means that "anything can happen," and one of those things is the loss of mobility rights for Syrians. We discuss this in particular with respect to the EU–Turkey Statement (commonly referred to as the EU–Turkey Deal). On 15 October 2015, the EU–Turkey Joint Action Plan was signed, which outlined cooperation around support for Syrians living under temporary protection (EC 2015). The Statement, signed on 18 March 2016, was intended to halt irregular migration to the EU, particularly of Syrians through Greece from Turkey (EC 2019). This Statement is an example of the EU's externalization policies, which are themselves, as Gökalp Aras (2019, 189) notes, part of "a long-standing and ongoing dynamic of the EU externalization towards Turkey in the field of immigration and asylum." Externalization refers to "extraterritorial State actions to prevent migrants, including asylum-seekers, from entering the legal jurisdictions or territories of destination countries or regions or of making them legally inadmissible without individually considering the merits of their protection claims" (Frelick, Kysel, and Podluk 2016, 190). The EU–Turkey Statement shifts the control of Syrians outside the EU to Turkey, making it much more difficult for Syrians to legally move to European countries in order to claim asylum. By placing restrictions on their movement (such as imposed exit visas), the Statement can push Syrians to undertake precarious journeys to reach Europe. Precarious movement also refers to the restrictions on mobility that can affect Syrians' ability to travel between and settle within cities inside Turkey, contrary to Article 26 of the 1951 Refugee Convention. These restrictions on mobility are detailed in chapters 2, 4 and 6.

Together these conditions – precarious status, space, and movement – describe in very concrete ways the impact of temporary protection on the daily lives of Syrians living in Turkey. We document these here to explain what the best conditions for Syrians who live in Turkey look like in order to ask whether we, as an international community, and those of us working in the field of refugee and migration issues, are accepting of such conditions, and temporary protection as a model more generally, as we respond to refugees fleeing protracted conflict and war.

The Tragedy of Lives That Continue to Be Lost

A principal reason to write this book has been to detail the impact of temporary protection status on the lives of Syrians living in Turkey. Another has been to document the tragedy of the lives that continue to be lost. According to the International Organization for Migration's (IOM) Missing Migrants Project, the Mediterranean is the deadliest region on earth for migrants, with 20,504 recorded deaths between 2014 and October 2020, compared to 9,244 in Africa, 4,288 in the Americas, 3,180 in Asia, 669 in the Middle East, and 652 in Europe over this same period. In the Mediterranean, the single largest cause of migrants' death is drowning at sea (IOM n.d., 2014). Recognizing the instability, inaccuracies, and politics around the counting of border deaths (Heller and Pécoud 2020; Weber and Pickering 2011; Tazzioli 2015),[3] the fact is that the comparative numbers showing extremely high fatalities in the Mediterranean compared to very low numbers in Europe point to the effects of Europe's externalization policies, which leave many to die at sea as they struggle to reach European shores. As Mountz (2020, 29) states, "To be clear, greater enforcement at sea correlates strongly with more deaths at sea." Here Alison Mountz refers to her work with Kira Williams (Williams and Mountz 2018) in which they "statistically analyse the relationship between increased border enforcement operations at sea and migrant losses of life around the EU between 2006 and 2015, and find them to be significantly and positively correlated." Mountz and Williams argue that "although discourse about interception and externalization has shifted to humanitarian rescue narratives, offshore enforcement by any other name continues to be highly correlated with migrant deaths." Migrants and refugees continue to flee the precarious conditions in which they have been forced to live, risking their lives in the hope of reaching countries in Europe where they can make asylum claims and start anew. As discussed in chapter 6, like other refugees – and like those of us who are not refugees – Syrians dream of a future for themselves and their children and of finding greater permanence and pathways to more permanent legal statuses such as permanent residency and citizenship.

The 1951 Refugee Convention was designed to help refugees by providing one of three durable solutions – third-country resettlement, voluntary repatriation, and integration with neighbouring host countries. Yet signatories to the Convention have been increasingly restricting access to resettlement as well as opportunities for asylum-seekers to reach territories where they might make claims to third-country resettlement. Less than 1 per cent of refugees have access to resettlement through the UNHCR (UNHCR USA). The *de facto* solution has instead become "temporary permanence," that is, living at best under conditions of temporary protection – and more often without even this legal status – in neighbouring host countries (such as Lebanon and Jordan). As we discuss in chapter 2, signatories to the Convention are putting in place more and more externalization measures and policies that have made reaching their territories increasingly difficult. These externalization policies encourage neighbouring countries (often in exchange for payment, as in the case of the EU–Turkey Statement) to host refugee populations. This situation raises the question as to whether the EU–Turkey Statement is yet another EU externalization policy. Does temporary protection, as the solution offered to Syrian refugees, undermine the promises made in the 1951 Refugee Convention? In this book we critically examine the concept of temporary protection within this broader discussion of refugee protection; we also try to answer a question that is continually asked: Why do so many lives continue to be lost? By detailing the precarious conditions of Syrians living in Turkey, and based on discussions with many Syrians about their lives, dreams, and reasons for leaving Turkey, we hope to explain why Syrians continue to risk their lives to seek asylum in Europe.

Alternative Realities

Over the past several years, the international community has recognized that the international refugee system is in crisis. High-level meetings on migration and asylum, led by the United Nations, led to the signing of the New York Declaration for Refugees and Migrants on 19 September 2016 (UN General Assembly 2016). This Declaration reaffirmed UN member-states' commitment to human rights and invited governments, together with civil society and private sector actors, to participate in multi-stakeholder discussions on two parallel processes: the Global Compact for Safe, Orderly and Regular Migration (GCM) and the Global Compact on Refugees (GCR) (UN General Assembly 2016a). Endorsed by the UN General Assembly on 17 December 2018, the GCR sets out a framework for "more predictable and equitable responsibility-sharing," noting that "a sustainable solution to refugee situations cannot be achieved without international cooperation" (UNHCR n.d., "The Global Compact on Refugees"). Based on eighteen months of consultations with UN member-states, experts, civil society, and refugees, the GCR outlines four key areas of commitment and cooperation to (1) ease the pressures on host countries, (2) enhance refugee self-reliance, (3) expand access to third-country solutions, and (4) support conditions in countries of origin for return in safety and dignity (UN General Assembly 2016b, C.7). One idea that is increasingly gaining traction is that if refugees cannot be repatriated and cannot be resettled to third countries, then they should be "made" to be resilient. We have provided a more detailed critique of the language of refugee resiliency elsewhere (Ilcan and Rygiel 2015). We should be concerned that in an age of neoliberal governments, self-reliance may come to stand for cuts to government investment in meeting the social needs of people like refugees and for a shift toward downloading responsibilities onto these groups so as to leave them responsible for their own protection and care.

As many of the chapters in this book show, Syrians actively address, negotiate, and *resist* their precarious conditions. In this regard, in chapter 6 we discuss precarious forms of resistance such as the undertaking of dangerous journeys to resettle in Europe. We also explore in chapter 5 the many other ways that Syrians are able to renegotiate their existence within their communities. This includes becoming active in cultural institutions, which provide them with opportunities to explain Syrian culture and identity to local populations in Turkey, as well as building and participating in various community initiatives, particularly in learning and social support, women's rights, and health care. These initiatives enable Syrians to improve their living conditions and to develop a sense of belonging in the country. Syrians are demanding that they be able to improve their lives in Turkey, which includes the right to be heard and counted *as political subjects*, something that critical citizenship scholars discuss as "acts of citizenship" (Isin 2008; Nyers 2008) and "acts of contestation" (McNevin 2011). Critical scholars note that when individuals and groups that lack full legal citizenship status claim rights they do not have but should have, they push the boundaries of citizenship beyond liberal aspects such as rights, status, and legal membership in a polity to include a performative aspect (Isin 2017), thus bringing about forms of "citizenship from below" (Nyers and Rygiel 2012). In other words, Syrian refugees are without a doubt resilient and already self-reliant, and their political engagement and claims-making are positive developments to be supported.

However, we should be more circumspect than this when talking of resiliency. That is, we should ask whether refugee self-sufficiency – a recent interest among scholars and academics – is something to advocate, or whether it distracts us from the international community's failure to provide assistance and a pathway to a meaningful new life to Syrians. During our participant interviews and conversations with NGO and business personnel in urban Turkey, we heard many positive stories about entrepreneurial projects undertaken by Syrians to open businesses and employ other Syrians, Tarbuş restaurant being one example (see chapter 5). However, we also heard about other proposals to create export zones in border and camp areas that would enable Turkish companies to hire Syrian workers. These proposals reflect a trend toward refugee self-reliance that is being promoted in academic and policy circles, one we should be wary of, given that the research to date suggests that these spaces are sites of labour exploitation (Arriola 2017; Esterling 2014). Scholars like Alexander Betts have applauded self-reliance strategies because they buttress refugees' market-based economic activities. As Betts and colleagues (2017, 5) assert:

> self-reliance offers the most viable way to address the negative consequences of protracted refugee situations. Even in the absence of durable solutions, empowering refugees to help themselves by giving access to the right to work, freedom of movement, and creating an enabling environment for independent economic activity can offer a better path to dignified and autonomous living than the status quo. Done well, such approaches have the potential simultaneously to benefit refugees, host communities, host governments, and donor governments.

According to these researchers, "refugee economies" are resource allocation systems conceived beyond the bounds of development assistance to include market-based activities. They add that the private sector, innovation, and recognition of the skills, talents, and aspirations of displaced populations may hold the key to opening up paths to greater self-reliance. But this replaces one solution – international protection – with resignation in the sense that it accepts that the international protection system has failed and that other countries are no longer upholding their international responsibilities to protect and resettle refugees. Instead, they look to the market to be the interlocutor between states, humanitarian assistance organizations, and refugees and advocate a new, fourth durable solution, that of integration into the capitalist economy. And here, while allowing that states play a crucial role in refugee protection, they assert that states need to create opportunities for refugees to integrate themselves into markets and that such integration will enable refugee autonomy and self-reliance (212).

Few would argue that states should allow refugees to work. But given the well-documented fact that export-processing zones around the world have long been notorious for their exploitative labour practices, especially in authoritarian countries such as Turkey, how will refugees be protected from that exploitation? Given that integration into the capitalist system is as much about some benefiting from the social inequities and divisions that capitalism also produces, how are we to ensure that hiring vulnerable populations such as refugees – who are living, at best, in the case of Turkey, with a volatile temporary protection status and subject to policies and conditions that can change at the government's whim – will be grounded in just labour practices? A commitment to refugee rights and protection must be the starting point whenever we think about reforming the international refugee system, and must be at the heart of any alternatives proposed. We hope that this book, which is based not only on policy and scholarly research, but also on extensive discussions with those who work daily to support Syrians, and with Syrians themselves, will illuminate the harsh living conditions of Syrians as they relate to precarious status, precarious space, and precarious movement. In this book we challenge the lofty proposals for alternative solutions that often do not take readily into account the very real conditions that people who live as refugees must endure. Refugees need to know that their already existing rights will be upheld in any solutions proposed.

This book is based on a four-year research project (2015–19, extended to 2020) funded by the Social Sciences and Humanities Research Council of Canada. Our research documents the precarity of Syrians' lives in Turkey and illuminates how that precarity changed over time. We have benefited greatly from the detailed research gathered under difficult conditions by Turkish scholars and Turkish humanitarian and rights-based organizations working in the field to support Syrians. This book is also based on site visits in several cities to NGO offices, community and cultural centres, workplaces, housing, schools and education centres, and shops and restaurants. We also conducted our work on the outskirts of several Turkish cities, in camp areas outside İstanbul, Ankara, Kilis, Gaziantep, and Antakya. In each of these cities we conducted extensive semi-structured interviews with key participants in UN agencies and national and international humanitarian organizations, as well as with scholars in the field of refugee and migration studies and those working in community and service organizations with refugees, including teachers, doctors, lawyers, translators, social workers, and human rights advocates. And we interviewed Syrians themselves – lawyers and doctors, artists and entrepreneurs, shopkeepers, construction workers, street vendors, and garbage recyclers, as well as those living hand-to-mouth on the street or relying on meagre aid assistance and soup kitchens. Interviews were also conducted with Syrians who had made the journey through Turkey to Stockholm, Sweden, in the summer of 2016. The overwhelming majority of interview participants were accessed by means of snowball sampling, with a small number accessed through our contacts with aid organizations. In order to get at grounded processes of precarity, we conducted forty interviews with representatives of international, non-governmental, and community organizations in urban Turkey that aid Syrians. These interviews focused on the types of services offered and the extent to which these services were changing the daily lives of refugees. With the aim of privileging Syrian voices, experiences, and knowledge, in addition to informal meetings and discussions with several Syrian refugees in each of the five cities where we conducted research in Turkey, we conducted forty-two in-depth interviews and several informal and formal focus groups, with refugees, twenty-seven in their homes or in public spaces in Turkey, and fifteen in their homes or in a settlement house established as temporary accommodation for refugees in Stockholm. The ethnographic skills of interviewing and probing, and of being attentive to cultural sensitivities and power dynamics in the refugee context, were imperative to our engagement with refugees. Like other studies that reveal refugees as meaningful and engaged subjects rather than victims (e.g., Biehl 2015; Oliveri 2012), our research emphasizes Syrian refugees' views on their precarious status and living conditions in Turkey, as well as their journeys from Syria to Turkey and onward in their search for greater protection and security. Almost all interviews were recorded and then transcribed, first into the original language of the speaker (Turkish or Arabic) and then into English. For this book, all names have been changed to protect the identity of the people who spoke to us. We recognize that given the daily realities of Syrians and those working to assist them, our interviewees' time was precious, and we are deeply grateful to them for sharing their time and knowledge with us. We hope we have done justice to the information

Introduction: Living under Temporary Protection

they generously offered about their lives and the precarious living conditions of Syrians in Turkey.

Overview of the Book

Chapter 1 sets out the conceptual background for understanding the precarious status, movement, and spaces of Syrian refugees arriving in, living in, and departing from Turkey. It begins by discussing humanitarian emergency responses to forced migration, emphasizing how, after the First World War, humanitarianism was institutionalized, refugee camps and massive urban refugee spaces were established, and policy around mobile populations began to develop. The chapter then conceptualizes humanitarian responses to emergencies as a mode of governance that can naturalize products of social action and conflict and steer subjects toward the "ambiguous architecture of precarity." It develops that architecture along three lines: precarious, short-term, or provisional *status*; precarious *space*, as refugees seek to make lives for themselves; and precarious *movement*, as authorities attempt to control where they live. Because refugees are not mere victims of governing efforts and precarious situations, the final section of this chapter introduces the idea of resistance as a form of political activism, as Syrians work to proclaim their dignity and invest in their own lives by participating in community-building initiatives, thus enabling them to claim the right to stay and the right to belong.

Chapter 2 examines Turkey's temporary protection of Syrians and situates this in the broader context of the international refugee regime and the role that externalization policies play in restricting access to that regime. Europe has moved toward employing externalization policies that enable the European Union (EU) and individual member-states to circumvent international commitments to protect refugees, often using third countries, such as Turkey, to resettle them temporarily – all of which makes movement more precarious for Syrians. Specifically, the chapter examines the EU–Turkey Statement (March 2016) and its impact on Syrians as an example of externalization policy.

Chapter 3 begins by tracing the development of Turkey's restrictive legal and policy framework and temporary protection regime and shows how it has contributed to the precarious living conditions of

Syrian refugees in three regards: residency, access to social services and education, and employment laws and policies. The chapter begins by outlining Turkey's approach to refugees up until its introduction of temporary protection in the autumn of 2014 and then examines the evolving status of Syrian refugees under that regime. It concludes by exploring the possibilities for citizenship that opened up in the summer of 2016. According to the Government of Turkey's DGMM, as of 10 July 2020 the number of registered Syrians in Turkey was 3,627,481 (Government of Turkey 2020). Of these, only 92,280 had been granted Turkish citizenship as of August 2019, according to a statement of the Ministry of Interior, Süleyman Soylu (*Turkish Minute* 2019). This means that a huge number of Syrians remain in limbo without a clear pathway to more permanent forms of settlement.

Chapter 4 delves into the impact of temporary protection status on the lives of Syrian refugees in Turkey, focusing on how that status has led to irregular access to work and to social services such as education, health care, and housing, to explain the diverse ways in which Syrian refugees negotiate and navigate daily life. Living under temporary protection and with no clear path to citizenship, Syrians must navigate a maze of ever-shifting laws and regulations and arbitrarily dispensed social services. These precarious circumstances operate at multiple levels of space, movement, and status. This chapter details how this complex and continuously evolving maze renders it very difficult for Syrian refugees to establish stable lives.

After ten years, many Syrians now realize that they will be living in Turkey indefinitely. Yet public discourse in Turkey still represents them as at best victims and at worst a burden on society. Faced with these negative perceptions and their precarious living conditions, Syrians must find ways to adapt. Many seem to be finding ways to take control of their lives, invoking their agency and making claims to belong in their new society. Chapter 5 explores how Syrians negotiate daily life in Turkish cities and interact with the larger society around them, as well as how they address, negotiate, and *resist* their precarious conditions. In the absence of a legal pathway to belonging, Syrians secure their place by demanding the right to belong and to stay. They do so in one of two ways. First, by representing themselves – that is, by taking an active part in cultural institutions in order to explain Syrian culture and identity to the larger Turkish society (here, we look at food and the arts). Second, by helping build community in order to improve their living conditions and strengthen their sense belonging in the country (here, we examine initiatives in learning and social support, women's rights, and health care).

Building on the more general discussion of refugee journeys to Europe in chapter 2, through in-depth interviews conducted and written up by Dr Maissaa Almustafa based on her research with Syrians, chapter 6 takes a more intimate look at what such precarious resistance looks like when it takes the form of refugee journeys and shows the toll it takes on people's lives. The chapter explores why Syrians make the difficult choice to leave Syria, and then Turkey, and describes the great risks they take as they make their way to Europe in search of protection and stability. The chapter narrates three journeys, representative of the many about which we heard, taken by Syrian individuals who travelled from Syria through Turkey to settle in Germany, Sweden, and Canada, providing details around decision-making, transportation, and networks. The stories explored here document the challenges and traumas these journeys presented; they are also testaments to the powerful exercise of agency that Syrians demonstrate as they claim their right to move – more specifically, their "right to escape" (Mezzadra 2004).

There is no end in sight to the Syrian war, which is certain to be remembered as a challenge to our times – one that revealed the shortcomings of the international refugee system and the lack of willingness on the part of many states to uphold their commitments to the 1951 Declaration. But it may also mark the beginning of a search for more compassionate and durable solutions to mass refugee movements.

CHAPTER ONE

Responses to Forced Migration: Humanitarian Emergency, Temporary Protection, and Counter-Responses to Precarity

The exodus of people escaping wars, major conflicts, ethnic cleansing, and other devastating circumstances has evoked national and international calls for compassion, incited surges of strategic calculations, and prompted emergency responses to forced migration. In the popular understanding, such responses involve humanitarian, state, non-governmental, and other actors, who provide assistance, care, and protection to these groups. Humanitarian emergency responses to forced migration are multifaceted and wide-ranging, and this chapter looks at their workings, their complexities, and the stakes involved and reveals their ambiguities – in short, it analyzes their social and political relations and how they affect the precarious lives of forced migrants, such as refugees and asylum-seekers. These people today are experiencing an intensifying detachment from state-based arrangements of rights and protections as well as protracted conditions of precarity. The term "forced migrant" may conceal as much as it expresses, but we find it useful, for it informs much policy and academic discussion (Darling 2017) and can illustrate how status categories can be ephemeral (Nyers 2011), create hierarchal systems of rights (Crawley and Skleparis 2018), link to issues of protection and distinct forms of precarity (Baban, Ilcan, and Rygiel 2017b; Ilcan, Rygiel and Baban 2018), and serve as a means of strategic contestation (Moulin and Nyers 2007; Sanyal 2014).

In this chapter, we pose the following questions: How do responses to forced migration emerge? How do they create precarious situations for forced migrants? And in what ways do migrants engage in counter-responses? To address these questions, the chapter draws on critical migration and precarity literatures to examine how social and political conditions, in past and present-day contexts, have framed responses to forced migrants in transit. It also discusses how, when these migrants are categorized as victims, they can be silenced or overlooked as advocates of change or as critical and activist subjects. The chapter discusses the changing approaches to governing people on the move, with a focus on forced migrants – refugees in particular – and the policies and practices of refugee management, including how humanitarian logics "construct" refugee populations. Specifically, with an emphasis on postwar humanitarian emergency responses, it highlights, first, the international coordination of displaced persons and refugees, and second, the expansion of refugee spaces. It also examines how the definition of *refugee* has shifted over time to create new forms of inclusion and exclusion and new forms of precarity and protection, all of which, we argue, link to the architecture of precarity. The latter term emphasizes that certain practices and policies involving forced migrants can compel them to live in a state of limbo, facing ambiguity around protection, living conditions, and mobility. This chapter sets the conceptual background for understanding the precarious status, precarious space, and precarious movement that we discuss in this chapter and in the chapters that focus on Syrian refugees arriving in, living in, and departing from Turkey (chapters 2 to 6).

In examining responses to forced migration, we will focus on three themes: postwar humanitarian emergency responses, including temporary protection; the intimate connections between humanitarian emergency responses and the architecture of precarity; and counter-responses to precarity. Instead of capturing the evolution of emergency responses, mapping innumerable processes associated with the 1951 Refugee Convention, or compiling a chronological account of events dealing with refugees and their precarity and counter-responses, the three sections highlight the discursive, programmatic, and governing dimensions of forced migrants in transit, with particular attention given to how issues of status and protection contribute to the precarity of refugees. To provide a critical historical framing, the first section outlines humanitarian emergency responses to forced migration. Here, focus is on the formation of the League of Nations after the devastation of the First World War; how the era of institutionalized humanitarianism led to the establishment of refugee camps and huge urban refugee spaces, besides initiating international coordination and postwar planning efforts; and, finally, how this era witnessed the development of policy for mobile populations.

After the horrors of the Second World War, there was large-scale repatriation of displaced persons and refugees to their home countries. Others were resettled to third countries. This era also saw the development of many new groups of refugees who were fleeing their homelands. All of this led to the creation of the UNHCR as an international agency to protect these people and to national and international schemes for controlling their movements. During these years, many displaced persons and political refugees experienced precarious status, inadequate protection, wretched living conditions, and restricted movement. Concomitantly, there emerged a new definition of the term refugee that prevented many people from obtaining refugee status and devalued refugees' political agency, all of which raised broader questions around classification schemes and frameworks.

The second section conceptualizes humanitarian emergency responses not as compassionate forms of intervention but as a mode of governance that produces precarity. This architecture is designed with little regard for the protection and care of human lives. It focuses on precarious, short-term, or provisional *status*; precarious *space*, as refugees seek to make new lives for themselves; and precarious *movement*, as authorities attempt to control where these people travel and live. Here, certain kinds of initiatives and practices aimed at controlling large-scale mobile populations can create ambiguous situations. For example, as we reveal below, temporary protection grants refugees some rights but not others, thus creating ambiguous moments of rewards, rights, and benefits (limited) even while denying these in other situations or places. And because refugees are not mere victims of governing efforts and precarious situations, the third section examines their counter-responses as forms of political activism, as they strive to proclaim their visibility and dignity, reconstitute a socially

Postwar Humanitarian Emergency Responses to Displaced Groups

Many actors participate in emergency practices, including states, international bodies, humanitarian organizations and NGOs, community groups, faith-based organizations, activist groups, for-profit companies, and philanthropic entities[1] (see also Hilhorst and Jansen 2010; Hilhorst, Desportes, and de Milliano 2019). Indeed, in the current period of uncertainty and political instability, Duffield (2018) reminds us that humanitarian responses to emergencies, including their diverse forms in the digital world, are often used to govern groups and populations and their movements throughout the world.[2] In his view, precarity "emerges at that historical moment when the economy becomes a site of permanent emergency" (Duffield 2019, 17). Our perspective is similar here but situates precarity within a discussion of postwar humanitarian emergency responses to displaced groups – responses that, we argue, link to the architecture of precarity. Specifically, this section provides a brief review of postwar humanitarian emergency responses in the twentieth century: the institutionalization of humanitarianism, the proliferation of refugee spaces, the redefinition of refugees that culminated in constructing them as victims and thus lessening their political agency, and the emergence of new practices and policies for protecting and managing refugees that underscore the architecture of precarity.

International Coordination and Coordinating Displaced Persons and Refugees (1914–1950)

The majority of the displaced persons who are now in Germany, Austria and Italy are expected to constitute the "hard core" of non-repatriables who are unable or unwilling for various reasons, chiefly political, to return to their countries of origin. These non-repatriables will become the concern of the proposed

International Refugee Organization, the new refugee body to be established under the auspices of the United Nations. (Office of Public Affairs 1946, 2)

After the First World War (1914–18), European states took greater control over their borders, extreme poverty became widespread, and millions of people found themselves unable to return home or find sanctuary. During the conflict, state and humanitarian bodies worked together, and the prevailing view was that such efforts would need to continue when peace came. Barnett and Weiss (2011) identify three wartime trends that help account for the formation of the League of Nations (1920) and its Nansen International Office for Refugees (1930). First, states and humanitarian relief organizations began to acknowledge the humanitarian principles of "impartiality," "neutrality," and "independence."[3] Second, states became more active in the delivery and regulation of humanitarian relief, which they began to fund in new ways. Third, states took on a greater role in developing international organizations and laws to spread the responsibilities and costs of providing aid. International sympathy for wartime and postwar suffering spurred this sea change: domestic groups were "lobbying their governments to show a little tenderness," and many people felt that "humanitarian emergencies were probably here to stay in one form or another" (Barnett and Weiss 2011, 43).

Shortly after the war, in 1920, the League of Nations internationalized this humanitarian impulse, and in 1921 it named Fridtjof Nansen its first High Commissioner for Refugees. Nansen negotiated a set of refugee rights, including rights to travel documents (the Nansen passport), education, and employment (Barnett and Weiss, 2011). However, in the interwar years, the discretionary power of states to permit or refuse admission to refugees varied over time and between groups of refugees. For example, Behrman reveals that the British government "allowed in only 11,000 Jews escaping Nazi persecution between 1933 and 1938; however, following the *Anschluss* [March 1938] and *Kristallnacht* [9–10 November 1938] up to 50,000 Jews were granted asylum in 1938–39" (Behrman 2014, 5). Public pressure, he asserts, forced this shift, and campaigns followed to admit other refugees, such as Basques fleeing Franco's Spain (Behrman 2014). Just before the Second World War in Europe, and during the war itself, Jews and other targeted "undesirable" groups such as Poles and Romas were sent to slave labour or to death camps, where millions were killed. Auschwitz-Birkenau, which opened in 1940, was the largest of the Nazi concentration and death camps during what became known as the Holocaust. In the immediate wake of the Holocaust, the plight of the millions of people who had been driven from their homes had to be addressed. Planning for this had begun even before the war's end.

During and after the war, growing international, humanitarian, and human rights concerns over the Holocaust and the massive wartime displacement of populations helped shape international planning for displaced persons and refugees (Frederiksen 2012). Such planning involved many Allied operations, supply and trade efforts, and paramilitary organizations, along with the formation of the United Nations Relief and Rehabilitation Administration (UNRRA). During UNRRA's five-year existence (1942–48), it relocated and managed millions of people within the occupied territories in Europe, Southeast Asia, and the Pacific. "It set up holding camps to care for the health, welfare, and wellbeing of displaced persons, fostered expert training of local personnel in war-torn countries, and aimed to define approaches to postwar planning, relief, and reconstruction" (Ilcan and Aitken 2012, 6). It also established a Central Tracing Bureau to trace missing displaced persons with the goal of repatriating them and, in some cases, reuniting them with their families. The bureau, for example, assembled and recorded information on displaced persons, including children; by 1946 it had 5 million cards on file in Germany (Shields and Bryan 2002).

These years saw the large-scale repatriation of displaced persons and refugees to their home countries and the resettlement of others to other countries (United Nations 1958). But for various reasons,[4] such as fear of persecution or even enslavement, some displaced persons and political refugees (including Jews, Balts, Estonians, Latvians, Lithuanians, Poles, Serbians, Ukrainians, and Yugoslavs) remained in Germany, Austria, Italy, and other territories occupied by Britain, France, and the United States. These people were sometimes referred to as the "hard core" of "non-repatriables" (Office of Public Affairs 1946, 2). It was also a period when international bodies and organizations, such as the International Committee of the Red Cross (ICRC), the International Planned Parenthood Federation, the International Refugee Organization (IRO),[5] and the International Union for Child Welfare, engaged in strategies that were about connecting people and places and linking the local and international. These strategies blurred separations and divisions among displaced groups and for that reason could not address the messier relations along gender, ethnicity, and national lines (Hyndman 2000). Likewise, they could not address the lack of protection and rights and the vast differences in living conditions that displaced groups and political refugees experienced, or the diverse ways in which they engaged in resistance to their precarity. In other words, such strategies flattened displaced persons and political refugees into generalized bodies without personal attributes, meaningful pasts, expected futures, or political agency.

Concerned about the precarious living conditions of immense numbers of displaced persons and refugees just after the war, some domestic groups began lobbying international organizations to address the exploitation, insecurity, and exclusionary treatment facing displaced groups. For example, in 1947, the Chair of the Joint Committee of Displaced Persons and Political Refugees wrote a memorandum to the ICRC regarding the status of displaced persons and political refugees who were still being held in camps and other locations in Germany, Austria, Italy, and elsewhere, outside UNRRA's ambit. This committee detailed the current status of these displaced persons and political refugees. It also noted its concerns regarding their lack of protection and "inhuman treatment," which had led to a recent protest by the inhabitants of DP camps. The committee demanded improvements to their precarious living conditions. Writing from Augsburg, Germany, in the American Occupation Zone, committee chair M. Grabinski stated:

> The problem of D.Ps. and Political Refugees [is] often being
> discussed in international assemblies as well as in the world
> press. On every occasion when the future of the world and peace
> is discussed, arises also this unsettled and painful problem to
> the detriment of the unfortunate human beings who, for no fault

of theirs, are compelled to live in inhuman conditions, clamouring for decision of their fates. For nearly two years they have been living in former military barracks or former concentration camps, their souls rotting in idleness. Now they have become a nuisance to everybody. They are in the way and they are treated worse than the Germans ...

In Kornberg ... many Ukrainians were denied D.P. status. The Agencies in charge of D.Ps. have distinguished themselves by inhuman treatment of the pople [*sic*] being in their power and authority, and, as a rule, started to evict all who did not pass the examination and sent them to unannounced destination.

As a protest, the inhabitants of D.P. Camps went on a hunger strike. After 5 days of hungering, the order to evict the Ukrainians was striped and delayed till such time when the temperature will be not so severe. The fight was won, but on the 27th of January, there were 142 sick persons sent to the hospital: 118 men, 19 women and 5 children. (Joint Committee 1947, 2)

The above memorandum, signed by the representatives of eight nationalities, not only problematized the poor living conditions of the detainees and their potential unruliness but also drew attention to their "precarious situation" resulting from a lack of DP status and to German authorities' refusal "to deliver them temporary or permanent residence permits" (1947, 3). The Joint Committee of Displaced Persons and Political Refugees recognized that one solution to this "precarious problem" would be to "send those hundred thousand of D.Ps. home." However, given that this solution was viewed at the time as unrealizable, the joint committee articulated other informal demands that focused on refugee protections and rights. These included providing displaced persons and political refugees with "remunerative, decent work," "legal advice in order to safeguard their interests," and "legal status as provided by International law defending their duties, rights and privileges" (7–8). Such informal demands for the protection and safety of displaced persons and political refugees were expressed by other concerned interest groups and domestic bodies across Europe, North America, Asia, and elsewhere. These interventions, however, were detached from others: they existed alongside the imminent development of a more precise definition of the term "refugee." This was a decisive moment for refugee law, for it led to the founding of the UNHCR and its laws to establish refugees' protections and rights.

From Political Actors to Helpless Victims in Need of Protection (1950–1970)

> There is no single, universally accepted definition of the term [refugee], which makes statistics difficult and uncertain. In its wider sense, however, it includes 1/ Refugees from the prewar period; 2/ displaced persons/D.P.s; 3/ Refugees according to the Potsdam Agreement; and 4/ Political Refugees. (Svensson 1950)

Population instability was a "global phenomenon" (Feldman 2007: 132) right after the war, yet it was European refugees who received the most sustained attention from many national governments and international organizations. The founding of the UNHCR in 1950 provided a framework for the world to protect international refugees and search for lasting solutions to refugees' issues. As part of a larger discourse of "UN humanism" (Hyndman 2000), the UNHCR mandate was broader than any one crisis. It was to help those "who have crossed an international border because of a well-founded fear of persecution" (Barnett and Weiss 2011, 67), in part by advocating for their rights. It was also to distribute and manage humanitarian assistance for forced migrants, provide legal advice, dispense travel documents, and help them attain the legal statuses being offered by states (Barnett 2011; Glasman 2017; Loescher 2000). It also monitored states' compliance with the UN 1951 Convention Relating to the Status of Refugees (Geneva, 1951), the body that had defined "refugee."

As one among many postwar humanitarian organizations, the 1951 Refugee Convention set in place a system of international and domestic laws to enshrine protections and legal rights for refugees, which formalized mechanisms for providing assistance to these large groups and for physically relocating them. Although some countries at the time, including Canada (see figure 1.1), initially raised questions about the 1951 Refugee Convention, it has since been endorsed by more than 140 states (Bastaki 2018), which have harnessed existing state institutions to ensure refugees' access to education, labour markets, social services, and police and courts, as well as their protection from refoulement. Article 1(A) defined a refugee as someone who, "owing to a well-founded fear of being persecuted for reasons of race, religion, nationality, membership of a particular social group or political opinion, is outside the country of his nationality and is unable or, owing to such fear, is unwilling to avail himself of the protection of that country." By this definition, it was departure from one's home country that largely defined refugee status. In legal terms, the definition disconnected the identity of the "refugee" from the identity of the "migrant" in an effort to protect those fearing persecution (Crawley and Skleparis 2018); it also separated the identity of the refugee from the identity of the citizen. As Barnett asserts: "Only a world of sovereign states that has categories of people called 'citizens' and were intent on regulating population flows could produce a legal category of 'refugees'" (2001, 251). Furthermore, the focus on persecution in the definition of refugee silenced many people and barred them from refugee status (Coutin Bibler 2003; McKinnon 2008; Wettergren and Wikstrom 2014) – for example, those fleeing natural disasters, escaping material deprivation, and experiencing internal displacement and persecution because of gender or sexuality (Behrman 2014; Hyndman 2000; Nyers 2006).

The UNHCR and the 1951 Refugee Convention kick-started a new understanding of the refugee in an era that focused on Europe and on anti-communist political discourses. Those people who qualified ranged from single, married, or divorced refugees, through those with refugee dependents and of a certain ethnic background, to refugees of European origin needing assistance (see, for example, Weis 1960). Popular opinion identified refugees as "heroes" who had fled Franco's Spain, Poland under Nazi control, or Soviet-subjugated Hungary in the 1950s. They were witnesses to the "evils" of communism and "ambassadors" praising the virtues of host states (Behram 2014, 8). Political agency became the "defining feature of the figure of the 'refugee' who was imagined as 'white, male and anti-communist', fleeing political persecution from the East" (Chimni 1998, 251, qtd. in Scheel and Squire 2014; see also Johnson 2014). On the basis of this view, many countries resettled hundreds of thousands of postwar refugees – Australia, almost 171,000 between 1947 and 1954 (McAdam 2013). These

THIS DOCUMENT ON LOAN FROM THE PRIVY COUNCIL OFFICE - CANADA

TOP SECRET

CABINET CONCLUSIONS

A meeting of the Cabinet was held in Room 201 of the House of Commons on Friday, June 29th, 1951, at 2.00 p.m.

Present:

The Prime Minister
(Mr. St-Laurent) in the Chair,
The Minister of National Defence
(Mr. Claxton),
The Minister of National Health and Welfare
(Mr. Martin),
The Leader of the Government in the Senate
(Senator Robertson),
The Minister of Justice
(Mr. Garson),
The Secretary of State
(Mr. Bradley),
The Minister of Veterans Affairs
(Mr. Lapointe),
The Minister of Citizenship and Immigration
(Mr. Harris),
The Minister of Mines and Technical Surveys
(Mr. Prudham).

The Secretary to the Cabinet
(Mr. Robertson),
Mr. Paul Pelletier, Privy Council Office.

United Nations; Convention on Refugees and Protocol on Stateless Persons; Canadian participation

1. The Minister of Citizenship and Immigration, referring to discussion at the meeting of June 26th, 1951, thought it would be inadvisable for Canada to accept in their present form, articles 26, 27 and 28 of the draft Convention on Refugees. These articles prescribed certain automatic rights which were to be granted to refugees, legally or illegally admitted, and also prohibited the expulsion to territories where the life or freedom of refugees was threatened on grounds of race, religion, nationality or political opinion.

1.1 | Cabinet conclusions (top secret). 1951 UN Convention on Refugees and Protocol on Stateless Persons: Canadian participation.

refugees were "heroic" and had certain rights and freedoms under the 1951 Refugee Convention; naming them as refugees defined them as political actors.[6] On a broader scale, refugee classifications, such as those embodied in the 1951 Refugee Convention, not only determine who qualifies (or not) for protection under international law but also link the "micro level of refugee registration in the field to the macro level of UNHCR global policy" (Glasman 2017, 2). Furthermore, they raise important ontological questions, have juridical and material consequences, and underscore how, since the Second World War, some humanitarian experts and refugee studies have essentialized those classifications (Malkki 1995). These classifications have resulted in the silencing or downplaying of the kinds of political and social practices and processes of which migrants are part and the different lived experiences they endure.

The world saw massive forced migrations throughout the 1950s and 1960s – most notably perhaps the mass exodus from Hungary after the Soviet invasion of 1956. It now became apparent to many states and humanitarian organizations that displaced people had become a permanent feature of the international system in Europe and elsewhere. Around this time, attempts were made to broaden the scope of the 1951 Refugee Convention so that non-European refugees could gain benefits and protections from the Convention. The UN Protocol Relating to the Status of Refugees (New York, 1967) expanded the notion of refugee so that it not long primarily encompassed post-1945 Europeans and instead covered the rest of the world, wherever displacement had occurred as a result of war and persecution (Glasman 2017; Wettergren and Wikstrom 2014). It removed temporal and geographical restrictions from the 1951 Refugee Convention definition of a refugee, thus allowing refugees from the South to seek protection in the North. For those states that removed the temporal and geographical restrictions, a new understanding of refugee imagined those from the South as poor and helpless, which served to downgrade their political agency (Nyers 2006; Scheel and Squire 2014). These refugees represented a "humanitarian emergency," which, for Nyers, further threatened their political agency and made them "a threat to world order and therefore of immediate political concern." "The refugee ... can only claim [but not exercise] membership to the elusive moral community of 'humanity'"

(2006, xvii). As Nyers aptly put it, "Refugees are silenced by the very discourses that attempt to provide solutions to their plight" (2006, xiv). Treating refugees as a humanitarian emergency produces them as victims (as voiceless and powerless to make decisions), thus denying them political agency and rendering them more vulnerable – or what Robbins (2013) calls the ultimate "suffering subject" (see also Kallius, Monterescu, and Kumar Rajaram 2015, 27). Such imaginings weakened refugees' capacity to protect themselves and to counter governing interventions of assistance. As Barnett (2013, 384) suggests, victim discourses can create new hierarchies and identity-based differences, such as distinctions by gender regarding who is a bona fide civilian and thereby deserving of protection.

Some states, however, such as Lebanon,[7] are not party to the 1951 Refugee Convention and have no national legislation dealing with refugees (see Janmyr 2016); other states have been reluctant to apply the full protections of the 1951 Refugee Convention to large numbers of refugees (see Bastaki 2018, 74); and still others, such as Turkey, have ratified the 1951 Refugee Convention but with a geographical limitation (see, for example, Aras and Duman 2018; Baban, Ilcan, and Rygiel 2017b; Korkut 2016; Strasser and Tibet 2019; Yıldız and Sert 2019).[8] For example, Turkey ratified the 1951 Refugee Convention after the UNHCR was founded and integrated it into national law in 1961, after a UNHCR office was established in the country's capital, Ankara, in 1960 (Kirişçi 2001). But it made a reservation to the 1967 Protocol – due to the region in which it was located, it chose not to remove the geographical limitation and would admit only refugees coming from Europe (Korkut 2016). For Syrian refugees in Turkey, this means that because they are not from Europe, they are ineligible to apply in Turkey for refugee status under the 1951 Refugee Convention. This has resulted in restricted status, mobility, and protections for Syrians residing in the country (see chapters 3 and 4), including those living in urban areas and in temporary refugee camps. Thus, on a broader scale, given that a number of countries remain non-signatory to the 1951 Refugee Convention and the 1967 Protocol, differences have been introduced regarding how *refugee* and *asylum-seeker* are defined, the types of mechanisms, policies, and discourses that are in place to shape their lives, how they negotiate these dynamics, and with how much success.

Temporary Holding Areas (1960–)

As refugee displacements shifted from the Cold War context of Central and Eastern Europe to a South–North axis, Western countries increasingly tightened their asylum policies (Chimni 2009; Fullerton 2001; Johnson 2014).[9] Some states developed an oppressive geography of walls, coast guard patrols, detention centres, safe zones,[10] and offshore processing (see Darling 2009; Hyndman and Mountz 2007; Lui 2002; Ramadan 2012). Some states have attempted to control the movement of mobile populations seeking refuge by detaining forced migrants, such as asylum-seekers, in foreign countries for refugee processing – referred to as "offshore processing" or "offshore detention" (e.g., Geiger 2016; Mountz 2020). This entails one country engaging another as its "agent" to implement its own obligations under the 1951 Refugee Convention, which insists that states help refugees find a durable solution. The assigning government is responsible for the conduct of its offshore agent. Offshore processing is part of some countries' domestic or anti-immigration policies for dealing with "unauthorized arrivals" – asylum-seekers arriving by boat without a valid visa. Authorities contend that this is an acceptable method that reduces refugee-processing costs, lessens people-smuggling and deaths at sea, and deters "illegal" migrants;[11] however, it badly fails to protect forced migrants and ensures precarious conditions for them.

For many decades, one prominent humanitarian response to forced migration has been refugee camps, where forced migrants' basic needs can be met, such as for food, water, shelter, and medical care. Supposedly, these are only temporary holding areas while durable solutions are found (see Agier 2011; Bulley 2017a; Chimni 2009; Hyndman and Giles 2017, 2011; Ilcan and Rygiel 2015; Johnson 2014). The proliferation of such camps in Asia and the Middle East in the 1960s and 1970s and on a massive scale in Africa in the late 1980s undercut the perception of the "powerful, political" refugee that had taken root in the decade following 1945. Instead, popular opinion perceived "an undifferentiated victim, voiceless and without political agency" and probably non-white (Johnson 2011, 1016; see also Hakli and Kallio 2020). Despite these people's marginalization, certain states and regions saw them as unruly and threatening and sought new ways at home and

1.2 | Zaatari refugee camp, Jordan, 2013.

abroad to manage and contain them. Some large refugee camps have become more or less permanent in these regions (see Ilcan, Oliver, and Connoy 2017; Johnson 2014) at a time when humanitarian emergency responses are expanding far beyond the earlier *ad hoc* aid (see Ticktin 2014). Refugees in these camps often lead "lives of waiting," sometimes for decades (Agier 2012, 274).

Placing forced migrant populations in temporary holding spaces or camps is common and often involves the UNHCR and its partners, including states, private sector organizations, faith-based bodies, and national and international NGOs. In both spatial and institutional terms, the refugee camp may indeed constitute part of "a tacit and unsatisfactory policy of containment," one that relieves the host state of its obligations toward refugees within its territory (Hyndman 2000, 140). Yet there are some exceptions. In some situations, such as Syrians escaping civil war, state or humanitarian authorities may not simply contain them in refugee camps, at least in the traditional way. For example, in May 2011, shortly after the Syrian war broke out, the Turkish government opened the first temporary camps for Syrian refugees near the Turkish–Syrian border. The initial open border policy, which referred to refugees as "guests," operated at first on the assumption that Syrians would reside only temporarily in Turkey. But as the number of Syrians in Turkey increased, registering under the temporary protection regime, more and more of them relocated to urban areas to the point that Syrians are now living in every province of Turkey (Saraçoğlu and Belanger 2019b). Currently, only around 3 per cent of Syrian refugees are living in government-controlled refugee camps (Kale and Erdoğan 2019), where the government works with humanitarian organizations, including the IHH, UN organizations that it allows in, and the Turkish Red Crescent, the latter of which is part of the International Red Cross and Red Crescent Movement and the largest humanitarian organization in Turkey. The Turkish government, not the UNHCR and its partners, is the main authority in these camps: it controls key administrative activities, decides who will be allowed in, regulates refugees' movements, and grants identity cards. Such camps are in effect state-run migrant spaces rather than "humanitarian space" in which international organizations institutionalize protection and relief for refugees in accordance with the humanitarian principles of neutrality, impartiality, and humanity (see Ramadan 2012; Spearing 2001, in Hilhorst and Jansen 2010). Furthermore, since the overwhelming majority of Syrian refugees live in urban areas in Turkey (93 per cent [Kale and Erdoğan 2019]), most national and international NGOs assisting them work in central urban areas, such as İstanbul, and in border cities in the southeast, such as Gaziantep, Hatay, Kilis, and Şanlıurfa (Aras and Duman 2018; Baban, Ilcan, and Rygiel 2017; see also chapters 3 and 4, below). Nevertheless, the growing international management of camps and the assumption that refugees should be largely responsible for their own futures (Ilcan and Rygiel 2015) have led to "refugee warehousing" for indefinite periods (Hyndman and Giles 2011, 362).[12] This may well be no mere passing phase. Mass displacement and forced migrations have transformed the post-1918 era into "a century of camps" (Agier 2011, 3–4), in the course of which the impermanent has perhaps become permanent. This is why Agier (2007: 171) refers to "camps-cities": "The camp is always a precarious place, but it is also a place where a relatively stable situation emerges ... The refugee camps agglomerate thousands of even tens of thousands of inhabitants for lengths of time that generally far exceed that of an emergency." Some observers in Africa, for example, have seen the refugee camp as part of a worldwide humanitarian/military effort to confine massive, "undesirable" populations, and as producing figures of victimhood that seem incompatible with citizenship (Fassin and Pandolfi 2010). In other cases, such as in Lebanon, refugee status has become a permanent temporary reality for millions of Palestinians awaiting resolution of their situation, and housing them in the country's refugee camps places them in what Ramadan (2012, 2) calls "permanent-temporary landscapes of exile." However, given Lebanon's perennial attempts to reduce the size of the country's Palestinian population, Palestinian Syrians fleeing from Syria to Lebanon during the recent war have been subject to entry and stay regulations. Such mobility control measures began in the summer of 2013, when the Lebanese government demanded that Palestinian Syrians possess a valid pre-approved visa, which required an application made by a guarantor in Lebanon. In 2014 the Lebanese government began permitting Palestinian Syrians from Syria to enter only if they had an embassy appointment and were transiting to a third country or with a pledge of responsibility (Janmyr 2016). Thus, Palestinian Syrians from Syria face grave difficulties accessing safety and protection in Lebanon's refugee camps and consequently face precarious situations.

In Europe, border zones have proliferated over the past few years as spaces of containment and control (Tazzioli 2020) and support has developed for large-scale reception structures. In Cara Mineo, Sicily, for example, around 3,400 people are living in overcrowded conditions, divided by ethnic and religious backgrounds. And the "jungle" makeshift camp in Calais, France, housed up to 6,000 people in appalling conditions before authorities demolished it in March 2016. Additionally, the EU and its member-states have promoted the confinement of thousands of refugees and migrants in Greece and the large-scale containment of refugees in Turkey (see chapter 2), while ignoring the gaps in protection in Greece's system of asylum and reception. Indeed, the European Court of Human Rights has repeatedly found Greece to

1.3 | Turkish Red Crescent, Kilis, Turkey, 2013.

have violated asylum-seekers' right to a speedy review of the legality of their detention before a legal body and of their conditions of detention (European Court of Human Rights 2018).[13] These and similar situations tell not only of precarity of movement but also of precarious living arrangements, often in deplorable conditions, sometimes without adequate food and health care and with little access to rights, benefits, information,[14] and freedom of movement. However, refugee camps are also political spaces in which diverse forms of solidarity-building and resistance develop (see, for example, Bulley 2016; Ilcan 2013, 2014; Ramadan 2012; Rygiel 2011, 2014b, 2016; Sanyal 2017). In this regard, Ramadan (2012) demonstrates that the camp can be viewed as a space where refugees engage in solidarity activities and exercise their political agency. Similarly, Bulley (2016) draws on many examples, such as UNRWA in Lebanon, to show that strategies of resistance can both challenge and bolster the governmental schemes and humanitarian ethos enacted by the "host."

The past few decades have witnessed an almost constant humanitarian emergency response to a seemingly endless series of crises that have devastated and uprooted masses of people: revolutions, wars, extreme conflicts, and famines, including the Hungarian Revolution of 1956, the Biafran Civil War of 1968–70, Sudan's civil war of 1983, the Ethiopian famine of 1983–85, the Liberian civil war of 1989–2003, and the ongoing Syrian war. Responses to forced migration have varied and, especially since the 1980s, have become progressively more restrictive, hypothesizing uncontainable "flows" of people and threats to receiving countries' security and stability (e.g., Chimni 2009; Fullerton 2001; Johnson 2014). These responses include new transit visas, new international obligations toward refugees, new agreements, such as the EU–Turkey Statement (see below and chapter 2), and temporary protection schemes.

Temporary Protection (1990–)

Different from other types of protection,[15] temporary protection grants a person or group the right to enter or remain in a country for a limited time due to the risk of serious harm in their home country. Many countries have applied this decades-old concept in several situations, especially during large influxes of asylum-seekers and cross-border population movements (Türk 2015, 41). Governments commonly grant it to large groups under accelerated processes and generally renew it (Orchard and Miller 2014, 5).[16] Although temporary protection is permissible under the 1951 Refugee Convention, states typically use it as a means to deter local integration: they provide only minimal protection and facilitate repatriation (Durieux 2015, 236). It is usually "return-oriented" and aims at repatriating the displaced person. For example, the 1990s conflict in the former Yugoslavia generated massive movements of people into Central and Western European countries, which tended to offer temporary protection, even though many migrants qualified as refugees (Orchard and Miller 2014, 29). During that conflict, the UNHCR for the first time called for "a flexible system of temporary protection," even for these convention refugees (Durieux 2015, 233). During NATO's 1999 campaign in Serbia and Kosovo, more than 900,000 Kosovar refugees moved across borders into neighbouring Balkan states, where they received temporary protection before later evacuation to countries of destination; however, a few months later the vast majority of the evacuated refugees returned to "UN-administered" Kosovo (Durieux 2015, 241).

In 1981, the 32nd Session of the Executive Committee of the UNHCR on the Protection of Asylum-Seekers in Situations of Large-Scale Influx emphasized the protection measures required to safeguard asylum-seekers in situations of large-scale influx. It was recognized that states might face difficulties in achieving durable solutions for asylum-seekers in large-scale influx situations, but it was nevertheless understood that states were obliged to ensure that basic human rights standards would be provided to them. The Executive Committee concluded, and Article 5 of the Temporary Protection Regime (TPR) reflects, that non-refoulement is a core principle: no one will be forced to return to a place where they fear persecution. The non-refoulement principle is guaranteed under TPR, yet some states, such as Australia, some EU member-states, the United States, and Turkey, do not abide by it. For example, the Turkish government has been accused of violating human rights and the non-refoulement principle (see below). These and similar kinds of temporary measures have long affected people's access to protection.[17]

In the past few decades, many states and international organizations have supported temporary protection schemes. The UNHCR's Standing Committee in 1997 emphasized that states can deny and "suspend access to individual status determination during the stay in the country of refuge" (Durieux 2015, 237). The EU's Temporary Protection Directive (TPD) of 2001 established a framework and minimum standards for such programs, which were applicable in the event of a "mass influx or imminent mass influx of displaced persons from third countries who are unable to return to their country of origin" (Orchard and Miller 2014, 30). The UNHCR's *Guidelines on Temporary Protection or Stay Arrangements* (2014a) conforms to the EU's TPD and presents temporary protection as a "pragmatic tool" for "offering sanctuary to those fleeing humanitarian crises" when assigning refugee status to people may be unsuitable or insufficient. Those guidelines encourage countries in the same region to harmonize their standards of treatment and thereby discourage movement outside the region. Türk (2015, 41) views the guidelines as "complementary to and building on the international refugee protection regime." Even so, the document raises critical questions about temporary protection.

On a broader scale, temporary protection often weakens refugees' protections, threatens their rights, and creates social and economic insecurity for them. Several countries offering it, such as Australia, Denmark, Germany, Israel, and Turkey, are in effect exacerbating refugees' social and economic inequalities. In Israel, for example, since 2005 around 60,000 Eritreans and Sudanese fleeing severe conflict have arrived to apply for asylum. Israel has refused to allow them to do so and has instead granted them all temporary protection. In doing so, it has denied them refugee status and left them more vulnerable and insecure. The newcomers cannot receive work permits, health insurance, social benefits, or any provisions for shelter and food. Extremely poor, they have since lived in inhumane conditions in poor neighbourhoods in south Tel Aviv, where they rely increasingly on minimal health care from NGOs (see Kalır 2015). In this case and similar ones, temporary protection leaves recipients more vulnerable to public scrutiny, police surveillance, and mobility restrictions (Ilcan, Rygiel, and Baban 2018; Menjivar 2006). As Menjivar (2006) suggests, these migrants enter an indefinite state of temporariness, or "liminal legality." Some states use temporary protection to control migrants' access to rights and length of stay, often by refusing them individual determination of refugee status and by withholding certain rights and benefits available to formal refugees. This type of protection tends to expose them to insecurity and exploitation, such as in Turkey (see chapters 3 and 4, below; see also, for example, Aras and Duman 2018; Ferris and Kirişçi 2016; Rygiel, Baban, and Ilcan 2016; Saraçoğlu and Belanger 2019b; Yüksel and İçduygu 2018), in effect contravening the 1951 Refugee Convention.

In the Turkish case, the government upheld an open-door policy with Syria, and consequently many refugees leaving Syria were able to enter the country. As more refugees arrived in Turkey, the Turkish government introduced the temporary protection regime and implemented formal regulations regarding refugees from Syria (see Bastaki 2018). Under the country's temporary protection regulations, there is no explicit right to work for Syrians, and even when they are given access to education and social services, their access to these is often uneven and tenuous. Over the past several years, these living conditions have been coupled with language barriers, gender divisions, various forms of anti-immigrant rhetoric and xenophobia, and restrictive employment policies that have prompted Syrians to engage in insecure and illegal work in order to survive. For example, many Syrian forced migrant women and young girls who live and work in countries such as Turkey are employed in temporary, poorly paid, and insecure work, such as informal garbage collection, cleaning, care, hospitality, agriculture, and food processing (see also Canefe 2018). In light of existing and precarious conditions of living, some Syrians choose to travel to Europe in the hope of finding safety and protection. Others, feeling the impact of the EU–Turkey Statement (see chapter 2), have found themselves confronting exploitation and trafficking, gouging by landlords, and social media bursting with anti-Syrian sentiment (see chapters 3 and 4). Humanitarian responses to emergencies may shape forced migrants' lives through encampment, victimization discourses, international agreements, and temporary protection schemes; they can also engender specific forms of precarity. We discuss this next.

Intimately Connected: Humanitarian Emergency Responses and Precarity

Considerable research emphasizes that humanitarian responses to mass movements of forced migrants can improve the lives of refugees, IDPs, and asylum-seekers as well as enhance human welfare, global civil society, and international standards governing states' conduct (e.g., Gunewardena and Schuller 2008; Lautz and Raven-Roberts 2006). While such responses provide food, shelter, and medical care, they also raise serious governance questions.[18]

We treat humanitarian emergency responses as more aptly a mode of governance. Didier Fassin (2011) argues that the politics of compassion – humanitarianism – profoundly affect populations in precarious situations. "On both the national and the international levels, the vocabulary of suffering, compassion, assistance, and responsibility to protect forms part of our political life: it serves to qualify the issues involved and to reason about choices made" (2011, 2). Peter Nyers (2006,

3) notes that "situations deemed emergencies ... bring to the forefront the unquestioned assumptions and tacit agreements that work to constitute the 'normal' state of affairs." Craig Calhoun (2004) finds that the notion of emergency shapes how we view the world so as to convert our resulting policy decisions about interventions into social problems. Humanitarian interventions, he suggests, lead us to view "disasters" not as matters of chance but as "emergencies that demand action" (2004, 380). In this and other literatures, scholars often tap Foucault's concept of governmentality when thinking about governance of migrant and other populations (e.g., Agier 2011; Fassin 2007; Walters 2011).[19] Some scholars see humanitarian governance in particular as a form of "mobile sovereignty" (Pandolfi 2003), as "the left hand of empire" (Agier 2011), or, more generally, as the employment of moral sentiments in the service of contemporary politics (Fassin 2011). Michel Agier (2011, 4–5) relates "humanitarian government" to policing and argues that "there is no care without control"; similarly, Ticktin (2005, 359) views humanitarianism and policing as "intimately linked."

Humanitarian emergency responses to forced migrants shape their lives and often make them more precarious; this fosters intimate connections between emergency responses and precarity. Scholars in fields as various as citizenship, education, employment, health care, housing, mobility, social protection, and social rights conceive of "precarity" as lack of security and stability in peoples' lives and explore how such experiences can displace people and sometimes unite them for collective action.[20] Human rights scholars, for example, emphasize the absence of adequate protection for refugees who live amid such situations and who deserve protection of their rights but do not always receive it (Hilhorst and Jansen 2012; Verdirame and Harrell-Bond 2005). Immigration researchers highlight refugees' place in the wider world of migration as one of particular vulnerability (Walsh 2008). Critical migration scholars focus on the discursive frameworks that exclude and politicize migrant and refugee populations (e.g., Agier 2011; Aras and Duman 2018; Hyndman and Giles 2011, 2017; Saraçoğlu and Belanger 2019b; Ticktin 2011a, 2014); the consequences of the use of security technologies to control refugees' movements (e.g., Jacobsen 2010); migration's often devastating effects on people who have to travel to reach a safe country, which often means dangerous journeys within and across internal and national borders (see chapters 2 and 6, below; see also Almustafa 2018; Crawley and Jones 2020; Ilcan 2018, 2020; Topak 2014; Yıldız and Sert 2019), journeys that have resulted in migrant deaths at sea (e.g., Albahari 2015; Rygiel 2014b, 2016; Squire et al. 2017; Williams 2015); and, in response to their vulnerabilities and forms of exclusion, migrants' community-building, protests, and solidarity efforts (e.g., Ataç, Rygiel, and Stierl 2016; Baban and Rygiel 2017; Basok and Candiz 2020; Lecadet 2016; Johnson 2016).

Forced migrants from Syria provide a good example of the close links between humanitarian emergency responses and precarity. The war that started in March 2011 has killed more than 500,000 people (HRW 2019d; *Al Jazeera* 2016) and displaced about 12.7 million (Mercy Corps 2020) and has led to intervention by states and international refugee organizations and by military and border-security personnel. It has also led to international and national policies on asylum and temporary protection that have made refugees' situations more precarious. As shown by the movement of Syrians into neighbouring and Eastern and Western European countries and their resettlement (e.g., Bulley 2017a; Fakhoury 2019; Janmyr 2016; Pollock et al. 2019), states have responded in diverse ways, ranging from providing the full protections of the 1951 Refugee Convention, to establishing temporary protection regimes, to outright rejection (see Bastaki 2018).

As noted earlier, Syrian refugees in Turkey receive temporary protection. Among other things, this often limits their access to legal employment and citizenship rights and forces them into often appalling housing (see, for example, Aras and Yasun 2016; Aras and Duman 2018; Bilecen and Yurtseven 2018; Erdoğan 2015; İneli-Ciğer 2015; Kirişçi 2016; Saraçoğlu and Belanger 2019b; Yıldız and Uzgören 2016).[21] Temporary protection shapes their ability to access social services, paid employment, and citizenship, as well as their capacity to travel and relations with their homeland. Such precarious status may increase their social vulnerability in urban spaces and prevent them from moving freely within the country (see chapter 3). Their status and living conditions reflect the failure of Turkish and EU temporary protection policies and of the EU's expansion of border controls to govern migrant movements (see chapter 2). Some Syrian refugees have responded by engaging in citizenship politics and community-building with help from local groups that inform them about their rights, encourage them to participate in the local economy, and involve them in social activities as they settle (see chapter 5). Other Syrian refugees (and people on the move) in Turkey and elsewhere exercise a form of political agency through dangerous travel, particularly on the Mediterranean and Aegean seas, in the hope of reaching safety and international protection in Europe (see chapter 6). In these and other contexts, Syrian refugees may challenge their precarious status and legal limbo and seek greater support, recognition, and protection. The literature on precarity enables an exploration of these diverse responses and actions. In this book, we approach precarity through a focus on forced migrants, particularly their insecure conditions of living and simultaneous inclusion and exclusion. In the following chapters, we provide an empirical analysis of Syrians living under temporary protection and experiencing precarious status, space, and movement in Turkey. Through what we term the architecture of precarity, we identify and analyze key dimensions of precarity.

The Architecture of Precarity

Scholars typically define and explore precarious situations in reference to marginal and casualized or contingent work in industrial branch plants; to post-Fordist capitalism in association with the rise of the service economy; or in connection with post-welfare states, especially in Western Europe and North America (Ettlinger 2007; Strauss and Fudge 2014; Waite 2009). They see precarity as a *condition* – insecure and unstable work – within specific labour markets (Arnold and Bongiovi 2013; Fantone 2007) that encompasses diverse processes and dimensions, such as the rise of temporary and intermediated forms of employment (Strauss and Fudge 2014), the changing nature and allocation of social and economic risks, the feminization of paid work, and the experiences of workers at the lower end of the labour market. Branch and Hanley describe such insecure work as "uncertain, unpredictable, and risky from the point of view of the worker" (2011: 569). Some researchers focus on exploitation relating to time (period in a job, length of working day, shift patterns) (Anderson 2007) in labour-market economies, which Tsianos and Papadopoulos (2006) view as "exploiting the continuum of everyday life." Such labour markets, mainly in advanced capitalist economies, seem to produce ever more precarious work (casual, short-term, illegal) that is unstable, lacking in protection, and socially or economically vulnerable (see Waite 2009). While this understanding focuses on vulnerable employment in labour regimes that capture the lives of many workers, including migrants, we dig deeper to explore both the relations of precarity and the underlying ambiguity inherent in migration. Our focus here is not on precarity as a coherent totality; rather, we view it in terms of a whole range of practices, conditions, and dynamics that are, in many ways, constitutive of certain *kinds* of precarity.

A growing literature is exploring precarity in migration to reveal the vulnerability and insecurity that migrants confront, including precarious conditions in relation to their socio-legal status, conditions of living, and mobility (Ataç et al. 2017; Basok et al. 2015; Dağtaş 2017; Janmyr 2016; Roy and Verdun 2019) and their gender and sexual orientation (e.g., Canefe 2018; Hersh 2017; Hodge 2019), and to their differing access to humanitarian assistance and protection (Aras and Duman 2018; Baban, Ilcan, and Rygiel 2017b), legal documentation (Goldring and Landolt 2011, 2013; Janmyr 2016), social rights (Gavanas and Calzada 2016), mobility (e.g., Bates-Eamer 2019; Paynter 2019), and stable and legal employment (Anderson 2013; Changia 2019; Kooy and Bowman 2019). In terms of the latter, precarious work in many labour markets is increasingly connected to shifting migration dynamics. For example, Anderson (2013) emphasizes the ways in which governments engage immigration controls to manage the flow of labour and shape what types of workers can enter the local labour market and under what circumstances. Her study demonstrates that the category of migrant is neither fixed nor straightforward, but somewhat ambivalent. She emphasizes that "the migrant" is both a political category and a legal one (since it does not concern simply a legal status, but also gender, race, and class), to such an extent that one could still be considered a "migrant" even after obtaining citizenship (see supposed second- or third-generation immigrants); meanwhile, not all foreigners are defined as migrants. Importantly, Anderson argues that "it is immigration of the poor that controls are generally designed to prevent, and 'poor countries' and countries whose citizenry are black are very likely to coincide" (2013, 123).[22] In other situations, authorities may force some migrant workers into certain spaces and dwellings, reconstitute them as a security threat (Hodge 2015), and punish or "illegalize" them (Aliverti 2012; see also Bauder 2014).

While precarity may resemble a broad array of conditions, such as those of risk and "risk communities" (see Waite 2009), we argue in this book that it uniquely encapsulates both vulnerability and ambiguity – simultaneous inclusion and exclusion. Precarity is highly mutable and thus unstable. Diverse actors, policies, and practices produce and govern it, and their interventions both include and exclude the migrant subject. These defining features arise in various domains (cultural, political, social), within and across scales (international, regional, national, local), and in distinct spaces and living conditions (neighbourhoods, cities, territories), and many actors animate them. More specifically, the features of precarity connect to wider social and political relations, manifest themselves particularly in the experiences of refugees, asylum-seekers, and other migrants, and endure through policies, programs, discourses, and practices that shape their daily lives. These features form part of what we call the "architecture of precarity" (Ilcan, Rygiel, and Baban 2018). Under this rubric, we identify three dimensions of precarity that encompass both vulnerability and ambiguity: status, space, and movement.

Precarious status refers to vulnerable and insecure conditions that emerge when governing authorities such as states assign members of vulnerable groups, such as refugees, a certain socio-legal status. This status can determine specific, perhaps limited rights to residence, health care, welfare, or work that may result in Standing's (2011) "shadow-economy precariat." This status can also reveal the gradations of precariousness that exist between status and lack thereof (Goldring and Landolt 2011, 2021; see also Bauder 2014). Accordingly, a refugee's legal status can shift, allowing varying degrees of agency and experience (Sigona 2012) for indeterminate periods (Goldring and Landolt 2013).

Temporary protection status is a good example of precarious status, one that affects hundreds of thousands of refugees around the world.

Because such protection is temporary, it can restrict access to rights in daily life, which in turn can lead to deeper poverty, exacerbate gender divisions (e.g., Canefe 2018; Kıvılcım 2016), and stimulate clandestine behaviour and social isolation (see Kooy and Bowman 2019; Menjivar 2006; Hallett 2014). Thus, temporary protection for Syrian refugees in Turkey affects their access to paid employment, education, housing, and health care (see Bilecen and Yurtseven 2018; Ferris and Kirişçi 2016; Memişoğlu and Ilgıt 2016; see also chapters 3 and 4) and can also affect their access to humanitarian assistance. With respect to the latter, as the Syrian war began, national and international NGOs began operating in Turkish provinces and districts where Syrian refugees were concentrating. Soon after, the Turkish government began introducing regulations governing NGOs' activities and requiring work permits for their staff for them to be able to work in the country. Some of these organizations, such as International Medical Corps, Mercy Corps, and DanChurchAid, were closed by the Turkish government "allegedly because they have been operating in Diyarbakır, cooperating with Syrian Kurds, and providing them with humanitarian aid" (Aras and Duman 2018, 2). Whatever the facts were, these shutdowns left some Syrian refugees under temporary protection without access to needed care and assistance.

Moreover, although Syrian refugees under temporary protection in Turkey have the same rights as refugees under international protection in terms of access to state-funded social services, including education and health care, that temporary status limits their access to full citizenship and employment rights. With regard to the latter, in January 2016, Syrians under temporary protection acquired the legal right to a work permit; but because of the highly restrictive conditions imposed on them, this right has led to only 15,000 Syrians receiving work permits as of January 2018 (Saraçoğlu and Belanger 2019b). Thus, temporary protection offers Syrians little or no long-term security (e.g., İçduygu 2015b; Kaya 2016; Korkut 2016; Şenses 2015; Yıldız and Uzgören 2016). Around the world, many recipients of temporary protection are not permitted, for example, to gain formal employment and thus participate in meaningful activities within the host country (Hallett 2014; ILO 2016). These barriers informalize employment, worsen the exploitation of workers (e.g., forced and child labour), and have a deleterious impact on working conditions and wages throughout the host society (ILO 2016).

Temporary protection can exacerbate differences between refugees and their hosts. For example, temporary protectees in Australia, Denmark, and Germany from 1999 to 2005 seemed to experience greater uncertainty, political exclusion, and social and financial difficulties (Mansouri, Leach, and Nethery 2009). A former Vietnamese refugee in Australia, Huy Truong, recounted that "it's completely demoralising, and in many respects inhumane, to not let people be productive with their hands, their head, their heart and to be feeling like this is a hopeless situation" (in Bleby, Fitzsimmons, and Khadem 2013; see also McAdam 2013). This "differential inclusion" points to the links between refugees and rights that create gradations of precarity and status, such as in relation to timing for access to social citizenship rights. It also points to how social exclusion marginalizes certain groups, injects new social divisions, and pinches off negotiated pathways to certain types of status. Everyday forms of precarity for vulnerable groups, such as refugees, stateless people, and non-citizens, affect how they handle daily life, including how they obtain social citizenship rights and humanitarian assistance (e.g., Ataç et al. 2017; Baban, Ilcan, and Rygiel 2017b), legal documentation (e.g., Canefe 2016; Goldring and Landolt 2011, 2021), and housing (Neilson and Rossiter 2005). These forms of precarity can also shape narratives of imaginaries and understandings of belonging (Casas-Cortes 2019; Sharma and Kunduri 2015) for various social groups, which in turn may help generate new kinds of activism in response to precarity. For example, Casas-Cortes (2019) has documented a multitude of activist efforts across Europe and how these have been developing under the rubric of precarity. She highlights the rise of "precarity activism" in Spain, focusing on feminist precarity collectives with their emphasis on "care-tizenship," to evoke a different understanding of political belonging that includes new forms of collective rights.

Migrants' precarious status can intersect with their precarity of space and movement. *Precarious space* is a multilayered concept that refers to those spaces that receive meaning through the precarious life experiences of marginal groups, such as refugees. These socio-spatial domains, which may entail squalid conditions in marginalized neighbourhoods, are not discrete and self-enclosed but are, as Massey (2005) highlights, spheres of coexistence comprising diverse trajectories and involving subjects and objects, and people and things, encountering one another. These spaces are not static, and their subjects, networks, and practices cannot easily be conceptualized as a whole (see Sanyal 2014). They can be sites of struggles and negotiations in daily life and reveal precarity and the interplay between the personal and the political. Precarious space resembles Banki's (2013) "precarity of place" – physical locations where vulnerable peoples can be subject to removal or deportation. As she says, it is a condition of "not quite, not yet," as in "not quite homeless, not yet deported or detained" (454), one that often affects people's choices and their responses to their situation.

In recent decades, as displacements have lengthened so as to underscore the geographic dislocation of forced migrants (e.g., Jacobsen, Karlsen, and Khosravi, 2021; Ramsay 2019), many refugees are looking to urban areas for economic opportunities that are restricted or unavailable in camps and similar settings. "Refugee" continues to invoke images of people living in tents or containers in isolated areas in the South, yet in 2020, of the roughly 26 million refugees in the world (https://www.unhcr.org/figures-at-a-glance.html), most were residing in urban spaces. According to the UNHCR, more than half of the world's refugees now reside in the poorest areas of some of the world's biggest cities, such as Amman, Jordan; Bangkok, Thailand; İstanbul, Turkey; and Nairobi, Kenya. Refugees fleeing war or persecution at home are today more likely to seek refuge in towns or cities. Some do so to find safety and economic independence, or to escape abuse or violence, while others seek specialized services, such as legal and medical, that may be unobtainable in refugee camps.

Cities and urban centres concentrate diversity and produce new and old types of social and economic inequalities (Butler 2012; Harvey 2012; Sassen 2000). They also generate precarious spaces as well as counter-responses to precarity (see chapter 5; Kılıçaslan 2016; Trimikliniotis, Parsanoglou, and Tsianos 2015). These spaces cast many refugees as outsiders and confront them with exclusion, discrimination, and perilous living conditions. For example, some non-legal refugees experience precarity of space through detention, eviction, and even refoulement (from the French, "force back") (see Zeter 2015), as well as through poor accommodation, marginalized neighbourhoods, and illegal work. In Turkey, many Syrian refugees dwell in urban spaces, largely in marginalized neighbourhoods, and can find only poorly paid work (see chapters 3 and 4; see also Canefe 2016; Erdogan 2015; Ataç et al. 2017). Canefe (2016) stresses the link between the precarious status of migrants (including refugees, asylum-seekers, irregular migrants, and stateless people) and the new labour laws in Turkey that have linked that country to the world's neoliberal economies. Turkey is widely viewed as a regional neoliberal economy of the "Global South," one that has been built on the shoulders of irregular migrants; in this, it differs from the more protectionist economies of the "Global North." In this context, Canefe defines refugees, asylum-seekers, irregular migrants, and stateless people as the "precariat" or "precarious proletariat" in that these groups eventually become employed under very unstable circumstances and thus are unable to demand their myriad rights, including those attached to citizenship, in the spaces and economies in which they find themselves. While we view precarious spaces as generating insecure life conditions, we also see their potential for fostering counter-responses to precarity, which involve an array of community-building activities that can create solidarity-building and new forms of politics (see chapter 5). This view somewhat aligns with Sanyal's (2014) assertion that cities are centres of heterogeneous mingling, conflict, and claims-making, in addition to being the emblematic sites where struggles take place. She views refugee spaces in cities as "archives of spatial and political histories" (2014: 561), which can produce and articulate new politics.

Precarious movement occurs when authorities apply governing practices to control the movement of marginal groups, such as refugees. When those practices deny migrant subjects rights in transit, detain them, or compel them to relocate, the migrants experience precarity of movement, which in turn can shape their social status and their residence. All of this evokes research by Loyd, Mitchell-Eaton, and Mountz (2016), who reveal that territorial control can rework the status of both people and places.

Many countries in the South are experiencing severe conflict and disruption, and large numbers of refugees are fleeing to Europe, the

Middle East, and elsewhere in search of greater protection and safety and to make new lives for themselves. Since 2011, for example, many Syrians have sought refuge in urban spaces in Egypt, Iraq, Jordan, Lebanon, and Turkey, where they often experience social exclusion, low-paying and insufficient employment, inadequate and overcrowded shelter, limited and uneven access to social services, and precarious status as temporary guests, temporary residents, or temporary workers. These conditions compel some refugees and asylum-seekers to leave the host countries, and some of them in turn encounter temporary roadblocks, mobility restrictions, and confinement. For example, EU member-states are calling for the confinement of thousands of refugees and asylum-seekers in Greece and the large-scale containment of refugees in Turkey. Such border and movement controls, which often jeopardize refugees' mobility, can stem from the politics of particular border zones, such as the Greek–Turkish border zone (see Topak 2014), projects of securitization (see Huysmans 2000; McNevin 2014), and regional arrangements such as the EU–Turkey Statement (see Bulley 2017b; Heck and Hess 2016; Karadağ 2019; Strasser and Tibet 2019).

Border and movement controls are subject to challenge. Some refugees are responding to their precarious movement, space, or status by engaging in collective action. In Turkey, for instance, some Syrian refugees are staying in the country and negotiating jobs, housing, and training (see chapter 3 and 4), raising consciousness, pushing for the right to stay and belong, and building community (see chapter 5). Others (and other people on the move) are engaging in the right to leave or escape and undertaking dangerous journeys across the Aegean and Mediterranean in search of international protection in an EU country. Though smugglers may assist them (see chapter 6), the decision to leave is theirs alone. Maurice Stierl (2016b, 566) views these refugees as thus becoming "subjects who enact the right to leave, move, survive and arrive" in the hope of gaining greater protection and easing their current precarious conditions. Likewise, with respect to acts of escape, Squire (2020) discusses the embodied experiences of migration. In analyzing the hidden geographies of the "Mediterranean migration crisis," she emphasizes the "*multiple* political interventions that the act of escape engenders" (5). These interventions, she argues, bring to the fore an appreciation of migrants' struggles against spatialized global inequalities and long histories of power and violence. They also highlight how migration can amount to a rebellion against the social relations they are escaping, against what she terms a "*non*movement," thereby exposing the hidden geographies of the supposed "crisis." This view of migration, Squire argues, guards against the unintentional repetition of abstract accounts of migration as a coordinated social movement; it also challenges assumptions that people on the move are victims who require both care and control, and emphasizes the diversity of migration experiences.

Everyday forms of precarity can also shape how certain marginalized and migrant groups share knowledge about how to find work and educational resources, identify local communities and social supports, and engage in social movements and "transformative nonmovements" (Squire 2020). Clearly migrants, as political subjects, respond in many ways to their precarious life conditions.

Counter-Responses

Researchers have shown that many refugees and asylum-seekers living in cities, towns, and camps are not at all passive victims. Many of them have set out to forge a socially and politically meaningful existence, proclaim their visibility and dignity, and invest in their lives through diverse cultural, social, and economic relations (see Agier 2008; Ataç, Rygiel, and Stierl 2016; Fresia and Von Kanel 2015). Many of those who live in refugee camps, for example, are not victims but political agents (e.g., Bulley 2016; Ilcan 2013, 2014; Hakli and Kallio 2020; Isin and Rygiel 2007; Malkki 1995, 1996; Rygiel 2011; Sigona 2015). Some of them are working to transform the space of these camps into new urban margins and to link them to the world's economies (Jansen 2014; Fresia and Von Kanel 2015). Some of them protest to demand recognition of their rights, such as Malian refugees in Mauritanian refugee camps (Fresia 2014), refugees from Palestine living in camps in neighbouring states (Ramadan 2012), and Roma inhabiting camps in Italy (Sigona 2015). For example, forcibly displaced Roma from the former Yugoslavia turned themselves into political subjects who shaped the political spaces of their "nomad camps." Nando Sigona speaks of "campzenship" to evoke the situated experiences of residents and their political membership in camps, where their everyday interactions reshape, adjust, and activate their rights, entitlements, and obligations. He emphasizes that these camps and similar institutions are contemporary spaces of politics (6).

The precarity of urban spaces, in which most of the world's refugees reside and which many move through on their journeys elsewhere, can lead to their participation in myriad counter-responses. For example, some forced migrants are challenging their precarious living conditions, including their inadequate housing and low social status (Banki 2013; Doerr 2010). Others are creating community organizations and community-based shelters and participating in various forms of political activism in urban settings of the Global South (Pascucci 2017; Şahin Mencütek 2020). Some are engaging in political acts such as building shelters for the precarious, as well as engaging in identity stripping, voluntary employment, "anti-deportation organizing and networking" (Darling 2017, 189), and social activism (De Genova 2010; Paret and Gleeson 2016). Still others are claiming the right to belong, to stay, and to leave (see chapters 5 and 6) – indeed, they are demanding the rights of citizenship, where citizenship is something performed (Isin 2017) in ways that can be ethical, cultural, social, and imaginative.

As they challenge their precarious living conditions, forced migrants engage with spaces from which they can expand their community-building and solidarity efforts. These spaces may offer them social support, jobs, a life with other people, and opportunities to raise families, participate in social activities, form networks as they work with various communities and engage as community members and political subjects, and make rights claims (see chapter 5). Political implications flow from the diversity and precarity of urban spaces. Trimikliniotis, Parsanoglou, and Tsianos (2015) see in urban spaces sites of "precarity-and-resistance." Migrants living in the precarious spaces of Athens, İstanbul, and Nicosia confront precarity as a key dimension of their daily lives and engage in struggles to claim their rights, which in turn fosters new forms of "commons through mobility," which are different from Lefebvre's (2003) "right to the city." Trimikliniotis, Parsanoglou, and Tsianos (2015, 6) suggest that while precarity can hardly be said to generate opportunities to rebel, its very liminality may spur an ever-increasing need and desire for "communing processes" (2015).

Such processes can help us understand the kinds of connections migrants make in their neighbourhoods and places of work and recreation and through their ties to community organizations and networks. In this regard, what interests Tazzioli and Walters (2019) about such alliances – which they refer to as "traversal alliances" – is "precisely the ways in which migrant solidarity practices to some extent manage (although often only in a very temporary and precarious way) not only to create connections between migrants and citizens but also to build common terrains – in terms of political claims and strategies" (182–3).

As they build common terrains, some migrants engage urban spaces through various forms of political mobilization. In the summer of 2015, more than 350,000 migrants moved through Hungary. The response to this was twofold: Hungarian citizens engaged in crisis narratives that sought to immobilize the migrants; and migrants and others engaged in tangible political mobilization that aimed to enable their mobility. Kallius, Monterescu, and Kumar Rajaram (2015) explore migrants' roles in urban Europe today and their horizontal modes of solidarity, which call into question the perceived "crisis" of violence they supposedly present to Europe and how that perception constricts their political agency. They contend that migrants' radical occupation of public spaces across Hungary has mobilized horizontal solidarities with them among EU citizens, activist networks, and NGOs. These solidarities took form as migrants and the treatment they received exposed the inequalities and exclusions underpinning public order and politics in Hungary. At Budapest's railway station and in other urban public spaces, supporters' chants echoed the pro-democracy protests in Syria, chants that called for mobility rights in the face of the Hungarian government's criminalization of people who helped migrants. Such solidarities "highlighted slippages between humanitarian and political action and led to the de facto collapse of the Dublin Regulation, the [restrictive] cornerstone of EU asylum legislation, which requires migrants to apply for asylum in the first EU country in which they arrive" (27).

Contra Trimikliniotis, Parsanoglou, and Tsianos (2015) and others, Şenses (2016) notes that Turkey has witnessed few "acts of citizenship" in the form of organized collective claims for justice or migrants' rights,

1.4 | Syrian refugees cross into Hungary, 26 August 2015.

unlike the United States, France, and other countries, which have seen many such acts. But he also notes that Turkey has experienced protests and awareness-raising activities, both negative and positive, especially vis-à-vis the growing number of Syrian refugees. For example, xenophobic actions against Syrians have inspired leftist political groups and pro-migrant civil-society organizations to launch street protests declaring, "Don't touch my brother/sister" (*Bianet*, 29 August 2014). More importantly, however, Syrian refugees are meanwhile participating in daily life as workers, pupils, business owners, tenants, teachers, community members, customers, parents, and university students. While enacting these everyday roles, they may question their precarious living conditions and challenge them; engage in activities that may disturb, even disrupt, routine practices of state agencies; participate in organized labour (see Şenses 2015); and form counter-responses that engage them in rights claims, such as the right to citizenship.

Every human being has a right to citizenship, which includes the right to mobility. In this regard, Balibar (2003) highlights the links between movement, claims, and citizenship:

> Surely freedom of movement is a basic claim that must be incorporated within the citizenship of *all people* (and not only for representatives of the 'powerful nations', for whom this is largely a given). But the *droit de cité* (rights to full citizenship) includes everything from residential rights as part of having a "normal" place in society to the exercise of political rights in those locations and groupings into which individuals and groups have been "thrown" by history and the economy. Let's not be afraid of saying it: these citizenship rights include the manner of their belonging in state communities, even, and indeed especially, if they belong to more than one such community. Given the above, the right to full citizenship is indissolubly linked to freedom of movement (42).

In other words, the experience of citizenship comprises an assemblage of activities that cannot be captured by legal definitions of citizenship. In line with the scholarship on critical citizenship, Isin (2012) asserts that migrant rights can be supported with reference to civil rights. Such rights-claiming activities are understood as enactments or performances of citizenship (Isin 2017). These performances focus on what people can do to achieve membership, inclusion, and participation in the political community. As Isin puts it, it is crucial to recognize "acts as those that 'create a scene,' which means both performance and disturbance" (2009, 379). They are embodied practices and play a crucial role not only in understanding the importance of acting with "dissent, resistance, or even disobedience" but also in interrogating whether it is possible to study politics "without its subjects, citizens, and their relational others, strangers, outsiders, and aliens" (2017, 520). In recognizing that non-citizens assert the right to claim rights, Basok and Candiz (2020) emphasize another type of right: the right "to move safely and securely within a territory without fear of being detained, robbed, assaulted or kidnapped" (2). They refer to this right as "a right to mobile citizenship." In the context of analyzing solidarity activism in

Mexico, they demonstrate how transit migrants, through their migrant journeys, negotiate border regimes, aim to avoid dangers and overcome obstacles, and receive aid and protection from migrant shelters and solidarity organizations.

Through their performances of citizenship, migrants and refugees have long been contributing to the building of new communities, new forms of belonging, and open spaces for fresh dialogue and engagement. Indeed, several studies of migration indicate that the migrant is one of the key protagonists of our time, directly part of economic and social transformations (Jonsson 2020), and scrupulously embedded in the histories of specific locations and in ongoing struggles for rights and recognition (e.g., Berg and Sigona 2013; Ilcan 2020; Khosravi 2011, 2021; Sanyal 2014). For us, it is crucial to understand how such struggles for rights and recognition occur within a field of tensions, such as precarious status, space, and movement. Doing so can in turn move the analysis beyond bounded views of counter-responses and solidarity practices.

Conclusion

This chapter has demonstrated that responses to forced migration consist of multiple and shifting actions and relations and involve numerous actors, authorities, and institutions within and across borders and territories at local, national, regional, and international levels. Such responses are enduring and commonly involve humanitarian and state actors (among others) effecting long-term change in a context in which discourses on forced migration are shaped by diverse authorities, practices, policies, and juridical arrangements and agreements. The result is often precarious conditions for forced migrants, namely refugees, asylum-seekers, and other migrants. But at the same time, these migrants are not silent: they respond through their participation in collective formations, struggles, and through claims-making.

The chapter began by examining historical responses to forced migration. After the destruction of the First World War, the League of Nations was founded, which launched the era of institutionalized humanitarianism and eventually led to refugee camps and massive urban refugee spaces. In the course of these developments, policies began to take form to address mobile populations. Around this same time, more and more international organizations began engaging in strategies that focused on relating people and places, connecting the local and the international, and linking the micro and the macro. All of this blurred the social divisions among displaced persons and raised the messier issues of protection and precarity confronting displaced persons and political refugees. This chapter also drew attention to how, after the Second World War, vast new groups of refugees fled their homelands only to find themselves trapped in legal limbo, without legal protection and enduring precarious conditions of life in camps and in various places in Germany, Austria, Italy, and elsewhere. Some domestic groups and bodies acknowledged their suffering and appealed to international organizations to extend protection to them. These appeals were articulated alongside requests by international organizations for an international definition of the term *refugee*. This led to the founding of the UNHCR as an international agency to protect refugees and of national and international schemes to control their movements (Barnett 2011; Glasman 2017; Loescher 2000). But the new definition of refugee, as established by the 1951 Refugee Convention, devalued refugees' political agency and blocked many groups from obtaining refugee status and thus from gaining access to certain forms of legal protection. That definition also downplayed the vast differences in living conditions experienced by refugees and the variations in their demands for care and assistance (Feldman 2007). This helped reduce them to generalized bodies, without personal attributes, acknowledged histories, or expected futures. Such have been some of the social and material consequences of refugee classifications.

Since 1945, the world has had to respond continuously to a seemingly endless series of crises – revolutions, wars, famines – that have displaced untold masses of people. The ongoing Syrian war is merely among the most recent. Responses to forced migration have varied, but especially since the 1980s, those responses have become progressively more restrictive, in rejoinder to the supposedly uncontainable "flows" of people and the threat they seem to pose to receiving countries' security and stability (Chimni 2009; Johnson 2014). Those responses have included new requirements for transit visas; new international obligations toward refugees; new agreements, such as the EU–Turkey

Statement (Heck and Hess 2016; Karadağ 2019; Strasser and Tibet 2019); and temporary protection. The latter, on which this book will focus, has reproduced refugee precarity. Although temporary protection is permissible under the 1951 Refugee Convention, states such as Australia, Denmark, Germany, Israel, and Turkey usually turn to it in order to deter local integration. It provides only minimal protection and expedites repatriation (Durieux 2015). This kind of temporary protection, we have argued, comprises many actors, policies, and practices in the production and governance of precarity, and the resulting interventions both embrace and disregard the migrant subject. We see all of this in diverse domains, within and across scales, and in distinct spaces and living conditions. The architecture of precarity, crafted with little commitment to the protection of human lives, takes three main forms: precarious *status*, precarious *space*, and precarious *movement*. Many of its practices aim to control displaced populations; they provide some rights to refugees but not others, and this opens the door to profound uncertainty. Having recognized that refugees are not mere victims of governing efforts and precarious situations, the last section of the chapter examined how counter-responses to conditions of precarity are a form of political activism. This discussion drew attention to how forced migrant groups have learned to challenge their living conditions and social status, to build community organizations, and to show they can mobilize politically and engage in rights-claiming activities.

CHAPTER TWO

Precarious Mobilities: Externalization Policies and the EU–Turkey Statement

The photograph of three-year-old Alan Kurdi lying dead on a Turkish beach made international news in early September 2015, galvanizing public outrage around the world at the ongoing plight of Syrian refugees (Mackinnon 2015; Kurdi 2018). Alan Kurdi, his five-year-old brother Galib, and their mother, Rehana, were among a group of Syrians whose boat capsized off the coast of Turkey near the Greek island of Kos, where they drowned.[1] While the Kurdi story is now well-known, it is but one of a multitude of tragedies that many Syrians, and others, have suffered while attempting to reach Europe by land or sea. Since the outbreak of the Syrian war in March 2011, many Syrian refugees, like the Kurdis, have undertaken precarious journeys (see chapter 6) in search of international protection, notwithstanding that most European countries have closed their borders, restricted access to asylum-seekers, and limited refugee resettlement rather than embracing their international legal obligations to protect refugees.

This chapter situates these precarious mobilities in the broader international context of the asylum regime and the European Union's (EU) externalization policies – specifically, through the EU's arrangements with Turkey as they relate to Syrian refugees. In response to the border and migration politics in play, Europe has moved toward enacting externalization policies whereby the EU and its individual member-states circumvent international commitments to protect refugees, often using third countries, such as Turkey, to resettle them temporarily. This has made movement more precarious for Syrians. More specifically, the EU and Turkey, in response to the Syrian refugee crisis, signed a statement on 18 March 2016 to manage irregular and refugee migration into

Europe (EC 2016b, 2019). This EU–Turkey Statement (more commonly referred to as the EU–Turkey Deal) is illustrative of what has been an at least decade-long approach to governing migration into Europe (Kale et al. 2018), including for asylum-seekers. As Gökalp Aras succinctly explains, "since the late 1990s, the EU has sought to develop an 'external dimension' of cooperation on immigration and asylum management with nearby sending or transit countries" (Boswell 2003, 619)." This external dimension is "motivated" by a "logic" of keeping "'unwanted' populations where they are" so as to "externalize European borders and policies beyond the EU." The point of doing so is to ensure that "transit and sending countries will act as the primary source – or at least, the first line – of control, through border management and visa policy, especially where third country nationals (TCNs) are passing through their territories. If these measures fail, these partner countries are expected to readmit unwanted migrants who have crossed to Europe through readmission agreements" (Gökalp Aras 2019, 187). This approach to externalization has enabled European countries to drastically reduce the numbers of refugees and asylum-seekers who arrive, while at the same time technically upholding their commitments to asylum (at least in theory) and the right to international protection, as outlined in the UN Convention Relating to the Status of Refugees (Geneva, 1951, hereafter the 1951 Refugee Convention), and the UN Protocol Relating to the Status of Refugees (New York, 1967, hereafter the 1967 Protocol).

The EU–Turkey Statement has enabled European countries to avoid being seen as circumventing their international legal commitments to protect refugees by framing Turkey as a safe third country that offers temporary protection (but see Lehner [2019] for a detailed critique of Turkey as a safe third country). The statement limits the resettlement of Syrian refugees in third countries in Europe; instead, they reside in Turkey under temporary protection. It has also made it harder for them to leave Turkey, except illegally, and as irregular migrants rather than as refugees (see below). In other words, the statement conveniently enables European countries to uphold an international refugee system and EU policies on asylum while, at the same time, making Europe more difficult to access, and for fewer people. This leaves many Syrians living in what are often dire conditions or risking their lives in an effort to reach Europe in order to claim asylum (see this chapter's final section and chapter 6).

The rest of this chapter examines the EU's increasing "externalization" of refugee policy and how it affects Syrians in Turkey by looking at the EU–Turkey Statement (March 2016) and how it has created precarious mobilities, as illustrated by some of the experiences of Syrians in their efforts to reach Europe.

Contextualizing the EU–Turkey Statement: Syrians as Neither Guests nor Refugees

Turkey hosts the largest number of Syrians in its region. According to the Turkish government, as of October 2020 some 3,626,734 Syrians were living in Turkey under temporary protection (Government of Turkey n.d.). When large numbers of Syrians began arriving in Turkey in 2011, the government quickly grew reluctant to recognize them as refugees; it received them first as "guests" and later under temporary protection (see chapter 3). As explained in the previous chapter, temporary protection is a mechanism for dealing with a mass influx of refugees by granting a person or group the right to enter or remain in a country for a limited time if they are at serious risk in their home country. However, temporary protection comes with the expectation that they will return home in the near future rather than resettle in the host country.

Turkey's restrictive policies[2] were such that prior to the arrival of Syrians, most non-European asylum-seekers who were deemed "conditional refugees" applied for refugee status determination (RSD) through the UNHCR in Turkey, which determined their eligibility for resettlement in a third country (Çorabatır 2016, 6). The UNHCR has a "mandate to conduct individual refugee status determination (RSD) interviews with asylum seekers originating in non-European countries" (6). After the 1994 Asylum Regulation was adopted, this practice, which was implemented in coordination with the Foreigners' Police – the national authority responsible for refugee and asylum issues – came to serve as a "parallel" procedure for non-European asylum-seekers. If eligible, the UNHCR, in coordination with the Foreigners' Police, sent the person's file to the embassy of a third country (e.g., Canada) for possible selection for resettlement. (In 2014, the Foreigners' Police was superseded by the Directorate General of Migration Management [DGMM] as the national authority responsible for refugee and asylum issues; see Biehl [2015, 61].) The mass arrival of Syrian refugees complicated this parallel process, creating what amounted to two processes for Syrian refugees. As President of the Ankara Research Centre on Asylum and Migration and former UNHCR spokesperson Metin Çorabatır explains, in the case of Syrians, one process for addressing their asylum claims was based on this individual RSD process. But now a second system had emerged for dealing with Syrians as a collective group based on their mass influx into Turkey.

As noted earlier, when Syrians began arriving, they were recognized as "guests" by the Turkish government. At the time, the Law on Foreigners and International Protection (LFIP) did not exist, and the Turkish government's plan was to contain Syrians in camps along the border. At first, the UNHCR refrained from processing individual asylum claims so as not to be seen as incentivizing people to leave the camps to make those claims (Çorabatır 2016, 8). Because of the rapidly increasing numbers of Syrian refugees, the UNHCR RSD process was unable to keep up. So the Turkish government issued a regulation in March 2012 extending Syrians' "temporary protection." This was meant to speed up the processing of large numbers of Syrians.

In April 2013, the LFIP further formalized temporary protection (Republic of Turkey 2013a; chapter 3). Eighteen months later, in October 2014, the Temporary Protection Regulation (TPR) was introduced. According to that regulation, prepared on the basis of Article 91 of the Law No. 6458 on Foreigners and International Protection, beneficiaries of temporary protection had a right to stay in Turkey until a more permanent solution was found for their situation. They were also protected against forcible return to Syria and granted most fundamental rights and needs such as for health care, education, and social assistance (Government of Turkey 2014). Thus Syrians had been granted certain rights and protections, though far fewer than had prescribed by the international refugee framework.[3]

Çorabatır explains that the TPR also "formalized the decision to refrain from registering individual Syrian asylum applications" and that this created "an alternative asylum system for large groups arriving in

Turkey that runs parallel to the asylum system for individual applicants." He notes that while "both are temporary in nature," the "one is a system of individual protection and UNHCR-coordinated resettlement and is largely inaccessible to Syrians," while "the other is a system of collective temporary protection within the country, for which Turkey is seeking international financial support" (2016, 8). As well, the system of individual RSD is based on the idea of third-country resettlement. In contrast, the second system is based on the idea that large groups of asylum-seekers will temporarily stay in Turkey but return to Syria before too long. Clearly, this second system hinders Syrians from making individual asylum claims through the UNHCR: "Syrian refugees do not, therefore, have the right to apply for individual asylum and, as a consequence, are excluded from the UNHCR resettlement program" (9). When greater resettlement quotas were instituted in 2014, resettlement was made available to those Syrians deemed the most vulnerable, based on UN vulnerability criteria and partial rather than full RSD procedures (9). But on 10 September 2018, the UNHCR stopped altogether the registration or referral of foreigners for international protection in Turkey (UNHCR 2018c). It had supported these processes in a limited way while the DGMM was still being set up, but only until the latter took over the entire process (UNHCR n.d., "Registration and RSD with the UNHCR").

As mandated by the 2013 LFIP, foreigners seeking international protection in Turkey are now expected to do so through the Provincial Directorate of Migration Management (PDMM) in the first city in which they arrive upon entering Turkey (UNHCR 2018c).[4] PDMMs oversee the registration of Syrians, issuing Foreigners' ID cards (*kimlik*) that give Syrians access to services (see chapters 3 and 4); these offices also oversee other processes related to providing international protection (UNHCR 2018c). Although it has halted registrations and referrals, the UNHCR continues to have access to information about those applying for international protection and to provide counselling services to anyone in need (UNHCR 2018c). Even so, according to the UNHCR's database, "while one in ten Syrian refugees met resettlement criteria in 2017, only one in 200 benefited from this opportunity last year (37,179 individuals were submitted in 2017, less than 0.7% of the total population)." These numbers were expected to continue to drop (UNHCR

2018e). The near impossibility of being resettled by the UNHCR in a third country was described to us by a Syrian lawyer in Gaziantep:

> The UNHCR established a number of centres in Turkey to receive refugees. There is a UNHCR centre here in Gaziantep. Syrian families register themselves as refugees at the UNHCR. After one year they hear from the UNHCR for an interview. First of all, not everyone is able to register. I do not know the criteria or the considerations. Until this moment, from all the people that I know, only two people managed to register and were called for an interview at the US embassy. They first registered at the UNHCR and after one year they were called for an interview with the UNHCR and then an interview at the US embassy. After the interview, it took one of them six months to obtain the US visa. The UNHCR centre in Gaziantep has been open for one year. I know many families who registered at the UNHCR and did not hear from the centre yet. I personally went to the UNHCR and they refused to register me, and I have no idea why. (23 June 2015)

We asked this lawyer why so few Syrians were able to register:

> The [UNHCR] interview was too short and brief. After this two-minutes' interview, they will tell you if you can register or not. They mainly ask about the reason for registering and leaving Turkey. After you explain your case, they usually say that there is nothing unique about your circumstances and they are similar to the conditions of other Syrian refugees in Turkey. They will tell you that you do not have a particular case.

As the lawyer's observations indicate, the UNHCR – and the international community more broadly – are willing, given the scale of displacement, to leave most Syrians under temporary protection in Turkey, which precludes them from seeking individual RSD for third-country resettlement as refugees.

Yet Turkey's temporary protection has made movement more precarious for Syrians. Syrians can almost never receive refugee status through the UNHCR. As well, in line with its own LFIP law, Turkey also rarely provides them with exit visas (Republic of Turkey 2013a). Moreover, if Syrians under temporary protection travel to another country and later return to Turkey, they *may* be granted temporary protection but this is not guaranteed. As Cavidan Soykan (2017, 90) explains, "Turkey added a temporary provision into the Temporary Protection Regulation on 5 April 2016 for Syrian returnees. Under this provision, after being readmitted, Syrians may be granted temporary protection upon request. However, this provision does not guarantee automatic access to the temporary protection mechanisms for Syrians." According to Article 12(1) of Turkey's Temporary Protection Regulation, temporary protection status ceases when a "beneficiary leaves Turkey voluntarily"; "avails him or herself of the protection of a third country"; or is "admitted to a third country on humanitarian grounds or for resettlement" (AIDA n.d.; Republic of Turkey 2013). A beneficiary of temporary protection who wishes "to exit Turkey permanently [must] obtain an exit permit from the Directorate General of Migration Management through the Provincial Directorate of Migration Management" of the city in which he or she first registered (UNHCR 2017d; Republic of Turkey 2013). As a result, many Syrians have found their mobility to be further restricted: without access to an exit visa and a legal way to leave Turkey, they are forced to remain in Turkey, living under temporary protection and precarious conditions (see also Baban, Ilcan, and Rygiel 2017b; Ilcan, Rygiel, and Baban 2018; chapters 3 and 4).

Many Syrians find this situation unbearable (see chapters 3 and 4) and attempt to cross into Europe in more clandestine ways, sometimes resorting to human smugglers and travelling in tiny dinghies. As the Syrian lawyer in Gaziantep stated:

Syrians do not feel secure or safe here. They do not feel that they have a future here. This explains the huge numbers of desperate Syrian families, young men, young girls who are willing to get on those "death boats" to leave in spite of the increased death toll. People were left with no other alternatives but to do this high-risk journey looking for secure places where they can have protection and [a] future.

The rest of this chapter explores the border politics between Turkey and the EU – politics that make movement even more precarious for Syrians (see also chapter 6).

A European Crisis: Failing to Protect Refugees

The majority of Syrians who have fled the Syrian war and sought protection in neighbouring countries, especially Turkey, encounter less than desirable living conditions. Social assistance is inadequate, work is poorly paid, and access to education and housing is minimal. These last are crucial to their efforts to rebuild their lives (see chapters 3 and 4). For many people, what they encounter in Turkey falls far below the lofty promises of the 1951 Refugee Convention (on refugee rights, see Hathaway 2005 and 2007). It is hardly a surprise, then, that some Syrians choose to cross into Europe by clandestine and often dangerous means. It should also be noted, however, that Syrians are motivated to cross into Europe, despite the risks, by other factors besides the harsh living conditions in Turkey: greater security; parents' aspirations for their children's futures, such as opportunities for education and employment, which may not be afforded to them in neighbouring countries; and a desire to be closer to family members who have already resettled in Europe (Almustafa 2019; McMahon and Sigona 2018). Syrian refugees may also, rightly or wrongly, imagine Europe to be a place of peace and wealth (*Telegraph* n.d.). Many expect to find a Promised Land, only to quickly discover of course that the reality is often quite different. Asylum processes differ enormously between European countries, as do opportunities for refugee status. Living conditions for newcomers also vary greatly, as does the welcome they receive and thus opportunities for social inclusion.[5]

In the first ten months of 2020, as many as 88,264 people crossed the Mediterranean land and sea borders into Europe (some 68,931 by sea, 19,263 by land) – a significant drop from previous years, which saw a total of 861,630 known crossings of those borders, and some 1,543 known deaths or disappearances (UNHCR n.d., "Mediterranean Situation").[6] Many scholars view this tragic death toll as the result of the EU's broader strategy for managing its borders (Brian and Laczko

2014; Mountz 2020; Rygiel 2016; Squire et al. 2017; Stierl 2016a, 2016b; Williams and Mountz 2018).[7]

Many European countries are deeply reluctant to resettle refugees. As Amnesty International (AI, n.d.) notes, "In total, 162,151 resettlement places have been offered globally since the start of the Syria crisis, which equates to a mere 3.6% of the total population of Syrian refugees in Lebanon, Jordan, Iraq, Egypt and Turkey." When refugee arrivals were at their highest in 2015 (what has come to be called the "long summer of migration" [Kasparek and Speer 2015]), it was Germany that accepted the greatest number of Syrians – "about 39,987 places for Syrian refugees through its humanitarian admission programme and individual sponsorship," or "about 54% of the EU total" (AI n.d.). Sweden came second, with some 30,000 (Migration Policy Centre n.d.). "The remaining 26 EU countries had pledged around 30,903 resettlement places, or around 0.7% of the Syrian refugee population in the main host countries" (AI n.d.). In April 2016 the European Commission (EC) called on EU member-states to increase their efforts at relocation and resettlement, labelling progress to date "unsatisfactory" and the situation "urgent." It added that "based on the information received from Member States and Dublin Associated States [Dublin Regulation of 2013], 5,677 displaced people in need of protection were resettled to 15 countries since the start of the EU resettlement scheme agreed on 20 July 2015." At its peak, the spaces offered to resettle Syrians and other refugees by European countries thus fell far short of the need. Even while the need continues to grow, the spaces for resettlement continue to shrink every year. For example, in 2018, UNHCR Turkey submitted the names of 16,042 Syrian refugees for resettlement; only 8,979 of them departed for resettlement. In 2019, 8,840 Syrian refugee cases were submitted; only 5,522 of them resettled (UNHCR n.d., "Resettlement Data"). More globally, the UNHCR notes that while the number of refugees in need of resettlement is projected to be about 1.4 million (in 2019), resettlement places in 2017 totalled a mere 75,000. Based on such figures, "It would take 18 years for the world's most vulnerable refugees to be resettled" (UNHCR 2018a).

But Europe's failed response is due to more than an unwillingness to resettle Syrians and others. It also reflects the EU's broader approach to managing its borders through externalization policies, of which the EU–Turkey Statement[8] is only the most recent example. As Kristen Biehl (2015, 66) notes, "Since the mid-2000s in particular, Turkey has also been cooperating extensively with the EU on issues of migration management, setting into motion the gradual 'Europeanization' of national immigration and asylum policies and border regime practices, which goes in tandem with securitization (Düvell 2012; Faist and Ette 2007; Hess 2012; Özçürümez and Şenses 2011)."

This "Europeanization," moreover, has embodied (especially since 2001) the securitization of migration and more restrictive border controls (Bigo 2002; Collyer 2006; Guild 2009; Huysmans 2006; Kale et al. 2018, 6). As many scholars have observed, this "Fortress Europe" approach, or the "external dimension" of EU immigration and asylum policy (Boswell 2003; Haddad 2008), involves policies and practices of "externalization" (Crépeau 2013; Frelick, Kysel, and Podkul 2016; Gökalp Aras 2019).

Externalization refers to "extraterritorial State actions to prevent migrants, including asylum-seekers, from entering the legal jurisdictions or territories of destination countries or regions or of making them legally inadmissible without individually considering the merits of their protection claims" (Frelick, Kysel, and Podluk 2016, 190). As many scholars have pointed out, countries that are signatories to the 1951 Refugee Convention thereby circumvent their responsibilities to protect refugees and their rights (Crépeau 2013; Frelick, Kysel, and Podkul 2016; Hathaway and Gammeltoft-Hansen 2015; Hyndman and Mountz 2008). The former UN special rapporteur on migrants' human rights, François Crépeau, criticized this approach:

> The European Union thus appears to be attempting to ensure that foreign nationals never in fact reach European Union territory, or, if they do so, are immediately returned. This is particularly troubling as it means that the responsibility for migration control is shifted to countries outside the European Union and that, consequently, the recourse of those migrants to human rights mechanisms within the European Union becomes legally restricted or practically impossible. (2013, 14)

But at the same time, it is important not to read the above statement simply as another example of the EU exerting its power to externalize its border control policies, for such interpretations "tend to reduce Turkey's role to a simple enlargement of the EU border regime and a passive object of the EU's externalization policies, [which is] insufficient when attempting to explain the current Turkish migration regime" (Heck and Hess 2017, 38). The statement needs also to be understood as reflecting Turkey's domestic politics and policies (see chapters 3 and 4) and its changing migration and asylum regime as well. According to Heck and Hess, "Undocumented migrants in Turkey have become a major theme of the accession negotiations with the European Union," and Turkey has emerged as "both a transit and immigration country." This has led to "a certain institutionalization of the migration and border regime in close interaction with the European Union since 2000" (2017, 40). As Karadağ (2019) illustrates in her examination of diplomatic relations and the practices of Turkish border guards, Turkey has also played the "constitutive role of the 'other' in shaping the framework of the process." The fact is that European externalization of migration policies requires ongoing cooperation with non-EU countries like Turkey and is driven by a desire for greater burden-sharing but also by Turkey's own domestic interests in using cooperation on the issue to further its own interests (Kale et al. 2018, 6).

Externalization policies and practices also reveal the convention signatories' contradictory approaches. They have pledged to develop rights regimes for asylum-seekers and refugees within their borders, yet they are working hard to prevent such groups from ever arriving there in order to be able to take advantage of those rights. As Frelick, Kysel, and Podkul explain, "Countries that have developed generally rights-sensitive standards and procedures for assessing protection claims of asylum-seekers within their jurisdictions have simultaneously established barriers that prevent migrants, including asylum-seekers, from setting foot on their territories or otherwise triggering protection obligations" (2016, 190). Externalization thus allows many signatories to pursue a Janus-faced asylum policy. The EU–Turkey Statement poses obstacles to Syrian refugees, who make risky journeys to Europe in the hope of claiming asylum in EU countries. By keeping Syrians in

Turkey and away from the EU, where they might claim refugee status, the EU–Turkey Statement places roadblocks on one of their very few avenues to a better life.

Externalization regimes, which are hardly unique to Europe, use a range of tools, such as visa restrictions; carrier sanctions; interdiction by third countries; offshore processing and detention of asylum-seekers (e.g., Australia) (HRW 2002 and 2014; Hyndman and Mountz 2008); bilateral and multilateral understandings, such as Readmission Agreements (Cassarino 2007; Migreurop 2005); and use of safe third countries, as in the US–Canada Safe Third Country Agreement (Macklin 2005). Other mechanisms push back asylum-seekers and irregular migrants along the routes they have already travelled, thus creating "paths of expulsion" (Mezzadra and Neilson 2003a). These latter may include formal deportation and detention but also informal mechanisms, such as "black deportations" along the Turkish–Greek land and sea borders. Between 2009 and 2010, the EU's European Border and Coast Guard Agency (FRONTEX, from French: *Frontières extérieures*) recorded a 45 per cent increase in migrants crossing at the Greek land and sea borders with Turkey (FRONTEX 2011, 44). At the time, estimates were that some 130,000 migrants crossed into Greece by sea or along the Turkish border every year, with as many as 7,000 arrests in September 2011 alone (Nielsen 2012). Migrants who attempted to cross the Evros/ Meriç River between Greece and Turkey were subject to unofficial and illegal "black deportations" – they were pushed back across the river, to border points such as Edirne in Turkey, and also off the Greek islands of Samos and Lesvos.

This unofficial policy allowed Greek border authorities to avoid processing asylum-seekers and irregular migrants. Instead, they were returned to Turkey, often by precarious means, such as in rubber boats with holes poked into their sides, leading to many drownings and deaths (Pro-Asyl 2007; see also Rygiel 2014a, 149–50). Though less common today, this practice still occurs. According to its "Desperate Journeys" report, the UNHCR and its partners received allegations of push-backs by state authorities, including in Bulgaria, Croatia, Greece, Hungary, Romania, Serbia, Spain, and the former Yugoslav Republic of Macedonia (UNHCR 2017a). As one Syrian man recounted to us regarding his family's journey:

2.1 | Evros/Meriç River, land border crossing between Turkey and Greece.

They had to cross a river that separates Turkey from Greece at that point of the borders. The smugglers put them in a small rubber boat. The boat is designed for 5 persons, but the smugglers forced 10 people inside. He then ran away. They crossed the river and reached the Greek side, where the Greek police, supported by the foreign police, most properly [sic] German, attacked the boat and hit the people and forced them to go back to Turkey in the same boat. Those who could not get inside the boat were beaten by wooden batons and were thrown in the river. They were all beaten, including the women, and were totally wet. They did not know where to go. They tried to call the smuggler, but his phone was off, and the network coverage was bad. They were lost. They tried to remember the way back through the forest, but they could not. So, they started shouting loudly, calling for help. After a while, the Turkish army came and took them to a military camp. (Stockholm, 8 July 2016)

After thinking they had reached Athens, the man discovered this was not the case. They were being kept in substandard detention conditions:

> The Turkish army took their travel documents and their mobile phones. They managed to call me from a mobile phone that was hidden by another detainee. The Turkish army did not treat them badly like the Greek police, but the conditions were terrible at the camp. The army divided them in groups and separated women from men. They put them in big rooms with no beds or mattresses. The floor was covered with dry hay and rotten grass, and they had some dirty blankets to use for covering themselves. The conditions were terrible, and the group was big.

The Foreigners' Police in Turkey ultimately registered the family members and sent them back to İstanbul, where they began the journey again, but this time from İzmir (see the final section).

While these examples of deportations may reflect a logic of security – closing the borders to unwanted arrivals – authorities sometimes justify externalization in more humanitarian terms (Frelick, Kysel, and Podluk 2016, 194). They may claim to be halting smuggling, which can risk refugees' and migrants' lives. They may talk about "capacity building" (i.e., developing human and institutional resources) in both countries of origin and countries of first arrival or transit (IFRC 2015). They may claim to be strengthening the rule of law, supporting human rights, or sponsoring better standards of living through economic development, thereby addressing the "root causes" of migration.

Notwithstanding all these claims, externalizing policies and practices are draconian and make it harder for asylum-seekers and refugees to resettle in places where they might claim refugee status and actualize their rights as refugees. Such policies and practices can also endanger refugees and asylum-seekers while they are on the move and prevent them from realizing a whole range of rights they have even during their difficult journey. First of all, they place refugees at risk of refoulement, in contravention of the 1951 Refugee Convention (Article 33). According to that article, no country may return a refugee to another territory where that person might face death, torture, or other cruel treatment. Signatories must provide access to safety for refugees and, when "mixed flows" of people are arriving, must properly screen them to determine eligibility for a claim to asylum. Failure to do so can place bone fide refugees at risk of refoulement, which can lead to torture and even death. Externalization jeopardizes refugees' rights throughout the migration process. As Frelick, Kysel, and Podluk (2016, 197) explain, this is because

> regardless of their status or location, migrants have a range of fundamental rights that can be implicated by migration-control externalization practices and which protect migrants against abuse throughout the migration process. These include rights that are implicated during transit, including while on the high seas and over land, if and when detained as well as during the expulsion or deportation process ... The perilous journey undertaken by many migrants, including on the high seas, as well as clandestine efforts by some to cross increasingly militarized (and sometimes closed) borders, can expose them to violations of the right to life and the right to seek and enjoy asylum and can additionally implicate their rights as victims of crime and abuse (such as by traffickers).

Thus, externalization policies make access to the asylum process more difficult, besides placing asylum-seekers at greater risk as they move in search of protection. Alison Mountz (2020, xxi) points to the emergence of "a proliferating series of spaces of confinement and limbo that migrants move through for years: the camp, the ship, the detention center, the island"; she refers to all this as "the enforcement archipelago" (xx), explaining that this "enforcement archipelago" is causing "asylum's death" – that is, the physical, ontological, and political death of asylum (5). She notes that "evolving and expanding state mobilities contribute directly to physical deaths through the global growth of offshore policing and detention" as well as to shrinking spaces of asylum or to its "ontological disappearance," meaning that "the very existence of asylum becomes threatened with extinction" (4). The shrinking of asylum spaces and the deaths of asylum-seekers together signal "the disappearance of asylum as a possibility worth fighting for: its political death" (5). The EU–Turkey Statement provides an important example of how externalization policies are impacting Syrian refugees in Turkey. Many of them are dying, and with them the very concept of asylum, as they undertake precarious journeys in search of safety in Europe.

The "EU–Turkey Statement"

The EU–Turkey Statement (18 March 2016) has set out various initiatives to address the so-called Syrian refugee crisis and to manage migration into Europe. These include important incentives such as EU visa liberalization for Turks (Kale et al. 2018) – a promise that has not been kept; a further promise of an initial 3 billion euros (with more to follow) from the EU under the Facility for Refugees in Turkey (EC 2018); and, most controversially, the "one-to-one initiative": for every Syrian who travels without authorization to Greece and is returned to Turkey, EU member-states agree to resettle one Syrian from Turkey (European Council 2016).

The "one-to-one initiative" is among the more controversial sections of the Statement. Under its terms, Turkey has agreed to (re)admit Syrians who have travelled as irregular migrants to Greece and, in exchange for each one, to send another Syrian in Turkey to resettle in Europe. The EC justifies this as a means to replace irregular migration along dangerous routes with more orderly resettlement. According to the EC, "This 1:1 mechanism aims to replace irregular flows of migrants travelling in dangerous conditions across the Aegean Sea by an orderly and legal resettlement process." This, it insists, is not a "collective expulsion":

All new irregular migrants crossing from Turkey into Greek islands as from 20 March 2016 will be returned to Turkey. This will take place in full accordance with EU and international law, thus excluding any kind of collective expulsion. All migrants will be protected in accordance with the relevant international standards and in respect of the principle of non-refoulement. It will be a temporary and extraordinary measure, which is necessary to end the human suffering and restore public order. Migrants arriving in the Greek islands will be duly registered and any application for asylum will be processed individually by the Greek authorities in accordance with the Asylum Procedures Directive, in cooperation with UNHCR. Migrants not applying for asylum or whose application has been found unfounded or inadmissible in accordance with the said directive will be returned to Turkey.

Yet despite this invocation of EU and international law and non-refoulement, some commentators have criticized the Statement precisely because it *does* contravene international law and threaten refoulement. For example, according to Amnesty International's Europe Director, John Dalhuisen, "The 'double-speak' this Statement is cloaked in fails to hide the European Union's dogged determination to turn its back on a global refugee crisis, and wilfully ignore its international obligations" (AI 2016a). He adds, "Guarantees to scrupulously respect international law are incompatible with the touted return to Turkey of all irregular migrants arriving on the Greek islands as of Sunday. Turkey is not a safe country for refugees and migrants, and any return process predicated on its being so will be flawed, illegal and immoral, whatever phantom guarantees precede this pre-declared outcome" (2016a).

Many scholars, refugee activists, and human rights bodies doubt whether Turkey is a safe third country for Syrian refugees (see, for example, AI 2016b; HRW 2016; Roman, Baird, and Radcliffe 2016; Ulusoy and Battjes 2017). As Ulusoy and Battjes (2017, 10) note, "The EU Asylum Procedures Directive requires that a person may only be readmitted to a 'safe third country' that guarantees effective access to protection." Scholars contend that the agreement risks violating the principle of non-refoulement and that Turkey's asylum system does not guarantee protection for returned asylum-seekers.[9] Moreover, according to Kemal Kirişçi, former director of the Turkey Project at the Brookings Institution – a public policy think tank in Washington, DC – while the EU may consider Turkey a safe country of asylum (see note 33 and

Ulusoy and Battjes 2017), many others have raised serious concerns about Turkey's commitment to democracy and the rule of law (Kirişçi 2016, 83). Alex Neve, the Secretary-General of Amnesty International Canada, notes that AI has repeatedly highlighted Turkey's inadequate protection of refugees' rights. Whatever the EU–Turkey Statement says, "Turkey is not a safe place for all Syrian refugees, and therefore … the right of Syrian refugees to seek safety elsewhere is totally understandable … It's something that needs to be respected." Furthermore, the Statement "decides that the refugee who has embarked on a journey is suddenly somehow now not a person with rights but a commodity that now can be swapped back into Turkey while we bring out another refugee." Thus, it "violates international law because of the notion that the refugee, who is being forced back to Turkey, is being forced back to a country which we do not believe can be considered safe" (interview, Waterloo, Ontario, 13 June 2016).

Like Amnesty International, the UNHCR condemned the agreement for potentially violating international law. The current UN High Commissioner for Refugees, Filippo Grandi, warned against returning people without ensuring protection for them within Turkey:

> [Any] asylum-seeker should only be returned to a third state, if the responsibility for assessing the particular asylum application in substance is assumed by the third country; the asylum-seeker will be protected from refoulement; and if the individual will be able to seek and, if recognized, enjoy asylum in accordance with accepted international standards, and have full and effective access to education, work, health care and, as necessary, social assistance. (Spindler and Clayton 2016)

The UNHCR's Europe Bureau director, Vincent Cochetel, echoed these remarks:

> The collective expulsion of foreigners is prohibited under the European Convention of Human Rights [Rome, 1950]. An agreement that would be tantamount to a blanket return to a third country is not consistent with European law, not consistent with international law. (Spindler and Clayton 2016)

Such sweeping criticisms from leading refugee officials and organizations are telling.

The Statement brings to the fore the risks involved in using externalization to handle Syrian refugees. Clearly, the EU risks shirking its responsibilities vis-à-vis the 1951 Refugee Convention. It may refoule Syrians to Turkey without first providing them with an asylum hearing. It justifies their return by taking Turkey's word that it is a safe third country. But as we saw earlier, that is highly questionable (see chapters 3 and 4 on living conditions facing Syrians there). Moreover, several court cases have cast doubt on the Statement's assumption. In a 2016 case, a Syrian man challenged his deportation back to Turkey under the Statement, and the Greek appeals committee in Lesvos ruled in his favour: "The committee has judged that the temporary protection which could be offered by Turkey to the applicant, as a Syrian citizen, does not offer him rights equivalent to those required by the Geneva convention [1951]" (quoted in *Guardian* 2016; Zalan 2016). Despite this ruling, however, the EC defended the Statement at the time, claiming that the ruling did not challenge the Statement, since it stipulated that all asylum-seekers must have the right to a hearing and that "there would be no blanket, no automatic return of asylum seekers" (Zalan 2016, n.p.). And in September 2017, in a case brought by two Syrian men, Greece's Council of State ruled their asylum claims inadmissible (AI 2017b). One was a twenty-one-year-old nursing student in Syria whom Turkey, after its police had arrested and beaten him, sent back to Syria; on his next attempt to cross into Turkey, a group of armed men attacked him and killed eleven of his companions (AI 2017b). Commenting on the ruling, AI's John Dalhuisen exclaimed:

> Today's ruling sets an ominous precedent for many other asylum-seekers who have fled conflict and persecution and are currently stranded on the Greek islands. Syrian refugees currently in detention following the rejection of their appeals are particularly at risk … These decisions breach a very clear principle: Greece and the EU should not be sending asylum-seekers and refugees back to a country in which they cannot get effective protection."

Worries over human rights were exacerbated after a failed coup in Turkey in July 2016 and post-coup arrests (such as that of German-Turkish journalist Deniz Yücel in İstanbul in February 2017 [Hauge 2017, 4]), at which time Amnesty International (2017a) issued a statement that "Turkey has become an even less safe space for refugees and asylum-seekers since the coup attempt." These individual cases may not, however, be the exception. As noted by members of the Greek Council for Refugees (GCR) Legal Unit, "From the launch of the EU-Turkey statement on 20 March 2016 until 31 December 2018, 1,484 individuals have been returned to Turkey on the basis of the statement of those, 337 were Syrian nationals. 36 of them have been returned on the basis that their asylum claims were found inadmissible at second instance on the basis of the 'safe third country' concept" (Kostantinou and Georgopoulou 2018, 14). Moreover, deportations of Syrians have continued; dozens were deported between January and September 2019 (HRW 2019c; and see chapter 3). Stories like these of Syrians detained, beaten, and deported suggest strongly that Turkey may not be a safe third country.

The Statement also proposes that Turkey open up its labour market to Syrians living under temporary protection. It also toughens visa requirements for Syrians and other nationalities, while liberalizing them for Turks entering the EU's Schengen area (EC 2016b). There was a time when Syrians did not need a visa for Turkey. The two countries had been mutually visa-free since 2009 (Heck and Hess 2017). It seems that Turkey's new visa requirements for Syrians followed the negotiation of the Statement.

These new visa requirements took many Syrians and aid workers by surprise; according to one relief worker, there was a widely held belief that many Syrians had gone home to visit family for the holidays, only to have Turkey deny them re-entry without a visa. "Last week is [the end of] Ramadan [the holy month of fasting] and Bayram and most of the Syrians came to ask that whether they can go to Syria easily or not. But we advised them to not go. Because then they return and the temporary protections expires and maybe they can't even come back because of these visa issues also. There is no open door anymore" (interview, İstanbul, 13 July 2016). As noted earlier, Article 12(1) of Turkey's

Temporary Protection Regime (TPR) states that temporary protection may cease when "a beneficiary leaves Turkey voluntarily" (AIDA n.d.; Republic of Turkey 2013). Furthermore, although Article 6 of the TPR guarantees Syrian refugees protection from refoulement, the government can suspend temporary protection on the grounds of a risk to national security, public order, or public health. Thus, Syrians under temporary protection live with uncertainty as to whether, if they cross into Syrian border communities for the holiday, they will be allowed back into the Turkey. In 2019, thousands of Syrians returned home for the Muslim Feast of Sacrifice, Eid al-Adha. According to the office of the governor of Kilis, 60,000 Syrian refugees were granted permission to return home for Eid al-Fitr and Eid al-Adh (Ahval 2019a). Border crossings were organized at Öncüpınar in southern Kilis province to enable Syrians to cross into places that had been liberated from Daesh with the understanding that they would be allowed back into Turkey after the holiday. One UNHCR official explained:

> Syrian citizens are still required to obtain a visa before travelling to Turkey; but it is exceptionally not requested for those who leave Turkey for seeing their relatives during the holidays that the Turkish government regulates their visits to Syria. However, we will monitor the returns from Syria after the holiday in August 2019 since there are now hundreds of people ... forcibly returned to Syria on the grounds of public security. (July 2019)

It seems that policy enforcement is left greatly to the discretion of officials. Reports suggest that about 2,500 Syrians returned to Turkey after the August holiday (Ahval 2019a). We can be certain, however, that the visa regulations arising from the Statement, which are now being imposed on Syrians, have greatly complicated Syrians' lives and made their movement more difficult.

Finally, in addition to opening up labour markets and imposing visa requirements, the EU–Turkey Statement called for an initial EU investment of 3 billion euros under the Facility for Refugees in Turkey (EC 2020), to support Syrians there with food, shelter, education, and health care. This was followed by a second allocation of another 3 billion euros in March 2018 (EC 2018). In return, Turkey would "take any necessary measures to prevent new sea or land routes for illegal migration opening from Turkey to the EU, and will cooperate with neighbouring states as well as the EU to this effect." It would increase "security efforts by the Turkish coast guard and police and enhanced information sharing"; take "the necessary steps and agree [to] any necessary bilateral arrangements, including the presence of Turkish officials on Greek islands and Greek officials in Turkey as from 20 March 2016, to ensure liaison and thereby facilitate the smooth functioning of these arrangements"; and firm up "measures against migrant smugglers and [welcome] the establishment of the NATO activity on the Aegean Sea" (EC 2016a). Turkey's greater role in border policing hit unaccompanied minors especially hard. According to Tibet (2017), the Statement further restricted mobility rights for Syrian youths: the government moved some Syrian teenagers to the Adana Sarıçam camp, who had been living in the İstanbul centre for youth asylum-seekers, Çocuk ve Gençlik Merkezi (ÇOGEM, Children and Youth Support Centre), run by the Ministry of Family and Social Policies. The Statement went on to encourage Turkey to control Syrians' movement into Europe even more tightly, share more information, and coordinate with Greek police to prevent, arrest, and detain Syrians (and others) arriving in Greece.

Regarding externalization, the Statement, instead of providing safe passage into the EU and resettling more asylum-seekers and refugees arriving from Turkey and other front-line states, limits arrivals to the EU, deters asylum claims, and controls refugees' mobility. It also normalizes Turkey's temporary protection as the best way to address the crisis. This has solidified a new norm: refugees are now treated not as political subjects with a "right to have rights," under the 1951 Refugee Convention, but as helpless victims, subject to temporary protection and dependent on humanitarian assistance from governments and NGOs, or as unauthorized travellers subject to security measures as if they were criminals (see chapter 1; see also Baban, Ilcan, and Rygiel 2017a). Legal scholar Audrey Macklin points out that externalization enables a kind of discursive disappearance of the refugee as a political figure:

> Refugees are vanishing from the territory of wealthy industrialized nations. I do not mean that refugees are literally disappearing. Despite the best efforts of western governments to deter them, thousands of asylum seekers do manage to arrive and lodge refugee claims each year. I refer here not to the legal and material reality of refugees, but rather to the erosion of the idea that people who seek asylum may actually be refugees. This dispiriting turn in public sentiment is enabled by a series of legal and popular conjunctions that produce what I call the discursive disappearance of the refugee. (Macklin 2005, 365)

In this sense the Statement "reconstitutes refugees," turning them from political subjects into humanitarian subjects, and thus eligible for humanitarian assistance rather than refugee rights (Baban, Ilcan, and Rygiel 2017b, 79).

In summary, the EU–Turkey Statement epitomizes recent externalization approaches that have circumvented international commitments to protect refugees. It deters their arrival in Europe and uses third countries, such as Turkey, to shelter them temporarily. Meanwhile, Europe resettles only a handful, thus paying lip service to its international commitments, while rendering most refugees precarious – irregular and *illegal* – as they make the dangerous trip to Europe to seek asylum and, if they survive, await their refugee determination. This process renders those who arrive in Europe much more vulnerable and subject to potentially greater abuse and exploitation. And it leaves those who reach Turkey and remain there much more vulnerable and precarious, with temporary protection and minimal rights and usually just getting by through underpaid and often exploitative work, as chapter 3 reveals.

Precarious Crossings

The difficulties for Syrian refugees living under temporary protection in Turkey compel many to try to reach Europe, despite the perils. In this chapter's final section, we discuss some of the conditions and realities of this journey (see also chapter 6, which offers first-hand accounts). Many Syrians who decide to leave Turkey locate smuggling networks in larger cities such as İstanbul, while others travel to the coast, often passing though İzmir. In the past, many refugees and migrants crossed the Turkish–Greek land border along the Evros/Meriç River. Since 2010, however, border police have detected large numbers of illegal migrants and refused entry to many. To deter further border crossings at this land border, a security fence was built along some 10 kilometres of a 12.5-kilometre stretch of land. Operation Aspida (Shield), conducted in 2012, deployed some 1,800 border police to the region, and FRONTEX led operations such as Poseidon Land and Poseidon Sea (now merged as Poseidon Rapid Intervention). In his end-of-mission statement, former UN Special Rapporteur François Crépeau noted that such measures "have resulted in a renewed influx of irregular migrants via the islands of the eastern Aegean Sea, with boats arriving on the different islands almost daily" (Frenzen 2012, n.p.). Thus, greater security has forced many more refugees leaving Turkey to attempt more precarious sea routes to Greek islands such as Lesvos. The EU–Turkey Statement, and parallel measures, have thus made their journey that much more precarious (see also Ilcan, Rygiel, and Baban 2018). As one relief agency worker explained to us: "We believe that travel restrictions are influenced by the new Statement with the EU, and they are in place to prevent Syrians to get to the coast easily" (İstanbul, 13 July 2016). Whether or not the Statement intended it, some refugees are experiencing more restricted mobility, and leaving Turkey has become more difficult for them.

Many refugees and migrants travel from İstanbul or other major cities directly to the coast, often using smuggling networks. One Syrian with whom we spoke described that journey to us:

> I found out from those friends and contacts about smugglers involved in facilitating the mobility of Syrians out of Turkey. Many of them were Kurdish or Syrians who live in İstanbul. So, I started collecting names and numbers and providing them to my in-laws, who in their turn managed to meet many smugglers at their hotel in the smuggling hub Aksaray [neighbourhood in İstanbul]. As you know, smuggling business in Turkey did not start with the Syrians. It has been there for the Afghans and the Iraqis. So, it was not a new business, but there were new people, the Syrians. (Stockholm, 8 July 2016)

Many migrants and asylum-seekers travel to İzmir on Turkey's west coast, where they seek out smugglers who will take them by sea (Yıldız and Uzgören 2016; Yıldız 2017). In İzmir they may make connections in cafés or hotels in the Basmane neighbourhood, and many stay for a night or two on "Otel Caddesi" (Hotel Street), relatively cheaply (back in 2013 for as little as ten Turkish lira [five dollars] a night). Many of the local hotel owners and employees have links to smuggling networks (Heck and Hess 2017; McNeil and Dlewati 2016).[10] The extensive network in Basmane charges about $2,000 per person (interview, Stockholm, 8 July 2018). One Syrian refugee described the process:

> We discovered later that all smugglers are connected through Turkish networks. You can't be involved in smuggling if you are not working with a Turkish boss. They take a percentage per passenger. The money paid by refugees is divided between the Syrian smuggler and the Turkish big boss. The Turkish smuggler provides the boat, secures the route, and decides on the point of departure. The Syrian or the Iraqi or the Afghani smugglers get the people and bring them to the meeting point.

Smugglers often take passengers at night to a more remote spot along the coast, somewhere between Ayvalık and Assos (the closest point to Lesvos, where one can see the lights from the main port town of Mytilene quite clearly).

More recently, however, many Syrians have crossed on their own. Many shops in Basmane now sell life jackets, floaties, and even dinghies directly to Syrians. Unfortunately, some sell substandard life jackets without sufficient foam to keep the wearer afloat. According to Katherine Hynes, a volunteer at the Moria first reception centre for refugees on Lesvos,

> These families are doing everything they can to have a safe trip over, so they go to the market and buy everyone in the family a life jacket but, little do they know, it's highly likely these life jackets are fake. I've seen life jackets ripped open and filled with packaging material – it's foam and it's porous. I picked one up and squeezed it, and water came out, so it's not buoyant,

it's actually absorbent. (quoted in Turnball and Shoebridge 2016, n.p.)

Clearly refugees, with or without smugglers' aid, and no matter what restrictions authorities devise, are still moving. The EU–Turkey Statement has not stopped people from crossing into Europe; instead it has generated a stronger and more diverse illicit economy helping people move clandestinely, and much more precariously. Refugees told, for example, of smugglers forcing them onto overcrowded boats, even at gunpoint (Turnball and Shoebridge 2016). As Hynes further explains:

These refugees are told by the smugglers, "You'll be fine, we'll give you a boat, it's designed for 30 people, you'll travel in a group of twenty-five," but when the refugees have given the money, they turn up and suddenly realize they're sharing a boat with 60 or 70 people … When they protest, and refuse to get on the boat, the smuggler then puts a gun to their head and says, "You get on the boat now, or your journey ends here" – they have no choice. (quoted in Turnbull and Shoebridge 2016)

Another Syrian woman with whom we spoke told us that smugglers, after putting them on the boat, suddenly "brought thirty-three Afghanis from the forest. This was against the plan, but we accepted it because we spent a long time in the forest and were desperate to leave. The Afghanis were families with kids" (Stockholm, 8 July 2016). She continued: "People felt sick and dizzy. They started vomiting … I took off my life jacket and covered my head with it because I was covered with water while the yacht was making its way through the sea. The waves were high, and the water was coming inside. We spent five hours until we reached Rhodes Island" (Stockholm, 8 July 2016).

Still others never make it even that far. Turkish coast guards catch and arrest them before they reach the boats (Kurian 2015; McNeil and Dlewati 2016). Many have to attempt the journey several times. As one Syrian man explained:

The journey from Turkey to the Greek islands is organized by one smuggler and from Greece onwards is organized by another.

So, you pay twice … I paid 2,000 euros as I was promised to have the safest journey in a safe wooden boat, not a rubber boat [*balam*]. But at the end, they are all liars. They trade with human lives … People complained when they saw the rubber boat, but the smuggler claimed that he was deceived by the big smuggler … After fifty metres in the water, the engine kept stopping, and we had to go back to the shore. After three failed attempts, it was too late for us to leave, and we had to stop because the sun rose. By the way, the balam is fifteen-person capacity while we were thirty-five people. (Stockholm, 6 July 2016)

Often, even while on a dinghy, Syrians risk drowning at sea. One Greek rescue worker on Lesvos explained, "The migrants come by dinghy from Turkey, with the smugglers putting a knife in their hands and telling them to slice the boat when they near Mytilene's port. Many cannot swim and drown. Rescue team members and others find the drowned washed up on the shore" (Rygiel 2016, 11).[11]

In contesting their precarious and vulnerable status in Turkey and elsewhere, Syrian refugees demonstrate their agency by engaging in such risky journeys (Almustafa 2019). These people are the fortunate ones with whom we could speak. Many more cannot share their stories because they never made it safely across to be able to claim asylum. As of October 2019, the number of people crossing from Turkey to the islands was 39,775.[12] Another 10,945 have to date crossed into Greece by land. Based on UNHCR data from 13 October 2019, around 36 per cent of those crossing from Turkey were children, 23.5 per cent were women, and 40.4 per cent were men (UNHCR n.d., "Operational Portal … Greece"). The growing number of unaccompanied minors raises serious concerns about their well-being as well as their vulnerability to human-trafficking networks.

Between 2014 and 2019, the highest number of refugees crossing from Turkey was in 2015, with 856,723 arriving by sea and another 4,907 by land.[13] Immediately after the EU–Turkey Statement was signed in March 2016, the numbers of refugees and migrants arriving at islands such as Lesvos fell dramatically. Arrivals at Lesvos were 42,601 in January 2016 and 31,416 in February. These figures dropped to 14,155 in March and only 1,766 in April (Pazianou 2016). According

2.2 | Dinghy washed up ashore on Lesvos, 2 August 2013.

to the EC's Seventh Report on the Statement (6 September 2017), irregular crossings along the eastern Mediterranean initially stabilized at an average of ninety-three per day (EC 2017b, 2). In the final analysis, though, the Statement has not had the intended long-term deterrent effect. The volume of people crossing is again on the rise: some

10,000 refugees – mostly Afghan and Syrian – crossed in September 2019, with the UNHCR noting this as the highest number in three years (*DW* 2019b).

Those refugees and migrants who do reach Greece are generally "locked down on the islands under very poor living conditions" (Heck and Hess 2017, 46; see also Heck and Hess 2016; Saranti 2019). Amnesty International documented how on the night of 19–20 March 2016, the Greek government turned reception centres on the islands into detention centres, changing its asylum procedures so that "asylum applications began to be rejected at first instance under a fast-track procedure; many of them were rejected without assessment of their merits on the assumption that Turkey is a safe country for asylum-seekers and refugees" (AI 2017, 6).

The EU is now concentrating its efforts on islands in Greece (and elsewhere, such as Lampedusa, Italy). Its effort to halt migratory flows is part of what it calls a "hot spot approach" (EC n.d.). The EC has described this approach as assisting "frontline Member States which are facing disproportionate migratory pressures at the EU's external border" by working with local authorities. EU officials, such as those from the EU Border Agency (FRONTEX), Europol, the European Asylum Support Office (EASO), and the Judicial Cooperation Union (Eurojust), provide local authorities with logistical and technical support in a variety of areas, including "registration, identification, fingerprinting and debriefing of asylum seekers, as well as return operations" (EC n.d.). Glenda Garelli and Martina Tazzioli (2016) more critically describe the hotspot approach as one that "works as a pre-emptive frontier, with the double goal of blocking migrants at Europe's southern borders, and simultaneously impeding the highest number possible of refugees from asylum claims." Tazzioli and Garrelli (2018, 2) note that islands like Lesvos have become "flexible chokepoints of mobility disruption." Detention centres and pre-removal centres on the Greek islands, such as Moria on Lesvos, are used to detain migrants and asylum-seekers in such a way that "Greek hotspots have become containment places for blocking migrants on the islands facing Turkey, hence preventing their arrival in Athens."

While many of the islands had reached their holding capacity well before the implementation of the EU–Turkey Statement, this hotspot

2.3 | "Moria refugee camp – hot spot – registration centre," Lesvos, Greece, 11 July 2018.

approach further increased pressure and numbers, since asylum-seekers and migrants effectively found themselves trapped on the islands, unable to move on to be resettled in a third country in Europe, given how few resettlement places were available (Garreli and Tazzioli 2016). In the case of Syrians, the intention was to return them to Turkey. But Turkey's designation as a safe country has come under increasing challenge, so that many Syrians have found themselves trapped on the islands, unable or unwilling to return. A case in point is the now infamous detention centre, Moria, on the island of Lesvos.

Moria was initially built to hold 1,500 people comfortably, with a maximum number of 3,500. Yet by 2018 it was holding as many as 8,500 – four times its capacity, according to the UN (Sanderson 2019). Other sources put this number in 2019 as high as 12,000 (DW 2019b) and as high as 22,000 in 2020 (Lindsay 2020). The conditions at Moria are notoriously poor, and this has led some NGOs, such as Oxfam, to close their operations there in protest against the woeful conditions, which have been caused in part by the EU–Turkey Statement (Chalaux 2018). According to a report by Human Rights Watch (HRW 2019a) summarizing the events of 2018 in Greece, refugees in reception and detention centres like Moria often face "severe overcrowding, unsanitary, unhygienic conditions and lack of sufficient specialized care, including medical care, trauma counselling and psychosocial support"; moreover, "physical and gender-based violence were common in asylum camps." The same report notes that children are often housed together with adults rather than in child-specific facilities and that "less than 15 percent of asylum-seeking children had access to education on the islands." Meanwhile, the high numbers of refugees arriving on the islands have spurred far-right groups to organize campaigns targeting refugees and migrants in the broader context of an increase in hate crimes in Greece (HRW 2019a).

By April 2020, overcrowding and unsanitary conditions were so bad that the UNHCR cut financial aid to people in Moria "after two centers on the mainland went into quarantine with coronavirus cases" (Lindsay 2020). As those familiar with camp life have noted, the preventive measures that people are being advised to take – social distancing and washing hands – are impossible in an overcrowded camp where there are only twelve water taps (Lindsay 2020) – that is, as many as "1,300 people per water tap" (Lovett 2020). In early September, the Moria camp was placed under quarantine when a Somali migrant tested positive for coronavirus; shortly afterwards, some thirty-five more cases of COVID-19 were confirmed (BBC 2020). The desperate conditions in the camp, including the outbreak of coronavirus there, may have contributed to the events of 9 September 2020, when at least three fires were set in the camp, which burned to the ground. There were conflicting reports of who was to blame. Greek Migration Minister Notis Mitarachi said that the "incidents in Moria began with the asylum seekers because of the quarantine imposed" (BBC 2020). Others suggested that the fires were arson, and still others, including some migrants living in the camp, blamed right-wing anti-migrant groups for setting the blaze (BBC 2020). On 16 September 2020, the

2.4 | "Third day of fire in Moria refugee camp on Lesbos Island in Greece, displacing 13,000 asylum seekers. The largest refugee camp in Europe completely burned down." Moria, Lesvos, Greece, 10 September 2020.

Greek government charged four migrant men from Afghanistan with setting the fire, claiming that it had been a deliberate act in protest of "confinement after the site was locked down following a coronavirus outbreak" (*New York Times* 2020a).

This account of Moria should serve as a lesson for the other Greek islands, where many asylum-seekers and migrants are similarly trapped in detention and awaiting processing or deportation to Turkey or elsewhere. A German politician who visited the islands reported that the Statement had created an "isolation policy," with refugees living "under inhumane conditions" (*DW* 2019a). One Syrian refugee summarized the Statement's impact for us, starting with how it has also changed the smuggling business in Turkey:

I am very interested in this Statement. I read it carefully and translated it into Arabic. I am actually surprised. It really affected people. Its impact is huge. Now, Syrians can't enter Turkey from Syria. A Syrian needs a smuggler to get him inside Turkey, and it is difficult to leave Turkey by boat because the Turkish police increased its control over the Turkish shores. In fact, there was no control, as the police knew about the smuggling operations and they ignored them deliberately. Now, things are under control, and only strong smugglers manage to get people out of Turkey. Those who reach a Greek island need a smuggler to get them out of the island to Athens, where mobility is very difficult because the Greek police are everywhere. (Stockholm, 8 July 2018)

The Statement has also had a significant impact on refugees once they arrive in Greece:

Syrians need to maintain [a] low profile in Greece. They can't stay in the hotels anymore and are forced to rent through the smugglers. So basically, people are hiding, and they depend on the smugglers who are hiding them until they find the right chance to leave. People became subject to exploitation and harassments and have to pay extra costs. In fact, some smugglers reduced their fees, but there are too many smuggling services involved in the process, which increases the total cost of the journey at the end. Most of those who try to leave from Athens using fake IDs or genuine European passports of people who look similar [are] caught by the police and are not set free like before. Greek police check their entrance point to Greece and send them back to the island they came through. In the islands, people are detained in mass detention camps.

With this reality facing them, some Syrians have decided to return to their homeland through the Assisted Voluntary Return and Reintegration program (AVRR).[14] Some 10,029 migrants used that program in 2016, its first year (EC 2017b, 5). Yet many Syrians and other refugees and migrants are still trying to leave Turkey. The Statement has made their movement much more precarious and created a buffer around Greece, particularly the islands. That buffer amounts to a trap for catching and detaining asylum-seekers. It has fulfilled its purpose: to discourage people from crossing into Europe from Turkey through Greece.

The Statement has thus diverted refugees to other, more dangerous routes, such as the one between Libya and Italy. In June 2016, in the immediate aftermath of the Statement, media and NGOs – such as Watch the Med, whose Alarm Phone rescues migrants at sea – counted at least three boats capsizing on their way from North Africa to Italy, drowning as many as 700 passengers; about 46,000 people made that crossing in the first six months of 2016 (Kingsley 2016). Watch the Med's Alarm Phone warned at the time about the impact the EU–Turkey Statement would have on people crossing:

> Nobody can still claim to be surprised, least of all those responsible for EU migration policies. But they refuse to abolish the deadly visa regime and to open up legal and safe routes. To the contrary: the Balkan route, which migration movements had struggled to open up last summer, was violently closed down. Among yesterday's victims in the Central Mediterranean Sea are now again Syrian and Iraqi refugees. As a result of the closure of the Balkan route and the inhumane EU–Turkey deal, refugees who arrive in Greece are being imprisoned on the Greek islands with the threat of being deported back to Turkey, while those on the Greek mainland are left without any perspective [sic] of leaving the country soon. These political changes force refugees onto the much more dangerous route via Libya. (2016, n.p.)

The story here is one of clear failure on the part of the international community, particularly European governments, to respond to the Syrian refugee crisis. This failure should be no surprise, however, for externalization and refoulement policies such as the EU–Turkey Statement have been developing since the 1990s. These policies, instead of protecting Syrian refugees, are making their lives and journeys more precarious, whether through temporary protection in Turkey (see chapters 3 and 4) or by forcing them to undertake increasingly dangerous journeys in search of protection as well as the recognition and rights they deserve *as refugees*.

Conclusion

The very concept of refugee is being erased as a consequence of "consign[ing] a growing proportion of entrants to the illegal category" (Macklin 2005, 365; see also Schuster 2011). In tandem with this, externalization processes such as the EU–Turkey Statement have resulted in more precarious movement for Syrians, making it harder for them to leave Turkey and reach asylum in EU countries. This reflects a failure by the international community and the EU – especially of signatories to the European Convention on Human Rights – to recognize Syrians as refugees. Instead, they have forced Syrian refugees to live under temporary protection in Turkey and – as we make clear in the next two chapters – to endure limited and temporary forms of humanitarian assistance instead of receiving rights as refugees and pathways toward more permanent resettlement. Syrian refugees desperately need aid and assistance, but the world has been all too willing to offer them merely short-term humanitarian relief instead of recognizing them as persons with a right to protection (in addition to other rights – see Hathaway 2005). The Turkish government's approach – temporary protection rather than refugee status – has restricted Syrians' ability to claim status and rights as refugees, without which they cannot claim the right to meaningful protection. Temporary protection blocks their path toward a new life in a third country, yet return to Syria is no longer possible.

CHAPTER THREE

Precarious Legal Frameworks in Turkey

When Syrians began fleeing their country in 2011, Turkey had little legal apparatus in place to handle large numbers of people seeking refuge within its borders, nor did it have the infrastructure to provide social services for them. Turkey began developing a legal framework for dealing with Syrian and other refugees nine years ago, in 2013, just after several hundred thousand Syrians crossed the border to escape civil war. By 2019, close to four million people had followed. The framework developed by Turkey is such that Syrian refugees there face precarious living conditions as they navigate changing residency regulations and inconsistently delivered social services. The laws and policies they must adhere to are in constant flux and imposed (often haphazardly) by a multitude of agencies.

Not knowing the Turkish language or how government services work makes it much harder for Syrian refugees to obtain social services and to access the job market. While civil society organizations ease some of these difficulties by helping them navigate the system, the legal framework and policies the Turkish government has adopted present serious obstacles for Syrian refugees who are trying to establish stable lives. The constantly shifting complexities of their rights in Turkey are such that they have to negotiate their rights and their conditions of existence. The restrictive legal and policy framework they face revolves around these three key issues: long-term residency, which is regulated by the "temporary protection regime"; access to social services and education; and employment laws and policies. This chapter examines Turkey's approach to refugees up until the autumn of 2014, the evolving status of Syrian refugees in that country, and possibilities for citizenship.

Long-Term Residency under Temporary Protection

Before Syrians began entering into Turkey in the spring of 2011, Turkey had 19,000 registered refugees, most of them from Afghanistan, Iran, Iraq, and Somalia (EU 2016, 130). When Syrians began crossing the border in flight from civil war, the Turkish government accepted them not as refugee claimants but as "guests" – an identity that has no standing in international law. Ankara had ratified the European Convention on Human Rights (Rome, 1951), the 1951 Refugee Convention, and the UN Protocol Relating to the Status of Refugees (New York, 1967), but with this geographical limitation: only individuals from Europe could apply for refugee status in Turkey.[1] This meant that until Syrian refugees started to arrive, the regular practice was that individuals arriving in Turkey from other parts of the world received temporary status until they settled in third countries. As İçduygu (2015b, 7) notes, "Considering its geographical proximity to conflict-ridden states, Turkey's geographical limitation disqualifies a vast number of asylum seekers and refugees seeking permanent protection from the Turkish state." Non-European asylum-seekers seeking refugee status had to have their status as refugees verified by the UN High Commissioner for Refugees (UNHCR) in Turkey.

Syrian Refugees and Turkish Law (2011–14)

Turkey initially accepted Syrians merely as guests. But their numbers rapidly increased until there were too many for RSD processing. So in March 2012 the Turkish government issued a circular defining their status as being that of "temporary protection." Thirteen months later, in April 2013, the national assembly passed the Law on Foreigners and International Protection (LFIP) (Republic of Turkey 2013), which the Justice and Development Party (Adalet ve Kalkınma Partisi, or AKP) had proposed. Prior to the LFIP (Law no. 6458), the 1994 Regulation on Asylum had provided the legal framework for refugee claims. Before that 1994 regulation was introduced, there had been two key pieces of

3.1 | Neither refugee nor guest poster from conference, İstanbul, Turkey, 2015.

legislation providing the legal framework for asylum claims: the 1934 Settlement Law, which regulated the immigration of people of Turkish descent, and the 1951 Refugee Convention and 1967 Protocol. As noted earlier, Turkey had ratified both, with a geographical limitation. This legal framework had provided very limited access to rights and services for refugees in Turkey (İçduygu 2015a, 3–4).

The arrival of Syrian refugees during the 2010s highlighted the urgency of establishing a legal framework for immigration policy. By then, the Turkish government was already working on a new immigration law and taking steps to harmonize its asylum law with the EU legal framework (3–4). In line with the EU policies, the Turkish government introduced the Action Plan on Asylum and Migration, which would revise the national legislation based on EU directives on asylum and migration. The LFIP was the country's first comprehensive law on migration management in line with international standards.

Turkey had received only 2 million migrants between 1923 and 2011. In that light, the new numbers were staggering – more than 3 million Syrian refugees in less than five years – and the legal system and government found it very difficult to cope with them. It took almost two years for the government to create a legal framework to address the needs of this sudden influx (*Diken* 2016). Until the LFIP came into effect, Syrians' legal status in Turkey was governed by the 1994 Regulation as well as the Interior Ministry's Circular no. 62 (issued on 30 March 2012). That circular, which declared the Syrians' status to be "temporary protection," was not made public (UNHCR 2014b). Officials determined initially that 100,000 people would be as many as the government could handle and as Turkish society could absorb (*Diken* 2016). A director of a humanitarian-assistance agency close to the government explained to us the initial confusion and the difficulty of defining the status of Syrian refuges:

> Because of the geographical limitation they [the government] in the beginning used the term "guest." In our culture, the guests stay in our houses three days and then they leave. After that, they are not guests, they are citizens or whatever. So, they [the government] could not even put a name, they could not match this term [guest] with an international one. In Europe you say refugee; here we say guest. In fact, they are the same people who left their homes because of the problems or because of the conflict. So, they [government] changed the term to temporary resident. (Interview, İstanbul, 6 December 2016)

This explains the Turkish government's reluctance to define Syrian refugees' legal status in Turkey in compliance with international law. The government saw itself as offering "traditional hospitality," as opening doors to people in need. Rather than treating the challenge within the framework of legal obligations, it relied on the ethos and language of charity and hospitality, a central tenet of Islam (Carpi and Şenoğuz 2019, 133–4). Government officials approached their responsibility toward Syrians fleeing the civil war by taking up the "Ensar" metaphor, in reference to Medinans who helped the Prophet Muhammed and his entourage escape persecution in Mecca (Kaya 2016, 15).[2] When Prime Minister Recep Tayyip Erdoğan addressed Syrian refugees on 10 August 2014, he used that metaphor: "In the last four years we have been having the honour of hosting you here. You became refugees and were forced out of your homes. We became Ensar and use all our resources to host you" (Haber 7 2014).

As more and more Syrians crossed the border, the government finished drafting the national legislation to align with international standards. The Turkish national assembly passed the LFIP in 2013, which established the Directorate General of Migration Management, which took over all issues relating to immigration from the Directorate of Security. It also formalized the terms "conditional refugee," "secondary protection," and "temporary protection," but without specifying the rights attached to any of these statuses. This new legislation did not solve a key source of precarity for Syrian refugees – it did not address long-term residency. Article 61 of the 2013 law reflected Turkey's long-standing geographical limitation to granting refugee status: it would still be restricted to individuals coming from Europe; all others would receive "conditional refugee status." The new law provided clarity and harmonized Turkey's immigration/refugee regime with international standards; however, the long-term status of Syrian refugees and the details of the "temporary protection regime" were left to the Temporary Protection Regulation of 2014.

Temporary Protection Regulation (TPR) (October 2014)

Article 91 of the LFIP provided the legal framework for the temporary protection regime. To further clarify the status and rights of Syrians in Turkey, on 22 October 2014 the government released the Temporary

Protection Regulation (TPR), which interpreted Article 91 of the LFIP. The TPR was to apply generally to forced migrants arriving *en masse* (Zeldin 2016; Republic of Turkey 2014; Baban, Ilcan, and Rygiel 2017b). According to Amnesty International, the UNHCR declared that the regulation met international standards, "in particular guaranteeing all Syrian residents (including Palestinians residing in Syria) access to Turkish territory, protection against refoulement and access to basic services." But, it added, "the regulation (as well as the meaning of 'basic services') was not communicated to Syrian refugees or civil society organizations working with them" (AI 2014, 20). Because the authorities did not actually publish the regulation, refugees and organizations working with them were unable to determine their rights.

While temporary protection grants certain rights and protections in terms of international legal norms, it falls significantly short of the protection the international refugee regime would normally grant to Syrians. It gives authorities greater leeway vis-à-vis residency, access to social services, and employment. This very arbitrariness, and indeterminate status in Turkey, serve as strong incentives for Syrians to make a perilous journey to Europe in search of refugee status. Many believe they can make such a claim in Europe and eventually gain a more stable future there. Furthermore, temporary protection does not offer pathways to citizenship, the prospect of long-term residency rights, or even RSDs. In fact, it stipulates that temporary protection will *not* lead to permanent residency or citizenship (Kutlu 2015, 4).

The Temporary Protection Regulation (TPR) of October 2014 describes the procedures for temporary protection (Articles 17–25), as well as the right to remain in Turkey (Article 25), and outlines access to various social services (Articles 26–31) and employment permits (Article 29). Article 54 establishes a framework for filing appeals with provincial officials and judges. More importantly, the regulation specifies the circumstances in which "temporary protection" may be terminated. According to Articles 11 and 12 of the regulation, temporary protection can be terminated only by the Council of Ministers, who may also grant status for persons who are under temporary protection (Turkish Government 2014). This regulation lays out the terms and conditions of temporary protection and grants certain rights to Syrian refugees, but it also eliminates the possibility of long-term residency. Moreover, the government still decides the duration of temporary protection and offers no clear pathway to permanent residency. While temporary protection is much more specific than the initial designation of "guest" and is embedded in a legal framework that itemizes claimants' rights and officials' responsibilities, it is ambiguous on permanent-resident status, and that is the main source of precarity for Syrian Refugees. In fact, Articles 11 and 12 of the TPR stipulate that the government can end temporary protection for any and all. The UNHCR's guidelines for temporary protection describe this practice as a short-term solution to meet the needs of large numbers of refugees (UNHCR 2014a). The Turkish government's decision to grant temporary protection was in line with the expectation that the conflict would be over fairly quickly and that Syrians would be able to return to Syria after a short stay in Turkey. However, what was expected to be a short-term solution under international legal norms has become a long-term uncertainty after nine years.

Many Syrian refugees in Turkey, especially those with a higher education, cited the uncertainty of temporary protection as their main reason for wanting to move elsewhere to seek long-term legal status and stable lives. One Syrian business owner in İstanbul explained to us that "many Syrians do not know whether they can have Turkish citizenship or not. Lots of Syrians do not want to stay in İstanbul and try to get to Europe because there is no legal status here. This is a good country and we are safe, but I do not have any rights here" (İstanbul, 14 July 2016). Another family receiving little assistance and with no resources to reach Europe told us that "all what we aim for is to eat, drink, and sleep with dignity. We are not aiming for houses or palaces. We know that we are not going to stay here, since there is no residency permission or citizenship status. All what we are asking for is an income to survive, nothing more" (İstanbul, 13 June 2015). This inability to gain legal residency makes Syrians feel precarious, for their presence is contingent on the government's goodwill.

Amnesty International reported that Syrians told its personnel that this lack of long-term legal status was devastating and that they preferred not to report any crimes against them or to seek government assistance because they feared deportation (AI 2014, 20–3). The same report stated that most government officials were unaware of Syrians' rights and entitlements, which led to responses contradicting government policy (20–3). Our interviews with Syrian refugees in İstanbul and Gaziantep confirmed the same point: uncertainty over their status – indeed, over their future – pushes them toward Europe, despite the perils the journey involves. The ambiguity surrounding temporary protection adds to that pressure. Many believe that in Europe they can at least claim refugee status and look forward to a stable future (see chapter 6). A Syrian refugee lawyer told us how temporary protection affects lives:

> There is no future here, and there is no stability. Syrians do not feel secure or stable here. This explains the huge numbers of desperate Syrian families … who are willing to get on those "death boats" to leave in spite of the increased death toll. People were left with no other alternatives but to do this high-risk journey looking for other destinations or try to apply for resettlement in other countries through connections, embassies, or through the UNHCR. Every day we see hundreds of young Syrians with high academic credentials willing to do this fatal trip. Here [in Turkey they] receive aid and assistance, and they have access to medical care and maybe education, but at the end, this is not a sustainable way to live. They make this trip, and many of them lost their lives before reaching their destination. (Gaziantep, 22 June 2015)

Precarity through Limited Access to Social Services

This denial of long-term residency is the main reason why Syrians in Turkey have precarious identity and limited access to social services, work, and mobility. We must distinguish two groups of refugees: those in government-run camps and those in towns and cities. The latter have much less access to government services (Akyüz and Coşkun 2014; Yıldız 2015). The former receive food and housing as well as social services such as education, entertainment, religious services, sanitary services, social activities, and translation services (USAK 2013, 26–8). Refugees in urban areas lack many of these services but may receive some social assistance from municipalities and non-governmental organizations (NGOs), including charities as well as social service centres operated through the Ministry of Family, Labour, and Social Services. The camps offer basic and social services, but they are also restrictive and seem not to lead anywhere, so around 90 per cent of Syrians in Turkey choose urban centres (UNHCR 2017e). Both groups of refugees, of course, face the same legal challenges vis-à-vis long-term status.

NGOs' reports and our interviews with Syrian refugees indicate that officials' contradictory interpretations of this framework, lack of information for refugees, and inconsistent application of laws and policies make it more challenging for refugees to chart a clear path forward in Turkey (AI 2014; HRW 2015; İGAM 2013). Temporary protection generates several levels of confusion for Syrians, starting with how they can register and whether doing so will prevent them from making refugee claims in other countries. In March 2013, Turkey's Disaster and Emergency Management Agency (AFAD)[3] began registering refugees living outside the camps for the purpose of providing them with an identification card (*kimlik*) that would entitle them to social assistance and access to certain government services.

Because Turkey had never processed large numbers of arrivals, the UNHCR provided it with thirty-four mobile registry stations, assistance with the registry process, and detailed information about what kind of data to collect; later the government stopped accepting the UNHCR assistance and developed its own forms, which omitted some elements of UNHCR forms (UNHCR field office, Gaziantep, 2015). The early stages of registration were chaotic, and government offices in different districts applied different criteria when registering Syrians. In the first months of registrations, officials collected only basic biographical information from arrivals, including name, country of origin, and contact details. According to Amnesty International, some officials (though not all) rejected a number of single men because they were not part of a family; also, some districts in İstanbul, and in other cities where many Syrians had gathered, processed applications quickly, while other cities created long delays. By the end of 2014 only about half of all refugees had been registered (AI 2014, 20–3).

The Turkish Medical Association (Türk Tabipleri Birliği; TTB) observed various government officials applying different criteria, asking for different documentation, and even telling refugees to register first with the police. Some local district administrators (*muhtars*) registered refugees themselves. Moreover, even though the government promised free registration, in some cities refugees were asked to pay a registration fee of between 170 and 200 Turkish lira YTL (TTB 2014, 31–5). Various NGOs reported chaotic registration and great confusion regarding Syrians' rights in Turkey (HRW 2015; İGAM 2013; USAK 2013). One humanitarian NGO told us that the arbitrary application of rules and charging fees for *kimlik* were both common:

> Sirkeci office [registration office in İstanbul] for Syrians' registration is mostly dysfunctional. People went down there with their families and were turned down and did not get what they needed. So, for the moment what everyone is telling us is that the best way to get the *kimlik* is to pay someone 200 lira and they will give it to you within the same day. This is what you have to [do], but most people do not have a spare 200 lira, and a family of five definitely does not have a spare one thousand lira. (İstanbul, July 2016)

The Turkish Bar Association (Türkiye Barolar Birliği; TBB) pointed to arbitrary and chaotic application of the TPR rules, pointing out that most officials, including those in the Migration Management Office, were unfamiliar with the regulation; furthermore, judges' rulings on cases related to it knew nothing about migration law and had received no special training (TBB 2016, 33–4).

New Kimlik and Mobility (Summer 2015)

In response to this initial chaos, the government declared in the summer of 2015 that Syrian refugees would receive new identity cards (*kimlik*). This resulted in further delay that limited Syrians' access to social services. The authorities explained nothing, and refugees with old identity documents could not obtain social services and did not realize they needed to reapply. We learned that during this eight-month transition, hospital workers and other government employees had to decide whether to provide services to Syrian refugees who lacked *kimlik*. Some turned a blind eye; many flatly turned these people down.

When we returned to Turkey in the summer of 2016, we found that the rules for registration and *kimlik* had changed yet again, placing

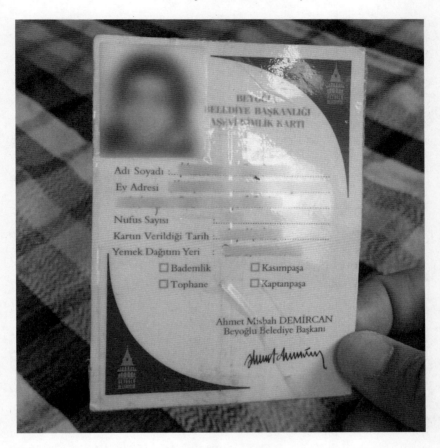

3.2 | Food Ration Card, İstanbul, Turkey, July 2015.

Syrians in an even more precarious situation. The uneven registration process and problems with identity cards had severely restricted some Syrian refugees' mobility. Syrians could obtain social services in the city where they registered. If they decided to move to another centre for work or family reasons, they had to re-register, which could take months, and meanwhile they were denied social services. Most officials with the Provincial Directorate of Migration Management were unwilling to receive referrals from other cities. In 2016 the government changed the rules yet again, requiring Syrian refugees to obtain new *kimlik* similar to those carried by Turkish citizens, but indicating their foreigner status and requiring them to obtain permission for intercity travel. In İstanbul, a humanitarian assistance worker explained to us that "if it is written 'İstanbul' in my protection ID, I should first approach PDMM[4] in İstanbul, then PDMM should let me travel to İzmir if I want to change my residence city to İzmir actually. Then when I … go to İzmir I should first approach PDMM in İzmir and change my residence city in my temporary-protection ID" (16 July 2016).

Syrian refugees told us about needing permission for simple travel to another city. One man, who had an established business in İstanbul and understood the system, complained, "I am running a business, but I cannot go to other cities to conduct business, because in some cases the bus companies will not sell tickets unless I have permission from the authorities. How can I run a business if I need a permission each time I need to travel somewhere else?" (İstanbul, 13 July 2016). This example may not reflect government policy, but rather, as one humanitarian worker told us, an "individual's arbitrary application of the rules" (İstanbul, 16 July 2016).

According to the Asylum Regulation of 1994, all asylum-seekers must register with the Foreigner's Police and with local governorates. Non-Europeans must also sign in with the UNHCR office, which directs them either to detention centres or to "satellite cities" (Article 6) (Soykan 2010, 13) – fifty-one places other than the three largest cities (Ankara, İstanbul, İzmir) – where they must "regularly report to local police for the duration of their residence in the city" and "may leave the city temporarily with written permission from the local police" (Article 6). Temporary protection exempted Syrians from these mobility restrictions. Yet it seemed that, following the EU–Turkey Statement of March 2015 (see chapter 2), the government was applying the satellite-city system to some Syrians, even vis-à-vis Ankara, İstanbul, and İzmir. The same humanitarian worker outlined the situation: "It is all about the readmission agreement [EU–Turkey Statement]. Because of the readmission agreement with Turkey, Syrians are now stuck in Turkey, and big cities such as İstanbul, Ankara, and İzmir are not satellite cities, and authorities don't want Syrians to always move around, because there is no signature duty for Syrians like other refugees in satellite cities – they can travel wherever they want" (interview, İstanbul, 16 July 2016). Humanitarian agencies and Syrian refugees informed us that such travel permits were becoming a requirement for Syrians, and some intercity bus companies insisted on them. As one interview participant stated, "They need the travel permit from the PDMMs in each city. For example, if a person who is registered in Ankara wants to go to İzmir, then he needs to go to the PDMM and then apply for travel permission. If they get this, it is like a paper; if they get it then they can travel. Some transportation companies don't even sell tickets to Syrians without this paper" (İstanbul, 16 July 2016).

Moreover, in the summer of 2016 the government stopped registering new arrivals, rendering them even more precarious, unable to claim even the minimal social services available to earlier Syrian refugees. Only in a documented emergency would local authorities register small numbers of them. Also in 2016, Ankara began requiring visas from Syrian refugees arriving from third countries, thus preventing Syrians from re-entering Turkey or relocating there from third countries such as Lebanon and Jordan. Rules and regulations on Syrians' status changed frequently, and many of them found out about this only when the new rules affected them. The government initially made no effort to inform them in their own language (Arabic), so most learned through conversations or social media, and that information was often inaccurate or incomplete.

The new visa requirement meant that even if refugees returned to Syria legally, they invalidated their *kimlik* in doing so and might not gain re-entry to Turkey. And if they did return to Turkey, they could not re-register, for the system had recorded them as having departed legally and hence giving up temporary protection. Put another way, they could no longer leave legally, and if they did they could no longer return; and if they did return, they had done so illegally and could no longer register for temporary protection (interview, relief agency, Ankara, 25 July 2016). Syrians unaware of these policy changes who went abroad to see relatives during holidays suddenly found themselves unable to return – stranded and in some cases separated from their families (interview, business owner, İstanbul, 3 July 2016; see also HRW 2015).

As a result of visa requirements and restrictions on internal mobility, many Syrians, especially those with higher education and professional degrees, stopped registering for temporary protection. They sought instead residency, just like any other foreign national, so that they could freely move within Turkey and travel abroad. An official short-term resident permit is harder to obtain than temporary protection and does not bring the latter's health and education benefits. Yet many Syrians now prefer it. One Syrian refugee told us, "I do not have access to health care, but I do not see myself here as a long-term resident. I would rather have my freedom of movement. I have family in Syria, and I need to visit them. Temporary protection comes with too many restrictions" (Gaziantep, May 2017).

During our interviews with NGOs and refugees, we noted a great deal of confusion about the *kimlik* and whether holding one would restrict domestic mobility. The *kimlik* is location-specific and requires refugees to notify authorities before moving to another city; if they do, the *kimlik* is cancelled and they must reapply for a new one in the new location. A representative of Mazlumder, an Islamist human rights organization, informed us that "they have a mobility problem. They can't move [from] city to city because they need to redo the whole process of the registry" (Gaziantep, 25 June 2015). So Syrians *may* move from one place to another, but the requirement that they cancel their *kimlik* and seek a new one in the next place creates another hurdle. Moreover, the confusion over *kimlik* makes some refugees understandably hesitant about obtaining one, because of rumours that authorities may share the information they provide with European authorities, who will place it in databases so that border agents can deport them back to Turkey should they leave clandestinely (Kutlu 2015; interview, Syrian refugee family from Tarlabaşı, İstanbul, 17 June 2015). Finally, some Syrian refugees, having lived in an authoritarian country, were uncomfortable about sharing their information with the government, while others had heard rumours that registered refugees would be the first to be deported once Turkey ended temporary protection (AI 2014, 20–3).

Clearly, ambiguities regarding the temporary protection regime, its duration, and its blocking of permanent residency have placed Syrian refugees in a precarious position. As well, temporary protection prevents Syrians from claiming international protection and the rights normally available to refugee claimants. Ankara's assigning Syrians this status instead of identifying them as "conditional refugees" has left them uncertain as to whether they qualify for legal employment and for resettlement in third countries under the international refugee regime, for their status indicates that they are not in immediate danger

(İneli-Ciğer 2015, 29). While temporary protection does not prevent them from applying for international protection, many doubt that they are eligible and fear deportation back to Turkey if they do apply later in Europe (Erdoğan 2015, 69).

Negative public opinion and growing hostility toward Syrian refugees in urban centres in 2019 resulted in government officials further restricting Syrians' mobility and implementing measures to reduce their visibility in cities. For instance, the İstanbul Governor's Office issued a statement on 22 July 2019 instructing Syrian refugees already registered in other provinces to return to those provinces by 20 August 2019; those who did not do so would be transferred there on the order of the Interior Minister.

On 23 July 2019, the Interior Minister, Süleyman Soylu, stated that 1,069,000 migrants had been registered in İstanbul, of whom 547,000 were Syrian nationals under temporary protection. In addition, there were 522,000 "other" foreign nationals registered in İstanbul. The minister also stated that there were many unregistered migrants, as well as others who had registered in other cities but were residing in İstanbul. The minister further added that identity controls would be established throughout the city, especially at the transportation centres (Bianet 2019).

Despite the Interior Ministry's announcement that unregistered migrants would merely be returned to their original province of registration, human rights organizations reported that Syrians were being forced to sign "documents of consent" for their repatriation to Syria because they had not been registered in İstanbul. According to Gerry Simpson, Associate Emergencies Director of Human Rights Watch (HRW), "Turkey claims it helps Syrians voluntarily return to their country, but threatening to lock them up until they agree to return, forcing them to sign forms, and dumping them in a war zone is neither voluntary nor legal" (*VoaNews* 2019). HRW reported that Turkish border guards had been pushing Syrians back across the border as early as 2015. By 2017, at least 330 people had died while crossing the border (HRW 2018c).

That report by HRW was confirmed by an official with UNHCR Turkey: Syrians living in İstanbul without registration or registered in other provinces were being deported, and these deportations were being conducted quickly, making it harder to intervene. The same UNHCR official added that most of these Syrians were being taken to southern Turkey by bus, where they were forced to go back to Syria (interview, UNHCR official, Ankara, August 2019).

Furthermore, an official from an İstanbul NGO reported that some Syrians who had been apprehended during the ID control when they left their house to go shopping were being processed by government officials for deportation even though they insisted that they *were* registered and could retrieve their ID from home (interview, NGO representative, İstanbul, August 2019). *Deutche Welle* reported that deportation cases increased significantly in July 2019, with some refugees being told by government officials that they would receive their new ID cards in Hatay when in fact they were scheduled for deportation (*DW* 2019a). A twenty-one-year-old Syrian refugee, Hisham El Muhammed, was one of the refugees who held an İstanbul temporary protection card. He was forcibly returned to Idlib province in Syria in June 2019. His father, wife, and three children were still in Turkey, and he was shot and killed while trying to cross the Turkish border illegally to return to his family in İstanbul (*Washington Post* 2019a).

Meanwhile, some Syrians are unknowingly "volunteering" to go back to the Syrian war zone. İstanbul police have launched a crackdown on Syrians working illegally or without residence papers; as a result, thousands of Syrians have been swept up and deported back to the war zone. Forced returns to a war zone are a direct infringement of the principle of non-refoulement and violate both international and Turkish law, which allows a fifteen-day window to appeal a deportation to the Constitutional Court, but Turkish authorities have been exploiting a legal loophole by coercing Syrian refugees to sign papers saying they are returning voluntarily (interviews in Kilis, Turkey, August 2019; see also *Guardian* 2019b; *Politico* 2019). These deportations and forced returns (see also AI 2019; DW 2019a; *Guardian* 2018; HRW 2018b and 2018d) are creating an environment in which some Syrians in Turkey are becoming more hesitant to register for temporary protection and to access health care, legal, and social services.

Lastly, the Turkish authorities have stopped registering Syrian refugees in İstanbul and in nine border provinces. HRW interviewed thirty-two Syrians in Hatay province, who confirmed that their efforts to register in those towns had been denied by officials (HRW 2018b). Unless they have a resident permit, being barred from registering prevents Syrian refugees from accessing social services such as education and health; it also places them at direct risk of deportation.

UNHCR and Turkish Refugee Status Determination (RSD)

Syrian refugees' confusion about applying for international protection arises partly because they lack full information about temporary protection, but also because international agencies such as the UNHCR are not prioritizing the registration of Syrians who have temporary protection for settlement in third countries, even if they may be eligible. Even some humanitarian organizations working with Syrian refugees are not fully aware of the legal intricacies of the temporary protection regime. A representative of Malumat (a humanitarian organization launched by Mercy Corps in Gaziantep) explained the confusion surrounding international protection:

> The UNHCR sometimes collects some names from some organizations but … not on a regular basis. Maybe [a] few examples: if they have the risk of dying, or something [else] … they need special treatment. The UNHCR registers these unique cases. Syrians fall into a separate category because they are considered as guests. Syrians are under special protection … [as] guests, [so] they don't qualify. If they get the Turkish *kimlik*, [this] disqualifies them from registering with the UNHCR. (24 June 2015)

Clearly, there is confusion over the difference between temporary and international protection. Article 16 of Turkey's Temporary Protection Regulation stipulates that individuals who are under temporary protection will be not be registered for international protection. In practice, this means that Syrians are confronted with two systems: individuals who *are* under temporary protection will not be registered for international protection, while those who are *not* will be (Çorabatir 2016, 8). But this only applies to the registry in Turkey; it does not necessarily erase the UNHCR registration process and the right to claim refugee status in countries outside Turkey. A former spokesperson in Turkey for the UNHCR explained:

> The UNHCR would like Syrians to be registered to have access to [UNHCR] services in Turkey, but ... we are not doing individual cases with Syrians. Syrians here are guests and ... assisted by the government. And the UNHCR supports the [TPR] registration process. The registration for temporary protection does not prevent them from anything; this is the response of the Turkish government to the refugees here. They register them legally, and they stay in the country legally and access every service legally. So, this is the kind of assistance provided by the government. But if any other country would like to take them, that's fine; you know, formally through the UNHCR or formally through family reunification. (Skype interview, Gaziantep, 25 June 2015)

Thus, temporary protection does not affect a Syrian refugee's right to apply, through UNHCR, to another country for international protection. However, UNHCR is registering Syrians in Turkey only in cases of emergency or family reunification, as it considers them otherwise safe under temporary protection. Yet temporary protection does not simply hinder Syrian refugees' ability to apply for refugee status within Turkey; in practice, because many Syrians seem unaware of their rights, it also undercuts their willingness to claim refugee status in third countries. Because temporary protection blocks them from long-term residence (and perhaps citizenship) in Turkey, they are in a precarious situation in terms of receiving international protection in third countries. This is a prominent reason why Syrians attempt treacherous crossings to make their refugee claims in Europe. As was explained in chapter 2, the UNHCR stopped carrying out its RSD activities in Turkey in September 2018.

Promise of Citizenship?

Neither the Turkish government's initial decision to allow Syrian refugees to enter Turkey in large numbers, nor its subsequent decision to grant "temporary protection," nor its changing attitude toward Syrians, can be understood in isolation from Turkey's domestic and regional politics. Changing domestic political parameters such as growing hostility toward Syrian refugees even among AKP supporters and the AKP government's broader geopolitical objectives in the Middle East and Europe have had an impact on the rules and regulations with respect to Syrians' mobility, employment rights, and citizenship prospects (Şahin Mencütek and Aras 2015, 201–4). It would be a mistake to analyze the Turkish government's policies for Syrian refugees as a simple application of legal measures without taking the larger political context into account.

Shifts in the AKP government's policies toward Turkey's Middle Eastern neighbours predated the Syrian war. Long before popular uprisings against authoritarian regimes in the Middle East erupted in 2011, the Erdoğan government and then Foreign Minister Ahmet Davudoglu were retooling long-held foreign policies to expand Turkey's sphere of influence and make their country a key player in the region (Davudoglu 2013; Gokay 2015). Some described this new direction as "Neo-Ottomanism" – that is, Turkey intended to carve out greater political influence in the former Ottoman territories (Atac 2018). Erdoğan's clashes with Israeli leaders, his vocal support for Palestinians in international forums, and the growing presence of Turkish state institutions such as Directorate of Religious Affairs and the Turkish Economic and Development Agency in the Middle East and in the Balkans, as well as his repeated mention of the former Ottoman territories in his speeches, were some indications that he was developing a new, more assertive foreign policy. Turkey's opening its doors to Syrian refugees was not simply a humanitarian response – it was also part of the country's efforts to establish itself as a regional power broker. Even while displaying its humanitarianism by accepting large numbers of Syrians on its territory, Turkey was inserting itself into the Syrian war. This was partly to display its clout in the region and partly to intervene in Syria's ethnic and religious cleavages so as to strengthen its position in an ongoing domestic conflict with Turkey's Kurdish population (Kösebalaban 2020). Furthermore, Turkey's opendoor policy toward Syrians was often at odds with its securitization of Syrians' mobility. It regularly conducted push-back operations along its Syrian border, which was fortified with a border wall, as well as along its western border, where large numbers of Syrians were crossing into Europe (Togral Koca 2015, 215–19). The following discussion examines citizenship rights for Syrians in Turkey in the context of this broader geopolitical background and Turkish domestic politics rather than simply as a legal matter.

In the same vein, and as we discussed in chapter 2, Turkey changed its policies governing Syrians' mobility within Turkey in response to its relations with the EU (Togral Koca 2015). Immediately after signing the EU–Turkey Statement, the Erdoğan government sharply restricted Syrians' mobility between Turkish cities. At the same time, it periodically threatened to open Turkey's border with the EU; in other words, it began using the Syrians as a bargaining chip (DW 2016). In March 2020, unhappy with the lack of European support for his military operations in Syria, Erdoğan did in fact open the Turkish–Greek border (*New York Times* 2020b). This caused thousands of Syrians to rush to that border in the middle of a global pandemic, only to find themselves stranded between the two countries. Clearly, Syrians' status in Turkey was hostage to shifting domestic and international political currents.

As we saw in chapter 2, the EU–Turkey Statement has made it harder for Syrians to claim refugee status in Europe and made their lives in Turkey more precarious. According to the Statement (text in EC 2016c), Greece must send back to Turkey all irregular migrants reaching the Greek islands. The EU will accept for settlement one Syrian for each refugee Greece has sent back to Turkey, up to 72,000 in total per year. For its part, the EU has promised Turkey 6 billion euros in assistance, visa-free travel for its citizens, and acceleration of EU membership negotiations. Recognizing that it could not undertake mass deportations of Syrians back to Turkey, the EU has also declared that people who apply for asylum in Greece will receive case-by-case treatment in line with international law and with the principle of non-refoulement – hence individual interviews and the right to appeal. However, the UN has challenged the Statement, and a high-ranking official there has stated that Greece lacks the organizational infrastructure to handle individual claims and that any mass deportation back to Turkey would be illegal (*Guardian* 2016b). After the agreement came into effect in March 2016 there was a dramatic decline in sea crossings between

Turkey and Greece. Within a month, arrivals on the Greek islands dropped by 90 per cent; yet the EU resettled only 177 Syrian refugees at that time as part of the one-to-one agreement (*Guardian* 2016a). The Statement severely restricted the ability of Syrian refugees in Turkey to claim refugee status in Europe. The EU had agreed to resettle 72,000 Syrian refugees but was doing nothing to relieve Syrians in Turkey or allow them to settle in Europe. Instead, it locked many of them into the legal ambiguity of temporary protection and denied them the long-term stability that international refugee law offers to victims of war and conflict.

Now that the European route has largely been eliminated, most Syrian refugees in Turkey continue to live under legal ambiguity, and the constantly changing and shifting legal framework is subjecting them to domestic political priorities and calculations in their host country. While temporary protection does not provide any promise of permanent residence or citizenship, there has been ongoing discussion about granting citizenship to Syrian refugees. Citizenship Law 5901 makes it possible for foreigners to be granted Turkish citizenship after five years of legal residence in the country. The principal requirements for that citizenship are: living in Turkey with a legal residency permit, documenting Turkish fluency, and having no criminal record. Also, the Citizenship Law 5901's Article 11 stipulates that the applicant should have no prior health condition, have "good morals" ("iyi ahlaklı" in Turkish), demonstrate a source of income sufficient to support himself/herself and dependants, and, finally, pose no danger to public safety and national security (Republic of Turkey 2009). These last two criteria – good morals, and not posing a danger to national security – are not clearly defined in the law, and this injects a great deal of arbitrariness into the process. And in the case of Syrian refugees, temporary protection status and the sheer number of Syrians living in Turkey has further complicated how and when and whether Syrians will be eligible for Turkish citizenship.

Government officials have added to the confusion. Prime Minister Binali Yıldırım[5] declared that Syrians who disturb public harmony and peace will not be eligible, and on the same day, Finance Minister Nihat Zeybekçi ruled out citizenship for Syrians who did not conform with Turkish ethical standards (*T24* 2016a). From time to time the

3.3 | Broken windows of a Syrian shop in Önder, Ankara, Turkey, 16 July 2016.

government has taken this issue into public debate, thus fuelling hostility against Syrians. On the night of the failed coup attempt of 15 July 2016, a large mob attacked and looted Syrian businesses in Ankara's Önder neighbourhood, home to more than 40,000 Syrians (for more on these attacks, see Baban, Ilcan, and Rygiel 2017b).[6] Provocateurs had organized that event through Twitter, inviting people to take revenge on Syrians at a specific time and place (Estukyan 2016). The human rights organization Mazlumder (2014) reported that police and other local authorities were aware of the threats, and many Syrians stated that police cars were patrolling the area but did not stop the looters.

During our visit to the area afterwards, we saw several hundred stores with shattered windows. Syrians we interviewed said that tensions had been growing in the neighbourhood for several months. Just days before the attacks, they had received messages from neighbours and through social media, warning them not to go out at night. One Syrian mother described the night:

> They hit our neighbours with stones, they broke the glass …
> and my son got sick because he was so terrified … The whole
> neighbourhood turned off the lights and hid. They broke [the
> windows] of all Syrian shops. Any Syrian they saw, they wanted
> to kill; that's what they said. They sent text messages [saying] to
> hide in your homes, stay at home and don't leave, there's a terror-
> ist gang going to do this, and, actually, that Saturday at 8:30 p.m.
> 60 to 70 men were there. (Interview, Ankara, 26 July 2016)

Similar attacks on Syrians have occurred in Gaziantep, İstanbul, İzmir, and Konya (Mazlumder 2014). This attack in Ankara, however, followed President Erdoğan's announcement on 5 July 2016 that it was time to start granting citizenship to Syrian refugees and that the Interior Ministry was working on this initiative (Arslan 2016). There was heated public debate about this as well as strong public opposition. For many Turks the announcement was a complete surprise, and it exacerbated the already rising hostility toward Syrians. According to the International Crisis Group (ICG):

> Surveys repeatedly find a widely-held view that refugees are a
> burden. In 2013 nearly 60 per cent of the population thought im-
> migration negatively impacted tourism, labour and the economy
> broadly. A seminal 2014 study underscored these findings as well
> as the cultural distance and other insurmountable barriers to
> integration host communities perceived. Over 80 per cent of re-
> spondents opposed citizenship; roughly 70 per cent wanted more
> restrictive policies, even sending Syrians home. (2016, 12)

One Syrian refugee summarized the situation: "Before President Erdoğan came up with this announcement, we had great relationships with Turks. Now everybody turned against us. These days when I take a taxi, I try to hide that I am a Syrian. As soon as they find out that I am a Syrian, they show great hostility. This was not the case before. Erdoğan made us more vulnerable than we were before. Why did he do this?" (interview, İstanbul, 14 June 2016).

The hostility toward and violence against Syrian refugees, fuelled by the president's announcement, is emblematic of the insecurity facing Syrians in Turkey, regardless which city they live in or what their living conditions are. Their daily lives are governed by and subject to the government's constantly shifting rules, whether through legal changes, government circulars, or bureaucratic procedures. As one representative of a well-established NGO summarized it, "One of the things we have been hearing is that there is a complete lack of clarity, especially for Syrians to find out what legal processes are changing. So, for them [there] is a great deal of difficulty in terms of navigating the bureaucratic procedure" (interview, İstanbul, 7 July 2016). Kristen Biehl (2015, 58–9) argues that "protracted uncertainty," associated with "indefinite waiting, imperfect knowledge, and the volatility of legal status" is a defining characteristic of being an asylum-seeker in Turkey, one that "invades asylum seekers' everyday lives" with a "powerful governing effect, serving to contain, demobilize, and criminalize them through the production and normalization of uncertainty." Temporary protection status for Syrians does nothing to alleviate this norm; rather, it institutionalizes uncertainty, the status of being in limbo, the challenge of waiting to return to Syria while enduring a temporary life in Turkey.

Citizenship for Syrians remains a deeply political issue, one that has become entangled in domestic political debates. In fact, Erdoğan made several conflicting statements about granting citizenship to Syrians, complicating the issue even further. After his 2016 statement about granting citizenship to Syrians, the public backlash was powerful (BBC 2016). In 2017 and 2018, as negative attitudes toward Syrians strengthened, the president declared several times that the Syrians would eventually have to return to their own country (*Cumhuriyet Daily* 2018). Finally, realizing that Syrian refugees were becoming a key issue in the local elections, he declared flatly that all Syrians would have to go back to Syria (*NTV News* 2018). The opposition parties contend that Erdoğan views Syrian refugees as natural supporters of his rule, which is why he wants to grant citizenship to them. Yet only 12 per cent of Turks approve of citizenship for Syrian refugees (İngev 2019).

A Pathway toward Citizenship

A citizenship process for refugees would normally follow this path: a government officially recognizes their right of asylum; a clear process is then outlined for them as to how they might obtain refugee status, with its accompanying rights as mandated by international law. Refugee-accepting countries then outline a process whereby they can obtain permanent residency and, in many cases, citizenship. But instead of outlining a clear process for Syrians to become citizens, Erdoğan's announcement seemed largely influenced by the political circumstances of the day. And once it became clear that hostility toward citizenship for Syrians was widespread, spilling over into social media through rapidly expanding Twitter campaigns, the government quickly changed its tune (Arslan 2016).

In the spring of 2017 the government launched a process for qualifying *some* Syrian refugees for citizenship. It did so without any announcement or explanation. In May 2017 in Gaziantep, Syrian refugees told us that some Syrians who had registered with the authorities were receiving text messages on their cell phones telling them to present themselves at a police station with certain documents. After doing that and going through an interview, they were told that another text message summons might follow. A successful second interview would lead at some indefinite future time to an interview in the office of the district governor, before a committee of local officials. Syrian refugees who had gone through this final interview told us that the Interior Ministry had received their file and would make the final decision. If it was positive, a text message would so inform the applicant: that person could now become a Turkish citizen.

This citizenship process lacks transparency and does not lay out an application process or provide any criteria for citizenship. Furthermore, negative decisions cannot be appealed. One Syrian refugee explained the process to us:

I go to the migration office with all the information I have. I submit all my information. My *kimlik*, passport, family card, whatever I have. I also give them my diplomas, high-school diploma, or student cards, and so on and so forth. I submitted all the information I had. Then you can follow up with a case number as you know. You go to an interview, a big commander interviews you. They ask about everything from your birth to the present day. They take all the information and review it. Then if they will give you the citizenship, they invite you to Ankara after a while. There is another interview there, but I don't know about the rest. (Interview, Gaziantep, 5 October 2017)

The same person added: "I had a friend in Gaziantep who went to the governor's office for an interview. His grandfather had an Ottoman identification card, from the Ottoman days. He showed that, and they really liked it. It seems like they will give him the citizenship. As you know, we [Syrians] used to be [Ottoman subjects]" (5 October 2017).

That Ottoman identity card may have had no bearing on the candidate's outcome, but in the absence of clear rules, any kind of rumour spreads among refugees and adds to the confusion. As this rumour circulated, many refugees travelled to İstanbul to search the Ottoman archives for a family connection. Another Syrian man told us:

They told me from time to time to check the Migration Office for an interview. I checked once, they said, "No, but you have to check again." They also said, "You are an engineer; we are asking for doctors and teachers now." I asked him why; he said, "We do not like engineers." He was just kidding with me. I was like "Ok. I'll wait until you love us." (Interview, Gaziantep, 5 November 2017)

In fact, our interviews with Syrians confirmed that there *is* no application procedure and that the process starts with a text message. Similarly, no one knows how the authorities select candidates, as they never advertise any criteria. In Gaziantep, refugees reported that the candidates had higher education as well as professional skills, which aligns with the government's later statements that most skilled Syrian refugees leave for Europe due to uncertain legal and living conditions in Turkey. As of October 2019, the citizenship process continued to follow the pattern outlined above. According to the Interior Ministry, by 1 August 2019, 92,280 Syrian refugees had been granted Turkish citizenship (Mülteciler Derneği 2020).

The president's announcement reflected short-term political interests and the influence of regional border politics as they played out through the EU–Turkey Statement. The EU and Turkey may well be competing for professional and otherwise highly skilled Syrians. Many Syrian refugees are aware that domestic politics in Turkey affect their legal status and possibilities for citizenship: "The Syrian file is now used as an element in the political game in Turkey and within Turkish election campaigns. So, Syrians do not feel secure here or safe here. They do not feel they have a future here" (interview, Syrian lawyer, Gaziantep, June 2015). Because clear policy direction is lacking, their situation in Turkey is deeply ambiguous. When large numbers of Syrians first crossed the border in 2011, Turkey had no legal framework or humanitarian infrastructure for processing and helping them. Now temporary protection has given them some form of legal status and provided them with social services such as health and education. But this legal framework has since evolved, confusing Syrians and leaving them unable to claim rights. Because the government bureaucracy is already byzantine – even for Turks – ever-changing rules and authorities' arbitrary application of them make Syrian refugees' lives precarious. One humanitarian assistance agency summarized the obstacles: "It is arbitrary interpretations, because one of the things we have been hearing is that there is a complete lack of clarity, especially for Syrians, to find out which and how legal processes are changing. So, for them of course it is a great deal of difficulty in terms of navigating the bureaucratic procedure" (interview, İstanbul, 2015). Moreover, the ping-pong politics of citizenship feeds into public hostility rather than offering a clear message supportive of Syrian integration. And as the attacks in Ankara showed, Syrians become the target of violence due to this policy ambiguity.

This ambiguous legal framework and arbitrary application of rules were on display in March 2020 when the Turkish government opened the border and encouraged Syrian refugees to cross into Greece. This was an effort to force Europe to support its Syrian policy. As we noted earlier, within a very short time thousands of Syrian refugees travelled to the Greek border in the hope that they would be able to cross the border to claim refugee status. Indeed, President Erdoğan had warned the EU to expect millions of refugees (*France24* 2020). The EU–Turkey Statement had drastically curtailed Syrian refugees' mobility rights within Turkey. As soon as the Turkish government signalled that it would no longer honour the Statement, thousands of Syrians, not knowing how long this opening would last, rushed to the border during the global pandemic. Only a couple of months earlier, Syrians had experienced a similar type of uncertainty when the Turkish government declared that it intended to create a buffer zone between Turkey and Syria and relocate one million Syrian refugees to the "safe zone" (*New York Times* 2019). This provoked a great deal of anxiety among Syrians, for very few of them were from the border regions; they did not want to be forcibly located to an unfamiliar area, and they feared that they would face hostility from the local population in those regions. Legal uncertainty under the temporary protection regime, changing and inconsistently applied rules, hostile public opinion, and the sense that they had become pawns in a larger international and domestic political game have greatly contributed to the precarity of Syrians' lives in Turkey. The lack of full legal protection as defined in international law and the very limited prospects of gaining permanent residency have prevented Syrians from making long-term plans and adapting to their host country.

Conclusion

Turkey's legal framework, which only partly complies with international law and norms, governs Syrians' legal status and rights (Council of the European Union 2001). In this chapter, we have explained that the reality of Syrians' lives is much more complicated than even this. Turkey now hosts one of the largest refugee populations in the world and had to rush to enact a legal framework that would allow Syrians rights to limited residency and to services such as health and education. However, the legal framework, which is defined by temporary protection and the domestic politics and foreign policy choices of the Turkish government, has led to severe instability and long-term unpredictability so that Syrians find it terribly difficult to start new lives in Turkey. Syrians often find themselves trapped between Turkish foreign policy ambitions in the Middle East and Europe. In Turkey, they are being denied permanent residency, so many of them risk their lives in search of long-term stability in Europe.

The temporary protection regime lacks specific measures to protect vulnerable groups such as refugee women and children. There are many documented cases of child marriage, sexual crimes committed against Syrian women, and child labour (Kıvılcım 2016, 201). As a result, Syrian women are ending up in polygamous marriages with Turkish men and experiencing sexual harassment in the workplace and in their neighbourhoods. NGOs have reported that Syrian girls as young as twelve are being forced into marriage as the second or third wives of Turkish citizens (ICG 2014, 21). They have very little legal recourse to this. The temporary protection regime defines access to services but does not consistently provide refugees with those services. This lack of defined rights within the legal framework has become the primary source of precarity for Syrians.

Uncertain legal status and lack of prospects for permanent residency have exposed Syrian refugees to the volatile ins and outs of Turkish domestic politics, leaving them vulnerable to changing public opinion, which has blamed them for economic difficulties as well as for social problems such as rising crime (Danış 2019a). Hostility toward Syrian refugees sharply increased in the summer of 2019 as Turkey's economic crisis deepened, so that Syrian-owned businesses in several cities found themselves under attack (*France24* 2019). One public opinion survey reported that 82 per cent of respondents wanted Syrians to be deported; the same survey reported that only 12 per cent of respondents approved of the government's Syrian refugee policy; even more alarmingly, 72 per cent of the respondents supported the decision made by some municipalities to bar Syrian refugees from public beaches (*T24* 2019). This growing hostility toward Syrians forced the government to sharply change its attitude toward all refugees residing in major urban centres. To calm the public, the government launched ID checks in cities and transported some Syrians back to their original city of registration; still others were deported outright even though they had registered with the authorities. The governor of İstanbul stated in August 2019 that the governorate was using thirty buses each day and sometimes chartering airplanes to transport irregular migrants to removal centres; it was using the same methods to send Syrian refugees back to their province of first registration (Ahval 2019b). As we mentioned earlier in this chapter, the government denies that it is forcibly deporting Syrians back to Syria, and claims that it implemented aggressive ID checks to take action against 12,000 irregular migrants residing in cities without proper registration. However, media and human rights organizations contend that forced deportations are indeed taking place (*Washington Post* 2019a; HRW 2019b; Refugees International 2019).

In this chapter we have sought to clarify the various legal and policy frameworks that have created precarious living conditions for Syrian refugees in Turkey. The government is trying to address some of the issues we have raised here, but the steady movement of refugees into Turkey has presented it with economic, social, and bureaucratic challenges that it lacks the experience to overcome. Among all the obstacles we have discussed, the ambiguous legal framework of temporary protection is perhaps the most significant, for it spills over into access to education and employment. Because it makes refugees' futures completely unpredictable and denies them a path to citizenship, most of them live in constant limbo, unable to make any long-term plans. A Syrian lawyer in Gaziantep explained: "Thinking about citizenship rights for Syrians in Turkey is still out of our imagination ... I learnt that, according to Turkish laws, there are many steps to pass in order to reach full citizenship and gain full citizen rights. This process is not applicable for Syrian refugees yet. It is not in the horizon" (interview, 22 June 2015).

CHAPTER FOUR

Precarity through Irregular Access to Social Services: Implications for Living and Working Conditions

Chapter 3 explained Turkey's system of temporary protection for Syrian refugees, introduced in the autumn of 2014, and its role in creating precarious conditions vis-à-vis status, mobility, and access to social services. In this chapter we focus on irregular access to social services such as education, health care, and housing, and lack of employment opportunities, to trace precarious conditions in the daily lives of Syrians in Turkey.

The Law of Foreigners and International Protection (LFIP) and the Temporary Protection Regulation passed in 2014 together establish the legal framework of Syrian's status in Turkey. However, the TPR says little about access to health care, education, and employment, leaving implementation to the discretion of the various ministries. Furthermore, the Temporary Protection Regulation of October 2014 does not lay down the scope and extent of rights for Syrian refugees, and this has opened the way for contradictory interpretations by government officials and for uneven access for Syrians (İneli-Ciğer 2015).

Syrian refugees must register and receive an identity card (*kimlik*) to gain access to social services. Our interviews with Syrian refugees and the civil society organizations that assist them revealed a great deal of confusion over how to apply for the *kimlik* and what social services refugees are entitled to receive. Furthermore, just as happens with registration, authorities apply the rules inconsistently, with much depending on the district (governorate). This link between *kimlik* and

126 THE PRECARIOUS LIVES OF SYRIANS

district of issue has helped create the precarious space that restricts Syrians' mobility as well as their ability to unite families. Chapter 3 explained how district-specific registration has effectively blocked full mobility rights for them. Any time they move they need to register again for a new *kimlik*, which usually takes several months, during which time they have no access to social services except for urgent medical care. As well, except for universal health care, Syrian refugees face variable access to social services.

A representative from the Islamist human rights organization Mazlumder explained the issues of *kimlik* registration to us:

> As for the urban refugees, the state provides some health care and limited access to education ... In terms of daily needs and what needs to be done for these people, the state is mostly absent, and it is left to civil society organizations to take care of [them]. For instance, a local business donates a certain amount of money through the *muhtar*.[1] And the *muhtar* gets grocery cards with these donations, and then those cards are distributed to refugees [for] 30 lira each. But it is arbitrary, and there are no established rules. The state has not been issuing *kimlik* and registering them for eight months now. What refugees hear right now is that the AFAD *kimlik* is ... not going to be valid anymore and ... the new *kimlik* [will be provided]. Also, the new *kimlik* are specific to the cities. So, if you register in Gaziantep, your *kimlik* is valid in Gaziantep. And then if you go to Konya it is not valid anymore, and then you have to register again, which creates a mobility problem. (Gaziantep, 25 June 2015)

A former spokesperson in Turkey for the UNHCR told us about problems of coordination:

> Local authorities develop their own assistance in İstanbul and in other border areas. Municipalities have their own systems. So ... coordination is a problem. So, if you are lucky that in the small district that you live in, the local government [or] municipality has a system, they may access [the] assistance. But in other districts, if you are unlucky ... there is no comprehensive system.

As far as the urban case is concerned, there is no coordination between the municipalities, government aid agencies, and charities. (Skype interview, Gaziantep, 20 June 2015)

In the early days, domestic and international NGOs played an important role along with municipalities with regard to distributing aid and assistance to Syrians. Because the government initially expected Syrians to stay in Turkey for only a short time and considered them "guests," NGOs filled the immediate need for legal aid, housing, and employment. NGOs' activities were not always coordinated, and they did not receive the same support and cooperation from government officials. Religious NGOs were quick to organize and receive government support; secular NGOs took much longer to become active and did not receive government support (Çorabatır 2016, 13). International NGOs were active during the first several years, even though the government did not permit them to organize relief efforts. However, several INGOs, such as Danish Refugee Council, International Medical Corps, and Doctors Without Borders, have established partnerships with local NGOs to organize relief work (14).

As the government became more active in coordinating relief efforts and access to social services, NGOs that were ideologically aligned with the government became an integral part of aid distribution and social services. As Danış and Nazlı (2019c) emphasize, these were more "pro-governmental organizations" than "non-governmental" organizations and worked as "auxiliary agents" alongside the state (145).

Access to social services such as health, education, and housing has class and gender dimensions, which left low-income Syrians and single women particularly vulnerable. Middle- and upper-middle-class Syrians who have transferred some of their savings to Turkey can bypass problems associated with accessing social services by sending their children to privately run schools. However, millions of Syrians have no access to any private wealth and depend on aid, low-paying jobs, and limited social assistance. Women and children are particularly vulnerable and end up working illegally for meagre wages and living in unsanitary housing. This chapter looks at three dimensions of social services for Syrian refugees in Turkey – health care, housing, and education – as well as employment.

Precarious Health Care

Upon receiving the *kimlik*, Syrian refugees are entitled to some social services, but these are not always readily available. The LFIP law leaves specifics to the respective government ministries. Health care is one of the social services to which Syrians have relatively easy access. The government services were organized quite efficiently from the start so as to include Syrians under temporary protection in the public health network. However, language barriers and unfamiliarity with the system block many Syrians' access to the health care system. Seemingly straightforward procedures such as making appointments, and registering their identity cards at a clinic to inquire whether public health care covers specific medical procedures, is difficult for Syrians who do not speak Turkish and are unfamiliar with the system.

Syrian doctors are not licensed to practice in Turkey. Even so, some have opened clinics without proper licensing and treat Syrian patients for a fee. We visited one of those clinics in İstanbul during our fieldwork, which served low-income Syrians who preferred to see an Arabic-speaking Syrian doctor. Many of these people found the Turkish health system too complicated to navigate. Some complained that Turkish clinics were hostile toward them. They said that some Turkish doctors refused to treat them and that others were impatient when they could not explain their problems in proper Turkish (interviews, İstanbul, 19 July 2016). The government eventually shut down Syrian-run clinics. Syrian refugees then started to use the Turkish health care system with more ease.

Syrians under temporary protection are eligible for the same health care and education as Turkish citizens. But these services are delivered by various agencies at different levels of government, and there is very little coordination between these agencies to help newcomers figure out how to access services. For instance, health coverage for Syrians under temporary protection includes visits to doctors, necessary surgery, and 80 per cent of drug costs (Kutlu 2015). Syrian refugees with *kimlik* can access public health services but encounter serious difficulties navigating the complexities of the health network. Public and private providers offer different levels of services, which government sources and private insurers pay for together. In addition, each hospital has agreements with public and private insurers for cost recovery and delivery of services. This complicated system is difficult for Syrians to navigate, and even with 80 per cent coverage, drugs are out of reach for those many Syrians who live in abject poverty. The Turkish Medical Association (TTB 2014, 17) reported uneven access to health care because of officials' conflicting interpretations of rules. Some Syrians had to pay social security premiums, which the government normally deducts from Turkish citizens' pay. However, if the medicine is covered under the Health Implementation Law/Budget Law (Sağlık Uygulama Tebliği), the total cost of the medication is covered by the Turkish government and refugees are not asked to contribute.

The TTB reported that, while government officials were learning how to provide health services to Syrian refugees, obstacles remained, such as refugees' lack of knowledge about rules and the location of facilities, language barriers, prohibitive drug costs, discrimination by providers, lack of ID, and requests to pay charges for previous visits (TTB 2014, 48). Some municipalities assist with drug charges, but Syrians may not know this. Lack of coordination between municipal authorities and health care providers, and language barriers, make it difficult for some Syrians to determine where to make claims for free health care and drugs (50). Changes to rules, long delays in registration, and the 2016 suspension of registrations for *kimlik* have troubled Syrians:

> We are able to get *kimlik* for people who need to go to the hospital immediately. There is a health clinic here, and they offer a month-long pre-registration document that gives access to emergency health care. However, once the month is up the ID is no longer valid, and they cannot receive services until they get their permanent ID. If family moves from another city, they need to get a new ID. But there has been [a] problem with issuing IDs for the last three months, and they cannot have their IDs. In those situations, we get these temporary IDs, but it does not solve their problem. (Interview, humanitarian relief agency, Ankara, 25 July 2017)

Sometimes even small changes in access to social services pose serious barriers for less affluent Syrians. For instance, the government had given *kimlik* numbers starting with "98" to Syrian refugees under temporary protection, to differentiate them from other refugees and foreigners (prefix "99"). Then without any announcement it rolled all "98" cards into "99," a change that Syrians had to implement online. As a result, many low-income Syrians who lacked internet access faced problems seeking medical help in government hospitals (interview with ASAM, İstanbul, 14 July 2016; see also Association for Solidarity with Asylum Seekers and Migrants [ASAM], the English name for Sığınmacılar ve Göçmenlerle Dayanışma Derneği). Because computer systems in government offices no longer recognized "98" ID cards, many Syrians could not obtain health services, and some could not enrol their children in school – yet the government kept issuing ID cards beginning with "98." Some Syrians only learned about this when they went to a hospital or to a school to register their children (interview with ASAM, İstanbul, 14 July 2016). Quite a few doctors and school principals would make the changes for them on the internet, but some would not, and denied them services. For precarious and vulnerable Syrians in Turkey, even a small bureaucratic change can bar them from basic services. One child died as a result. In January 2017, in the province of Antalya (Anatolia), a young boy, Ali İzzettin Ahmad, developed a high fever, and his parents took him to the hospital. The first facility refused to admit the child, for he did not have a *kimlik*. The father tried three other hospitals, to no avail. The distraught father took his child home, where he died the next morning (*Diken* 2017). During fieldwork we heard that hospital personnel usually assisted Syrians who lacked a *kimlik*. In this particular case, however, arbitrary decisions and bureaucratic obstacles proved to be fatal.

Language barriers are another serious obstacle for Syrians who are seeking access to health services. Many do not speak Turkish and find it very hard to communicate with Turkish doctors in hospitals where translation services are almost non-existent. To address overcrowding in hospitals and the language problem, in 2016 the government allowed Syrian doctors to practise in Turkey through the use of work permits related to foreigners under temporary protection (*Memurlar Net* 2017). This policy change allowed Syrian health professionals to work in the Turkish health care system. With the assistance of the EC Humanitarian Aid Office (ECHO) and the World Health Organization

(WHO), the Turkish Ministry of Health designed and implemented a training program for Syrian health practitioners, including doctors, nurses, and midwives. After training, Syrian health practitioners were certified to work in Migrant Health Centers (MHCs) established by the Turkish Government for Syrian refugees (WHO 2017).

As of January 2019, 527 migrant health units were operational in 154 MHCs; most of these employed Syrian health practitioners. The government plans to increase the number of migrant units to 805 practitioners in 180 MHCs (Eğici 2019, 9–10). Most of these health centres are in cities where Syrian doctors are strongly concentrated, and they employ Arabic-speaking staff. These MHCs have reduced overcrowding in public hospitals, which had been a cause of tensions between Turkish residents and Syrian refugees. Furthermore, MHCs have eased the language problem, for Syrian refugees are now able to explain their health problems to Arabic-speaking staff. However, the separate health centres may pose problems related to the incorporation of Syrian refugees into Turkish society in the long term and may lead to a two-tier health care system in which Syrian refugees have access to health care in their native language but receive second-rate care because equipment and qualified personnel are limited by comparison to other public health care facilities.

Precarious Housing and Social Assistance

It is a challenge for Syrian refugees to obtain other social services, such as housing and food stamps. These services are informal, and because they are supervised by municipal and local authorities, such as *muhtars*, they vary from place to place. Turkey offers no housing allowance or government-arranged housing services for refugees. As there is no government-supported housing or housing allowance, finding proper accommodation became a severe problem for Syrians. As Syrians started to arrive in large numbers in 2011, a housing shortage emerged, and rental prices increased in cities close to the border. Furthermore, Syrians tend to rent houses in neighbourhoods where other Syrian refugees live, and Turkish people living in those neighbourhoods started to move to other areas, creating segregated communities (Balkan et al. 2018, 3). Single women are particularly vulnerable for it is much harder

4.1 | Syrian accommodation, Gaziantep, Turkey, July 2015.

for them to find houses to rent on their own and to afford the rent even when they do find willing landlords. One civil society organization representative told us that religious charities organize housing for women only, which breaks up families: "When people cross the border with nothing and have no money to rent houses, sometimes they have no choice but to accept offers from religious charities running women only housing facilities. Some families send their daughters to these houses. They are traumatized by war and they get traumatized [a] second time when their families break up like this because they cannot afford housing" (Gaziantep, 17 July 2015).

In cities such as Gaziantep, Kilis, and Antakya, landlords started to increase rents, making it very difficult for Syrians to afford housing, thus forcing them to live in communal houses with poor sanitary conditions. In these communal houses, sometimes as many as fifteen people were forced to live together, sharing close quarters with strangers (*Reliefweb* 2015). Men find it easier to find accommodation in

Precarity through Irregular Access to Social Services

communal houses and live with others; for women and LGBTQ individuals, it is almost impossible.

Community agencies such as the General Commission for Palestinian Refugees in Syria arrange housing for members, with free rent to start:

> They rented some houses for us and provided us with some aid. It lasted for six months. They rented one building for twenty-four families and other families stayed in other buildings ... Some families had to share an apartment ... and the rent is usually paid through some aid organizations, friends and relatives. We now pay 500 lira per month, and the apartment consists of a living area and two small bedrooms. (Interview, Palestinian family, near Kilis, 24 June 2015)

We visited this family's apartment, which was in a housing complex with no public transport to the town centre and with very poor infrastructure. The complex housed mostly Syrian refugees and low-income Turks. The family of six shared the two-bedroom apartment. The rent subsidy had ended, and the father and younger son were working to earn the rent. In the last week of June, they did not yet have the July rent and the father told us that every month brought the same stress and uncertainty and the possibility of eviction. Another Syrian family, in İstanbul, told us that despite four members having odd jobs, their total income barely covered rent, leaving little for food and other basic needs and forcing them to rely on food assistance from humanitarian agencies and the municipality (17 June 2015).

We observed families with four or more members cramming into small rooms and sharing washroom facilities with others. Some people living in small rooms with inadequate, outdoor kitchen facilities were paying exorbitant rents to landlords who knew about many Syrian refugees' desperate need, and so rented out squalid spaces that violated health and sanitary regulations. Some Turkish landlords are prejudiced against Syrians and refuse to rent their properties to them. One refugee told us about his situation: "The most difficult thing I experienced is renting a house. Not all Turkish people want Syrians in their house. I think they do not look at us like moderate Muslims, or they look at

Syria like it is a desert area and we used to live in tents. They feel like we are noisy people" (Gaziantep, 17 July 2016).

Certain groups such as single women and LGBT individuals experience housing problems more acutely than other groups. These problems were emphasized to us in informal conversations with NGO personnel. A director of ASAM provided some critical insights into these issues:

> It is much harder for LGBT individuals. When they share housing with other men, they have to hide their identity, and if they are open with their sexuality, it is a big problem for them ... We do not have a proper solution for this situation, but we have a kind of close relationship with [the] LGBT refugee community, so when a new LGBT applicant comes to this office, and if we do not have a place to offer, we refer them to the local LGBT refugee community to see if they can host the newcomer for a while.
> We also have a close relationship with local LGBT organizations (LGBTI İstanbul) and sometimes ask them to provide shelter. But all of these measures are short term, and we do not have long-term solutions for vulnerable groups such as LGBT individuals. (Interview with ASAM director, İstanbul, 14 July 2016)

Precarity derived from poverty, lack of language facility, and uncertain legal status is dramatically worse for single women and LGBT individuals. Women's shelters are available under the Ministry of Family and Social Policies that provide services specifically for survivors of sexual and gender-based violence; but because so many Turkish and Syrian women qualify for them, capacity is very limited. There are also smaller initiatives that provide accommodation to single women at risk, such as the Şefkat-Der and Sultanbeyli Municipality Women Centre, but these offer only short-term accommodation. The AKP government administers social assistance – to Turks and Syrian refugees alike – largely through informal channels, local municipalities, and charities. However, this network's communal and clientelist ties inhibit access for Syrians. The Turkish Medical Association (TTB) provides anecdotal evidence about how arbitrary these services can be. In Şanlıurfa, for instance, one Syrian family received 400 lira monthly from a social solidarity fund, but a family in another district received only 300 lira and food stamps, and one in another district, nothing (TTB 2014, 67).

As well, newcomers can feel overwhelmed by the large number of actors and agencies with different capacities and missions. For instance, social services such as income support and food and clothing banks fall usually to AFAD, the Turkish Red Crescent, municipalities, and district administrators and religious authorities (*müftülük*). Civil society organizations such as İnsani Yardım Vakfı İHH (Humanitarian Assistance Foundation), İyilikder, and Cansuyu Yardımlaşma ve Dayanışma Derneği (Cansuyu Assistance and Solidarity Association) provide these same services (Bezmialem 2015, 10). These latter groups work with government agencies to provide grocery cards, cooked meals, and clothing, but often without coordination, thus baffling refugees. Each organization raises money and receives government support, but refugees must rely on information from friends and neighbours to actually locate these resources. The director of an arts organization in Gaziantep informed us that faith-based charities work closely with the government and support the Syrian opposition group that has aligned itself with the Turkish government. This creates problems for Syrian refugees with different allegiances:

> The state organized help to Syrians through Islamic charities. For instance, as a businessman, a business person in Gaziantep, if you wanted to donate to refugees, you first had to go the municipality. The municipality does not take the donation from you, but it directs you to Islamic charities, like the Bülbülzade, İHH. And also, for refugees as well, to get help from the municipality they have to go through Islamic charities, get a paper stamped from the charity, and only when they bring that stamped paper do they get food assistance from the municipality. (Interview with the director of Kırkayak Cultural Centre, Gaziantep, June 2015)

According to the Asylum and Migration Research Centre (İltica ve Göç Araştırmaları Merkezi; İGAM) in Ankara, faith-based charities organize most of the aid to Syrian refugees but do no long-term

4.2 | Food ration for a Syrian family, İstanbul, Turkey, July 2015.

planning and do not cooperate with one another, experienced charities, or international aid groups (2013, 20).

Our interviews with Syrian refugees confirmed that the social services available are both informal and arbitrary. For instance, charities and local district administrators (*muhtar*) distribute monthly, preloaded grocery cards to individuals who need food. But the cards are distributed unevenly to Syrian families and are strictly rationed. Some local charities stop providing these cards if they learn that families have children of working age, telling them to send their offspring to work. One family in Kilis lacked continuing access to a card or any other form of food support and so had to go into debt to buy food:

> Upon our arrival, we were supported by some aid agencies here – Turkish, regional, and international relief agencies and NGOs. Some of them were official, and others were civil agencies. They used to provide us with fast [clear?] food on a daily basis for a short period of time. I am now in debt [for] about 600–700 dollars, and I am not the only one … All the families here are suffering and are in debt with food bills. I was supposed to pay

the rent two days ago. I do not have the money for that. (Interview with Syrian man, 24 June 2015)

Precarious Education

Education is another major point of precarity for Syrians in Turkey, even though by law all children in Turkey, regardless of their nationality, have the right to education. In 2015 there were 746,000 school-age Syrians in Turkey, of whom 451,000 were not attending school (UNICEF 2015, 1). Human Rights Watch (2015, 2) reported that 90 per cent of Syrian children in twenty-five government-run camps were attending school regularly, but they were only 13 per cent of all school-aged Syrians in Turkey. AFAD runs seventy educational facilities, while the Ministry of Education has been schooling 75,000 children in seventy-five locations across Turkey (Kanat and Üstün 2015, 23–4). Some 200,000 Syrian children attend temporary education centres (TECs) and regular Turkish public schools. According to the Education Ministry, as of April 2019, there were 1,047,536 school-age Syrian children; only 62 per cent of them (643,058) were enrolled in Turkish schools. Given that in 2015 only 37 per cent of school-age Syrian children were attending school, in four years there has been a significant increase in the schooling of Syrian children (Ministry of Education 2019).

Methods for schooling Syrian children in Turkey have changed significantly over the years. On the assumption that the Syrian war would be over quickly and that most refugees would return there after a short stay in Turkey, the government left the education of Syrian children to private initiatives, mostly organized by Syrians themselves and by international NGOs. Syrians, too, assumed that they would soon be returning to Syria, and they wanted to educate their children in Arabic and in line with the Syrian curriculum to make sure that when they did return there, they would be able to continue their schooling without interruption. But as the war dragged on and it became clear that they would not be returning to Syria in the foreseeable future, the Turkish government changed its approach to the education of Syrian children and identified the incorporation of Syrian children into the national education system as a security issue. It was concerned that unregulated schools would function as spaces of radicalization, recruiting Syrian children into radical organizations (Unutulmaz 2019). On 23 September 2014, the Education Ministry tabled Circular 2014/21, "Education Services for Foreign Nationals," which introduced the concept of Temporary Education Centres (Geçici Eğitim Merkezi; TECs) and provided a legal framework for the monitoring of private schools run by Syrian charities or individuals.

This was the first attempt to bring all Syrian-run education centres under the supervision of the Education Ministry and to introduce Syrian children to the Turkish curriculum. According to Aras and Yasun (2016), the ministry accredits TECs, which offer an Arabic-language curriculum from the Ministry of Education of the Interim Syrian Government, and 78 per cent of Syrian children attend these TECs (3–4). Students may transfer from TECs to Turkish schools after appropriate assessment, but language barriers and differences in curriculum are such that few do so (2016, 3). Many TECs have been established in office buildings (including in NGO offices) or in public schools (for evening classes). Most lack adequate funding and seek funds from well-off families and humanitarian agencies (5). For a while, the Directorate of Religious Affairs ran schools in mosques that offered Koranic instruction and other subjects (interview, humanitarian relief agency, Ankara, 25 July 2016). TECs impeded the long-term integration of Syrian children into the Turkish education system, for the families that sent their children to these centres preferred to have their children educated in Arabic and in a familiar cultural context (Çelik and İçduygu 2019, 258–9). TECs, however, were not effective in delivering consistent education. They charged fees, which made it difficult for poor children to attend. They also offered an inconsistent quality of education, for they lacked a unified curriculum (258).

The multitude of TECs with differing objectives and uncoordinated curriculums sowed confusion among Syrian refugees. They also reflected Syrians' own early expectations about their future in Turkey. Initially, many Syrian parents chose to send their children to TECs and other Syrian-run private schools: they expected to return home soon, and schools with a Syrian curriculum would prevent a gap in their children's education. Ankara shared the same outlook and so did not develop a long-term education policy for Syrian children. Once it became clear that the Syrians would be staying much longer, perhaps even permanently, it began planning to teach the children Turkish and to introduce the Turkish curriculum into their schools. TEC schools have since been adopting Turkish standards and receive accreditation once they meet the Education Ministry's criteria.

However, despite Ankara's standardizing efforts, variety, inconsistency, and lack of coordination continued until recently. One humanitarian relief agency told us: "While the ministry controls all efforts related to education, there are independent schools operating on their own. For instance, there is a Libyan school here operating a branch. There is another school run by the Saudis. I don't know how they come here but they are here running schools. Sometimes they make an agreement with the ministry to get accreditation but not always" (Ankara, 25 July 2016). Setting aside the obvious educational confusion, most Syrian children in urban areas do not attend school regularly, and given that quite a few of them have been in Turkey since 2011, many lack formal education. According to Human Rights Watch (HRW 2015, 3), three main factors keep Syrian children out of school: lack of Turkish language, financial hardship, and problems with social adaptation.

Several families we interviewed confirmed that they faced multiple barriers. Some did not even realize that their young people could attend public schools. Others felt intimidated by the school system because they could not speak Turkish; lacking language support, children stopped attending school (Kilis, 24 June 2015). Having no Turkish left some children feeling alienated by the Turkish school system, and discriminated against when they did attend, so some families preferred the TECs, which taught in Arabic and offered a more hospitable environment (Kilis, 24 June 2015). Some Syrian children experience significant bullying and exclusion in Turkish schools and so prefer not to attend them (Unutulmaz 2019, 2380). Finally, many children have to support their families by working in textile factories or car repair shops, coffee shops, restaurants, and other services (Kaya and Kıraç 2016, 27). A former president of the Research Centre on Asylum and Migration (İGAM), an Ankara-based think tank and NGO, told us:

> The education sector does not work as well as the health sector. Syrians have a right to send their children to Turkish schools, but

they don't always do so. First of all, there is a language problem. Kids do not speak Turkish. In some areas the Turkish schools are not willing to receive Syrian kids, especially in border towns where numbers are large. Last year the government issued a circular to force Turkish schools to accept Syrian children, but it did not work ... Some people are mobile and do not stay in one area, so their children end up leaving their school, and finally there is poverty, and many Syrians cannot afford to send their children to school. [The] education sector is complicated and riddled with many complications. (phone interview, Gaziantep 20 June 2015)

Turkish and international humanitarian relief agencies offer basic instruction and language training, as well as a safe environment, for small numbers of traumatized children. For the daughter of one very poor Syrian family in İstanbul, one such centre was the only positive thing in her life:

They work with my daughter to help her overcome what she witnessed in Syria and the postwar trauma. They have two rooms where they work with kids in order to prepare them for the Turkish school next year. My daughter is really enjoying the classes as people there [are] so nice and there are many Syrians. They take them on trips and have lots of activities. My daughter is really keen to stay with them more than going to an official school. (Interview, 17 June 2015)

According to statistics provided by the Education Ministry, which carries out the Turkish government's decision to incorporate Syrian children into the Turkish school system, the number of Syrian children attending TECs declined to 90,512 in 211 TECs in eighteen cities (Ministry of Education 2019). TECs today are now functioning to teach Turkish and prepare Syrian children for the Turkish education system. Most Syrian-run TECs have been relocated to Turkish school buildings. The EU has launched a project with Turkey's Education Ministry to facilitate the integration of Syrian children into the national education system. It has provided the ministry with a direct grant of 300 million euros for a project named "Promoting Integration of Syrian

Children into the Turkish Education System." The core objective of this program is to train 5,600 Turkish-language teachers to quickly teach Syrian children Turkish and to facilitate those children's enrolment in the national education system (Delegation of the EU to Turkey 2017).

Long-term uncertainty under temporary protection has made it significantly more difficult to increase Syrian children's school attendance. Assuming that permanent residency was unobtainable, many families had planned to return home eventually and saw no need for their children to receive a Turkish education. Their stay has since become indefinite, but barriers to permanent status discourage parents from investing in their children's education and integration. In recent years, though, a changing outlook among Syrian refugees and the Turkish government's persistent efforts have reversed some of these obstacles; Syrian families are now being encouraged to send their children to Turkish schools. As Çetin and İçduygu (2019) observe, the incorporation of Syrian children into the national education system is a positive step toward improving the long-term prospects of Syrian youth in Turkish society, provided that the national education system develops "an intercultural and inclusive habitus for the incorporation of the incorporation of students coming from non-Turkish backgrounds" (263).

Precarious Employment

The patchwork of social rights available to Syrian refugees in Turkey under temporary protection can help them establish some short-term stability. However, those rights are complicated and incomplete, which renders Syrians' living conditions even more precarious and inhibits longer-term stability. Also, there is no firm legal entitlement underlying these rights that can lead to refugee status or eventual citizenship. Temporary protection means that whatever rights Syrians have in Turkey, they are more arbitrary than those enjoyed by conditional refugees. That is why so many Syrians attempt to enter other countries – they hope to find international protection.

Uncertain social rights disrupt Syrian refugees' lives perhaps most clearly in terms of employment. Turkey's LFIP of April 2013 regulates work permits for those under temporary protection. That law limits the types of work Syrians can do; it also results in precarious workspaces, many of them informal. The jobs available to them may be illegal, exploitative, and provide minimal social security and job protection. As we saw in chapter 3, registration for temporary protection did not initially bring employment rights. The Temporary Protection Regulation (TPR, October 2014) allowed the Ministry of Labour and Social Services to prescribe working conditions. The Council of Ministers has the authority to allow Syrian refugees to work in specific locations and sectors, but it has issued them very few work permits. While they may, under LFIP, apply for a work permit, their sheer numbers and circumstances make the process impractical. Also, such a permit is valid only for a specific workplace. Syrians may not comprise more than 10 per cent of an employer's personnel; they must secure fixed-term contracts; and they may work only in the province specified on the permit. To work in another province, they must apply to do so; that means paying an application fee of 600 lira per year of prospective work; and their initial one-year permit is renewable for only three years (Republic of Turkey 2013).

As of April 2020, 34,573 Syrians under temporary protection had been given work permits (Mülteciler Derneği 2020). It's not easy for foreigners to obtain an employment permit: they need a valid passport, a residency permit, and a job offer indicating that no qualified Turk is available (except in certain sectors; see below). The director of the Syrian Economic Forum outlined the process to us:

> First, you have to find an employer, and the employer should apply to the Ministry of Labour, showing that instead of hiring a Turkish national, he or she should hire this Syrian or this foreign person because of certain reasons. There should be a justification to prefer a foreigner [rather] than a Turkish national ... Also, the same law obliges the employer to hire five Turkish nationals in order to hire one foreigner. (Gaziantep, 22 June 2015)

A draft circular from the ministry spelled out sectors and locations for Syrian refugees to work under temporary protection (Kutlu 2015, 7). It went into effect in February 2016, allowing them to apply for a permit six months after they had received a *kimlik*; that permit, though, would be restricted to a specific location. Syrians could comprise no more than 10 per cent of a business's workforce (*Hürriyet Daily News*

2016). (Turkish workers had expressed their fears – loudly – that they would lose their jobs if Syrians accepted lower wages.) Under the new regulation, Syrian applicants would no longer need a valid passport or a residency permit and could apply for a work permit with only their *kimlik*. However, like other foreigners, they still needed a job offer from a business where less than 10 per cent of the employees were Syrian.

Under the LFIP, a workplace must have at least ten Turkish employees before it can hire one Syrian under temporary protection, instead of the usual five. Quite probably, this is meant to address concerns that Syrians are taking jobs from Turks. As well, a Syrian needs a job offer before the employer may apply for a permit on his or her behalf. This is perhaps a reasonable rule, given how few foreigners are looking for jobs in the country, but with the influx of Syrian job-seekers, it has become prohibitively expensive for employers to hire Syrians legally and apply for work permits for them.

Yet simply obtaining a permit does not guarantee work. The director of the Association of Ankara Solidarity, a Syrian-run organization trying to improve Syrians' relations with local residents, explained to us: "Currently not getting a work permit is an advance for Syrians. Once they have the permit, they have to pay for social insurance and their employers also have to contribute to their payment. Then the employer says, if I have to pay for social insurance, then I will hire a Turkish worker. Why would [one] hire a Syrian worker and put up with cultural differences and language barriers?" (25 July 2016). Another Syrian in Gaziantep concurred: "Work permits are not an issue for Syrians; lots of them cannot get legal jobs. Even for those who can get legal jobs, it is too costly to get it so usually people do not bother with [a] work permit. It is much easier to find a job without [a] permit, and it is cheaper" (interview, 12 July 2017).

Apparently, it is easier for Syrians to find a job without a work permit, so that employers can pay them less, under the table, and skip social security and job protection. This situation has created precarious conditions for Syrians, leaving them at the employers' mercy and compelling them to work for low salaries and with no legal protection against workplace abuses. One Syrian told us: "The major problem here in cities like Gaziantep is when you have poor Syrians competing with poor Turks. Hardly making minimum wage here and having an apartment, and then suddenly [the arrival of] Syrians, and now a person is working for an even lower wage and rents are much higher. That is too much pressure on the Turkish community" (12 July 2017).

The LFIP system has minimal impact, however, because many Syrian refugees already work illegally in sectors such as construction, restaurants, and textiles. One interviewee lamented: "There is the language barrier, and they exploit us. They pay minimum wages, or they do not pay at all. For example, the daily wage of a Turkish construction worker is 100 lira, whereas they pay the refugee or the displaced worker 40 or 50 lira for the same kind of job, and sometimes they do not pay him at all" (Kilis, 24 June 2015). He added: "There are some small factories that are involved in making coffee and pickles. They pay around 10 lira per day, and the shifts are more than 12 hours. It is complete exploitation." Because of such conditions, "some of the young guys were reluctant to look for work, since they might not receive any money at the end of the day."

BETAM (Bahçeşehir Üniversitesi Ekonomik ve Toplumsal Araştırmalar Merkezi) reports that young Syrian workers between eighteen and twenty-nine receive only 79 per cent of what their Turkish counterparts receive (2018, 7). They tend to take low-wage jobs, such as seasonal agriculture, thus displacing workers already at the bottom of the wage scale. In Gaziantep many Syrian refugees recycle garbage, replacing the Kurdish migrants who have moved into the cities over the past twenty years. An interviewee from Mazlumder in Gaziantep referred to this as "shift poverty," that is, one precarious group gives way to another, slightly more vulnerable. Such willingness to work for even less pits newcomers against poor local workers, creating tension (*Ege Postası* [*Aegean Post*, Basmane, İzmir] 2015). Similarly, in southern, seasonal agriculture, Syrians may be willing to accept 20 lira per day instead of the already low 60 lira (*Özgür Düşünce Gazetesi* 2016). Adding to Syrians' precarity, police often raid locations that they know hire Syrians illegally. One refugee explained to us: "They entered the restaurants and took all the Syrians who work in the kitchens. I used to work there. I managed to escape [through] a back door. I was smuggled with others at that time" (İstanbul, 17 June 2015).

Despite heavy fines for hiring Syrians illegally, many businesses find the lower wages irresistible (Kutlu 2015). According to another interviewee, "My son is frustrated because he is unemployed. We know

4.3 | Syrians working in a workshop in Gaziantep, Turkey, October 2019.

that we are not going to build houses or establish real communities … All … we are asking for is an income to survive, nothing more" (İstanbul, 17 June 2015). A compatriot in Kilis remarked, "I do not work. Our situation is really difficult here. From a humanitarian point of view, this is not an acceptable situation. We face a big dilemma at the end of each month, which is how can we pay the monthly rent?" (24 June 2015). In the words of yet another, "Syrian businessmen or professionals who managed to establish a business here are interested in settling permanently in Turkey, but this is not the case for the huge numbers of refugees who are unable to find a job or a sustainable income. Syrian families are usually big." One Syrian lawyer observed, "And now we see that in some cases all family members are involved in working, including young girls at the age of thirteen, who try to find jobs in factories and workshops like their brothers. This is a new social phenomenon, since these jobs have never been practised by girls before" (Gaziantep, 22 June 2015).

It's unclear how these challenges affect Syrian women. However, Mazlumder reported (2014, 41) that 80 per cent of female Syrians who responded to its urban survey did not work, and those who did were usually in services such as cleaning, elder care, or restaurant kitchen work, all potentially precarious positions where they are vulnerable to sexual harassment. As well, they fared worse than their male compatriots – for instance, earning perhaps 10 to 15 lira per day for cleaning house, while a Turkish counterpart took in 75 to 100 lira. These dreadful conditions, along with legal uncertainty, force the most vulnerable of Syrian refugees (such as members of the Dom community) into selling trinkets or collecting garbage on the street (interview, Mazlumder, Gaziantep, 25 June 2015). A few NGOs with scarce resources try to find work for Syrian women. One such NGO, the volunteer group Small Projects, organizes women's workshops in İstanbul. Its director outlined its mission:

> We are obviously not in a position to find employment for fifty to a hundred women, and we are also not really in a position to employ fifty to a hundred women. We basically are in a point of where we can turn ourselves into a small business running a women's handicraft collective kind of thing, which was like, 'We can string together bracelets, and people would buy them – it would be lovely.'
>
> Very complicated and time-consuming project to be doing, but it is evolving and improving, and it had some really good support from other organizations, and people are doing similar things to help us with product design and development, training process, internal management, and administration kind of development. People buy in a semi-bulk quantity, because one of the things about the economy of the world is that we can sell things to America for a much higher price than we can sell things in Turkey.

We fund this project out of our pocket, because it is not that expensive to buy bits and pieces in Turkey. And then once you sell something, there is a bit of a return that goes back into the operation. (İstanbul, 14 July 2016)

Given that the number of Syrian refugees in Turkey is currently 3.6 million and that only around 30,000 work permits have been issued to them, most Syrians work illegally and in precarious conditions. While there are no established numbers, child labour is fairly common among Syrian refugees; these children work mostly in agriculture, garbage recycling, and textiles (Tarlan 2016). Estimates are that there are 1,645,000 Syrians who could be incorporated into the workforce; also, that around 600,000 of them are working illegally (Kaygısız 2017, 8). They are willing to accept lower wages and unfavourable working conditions. This places them in direct conflict with other low-wage workers and fuels intercommunal tensions. According to one survey, 69 per cent of Turkish citizens living in five cities where Syrians live believed that Syrians were contributing to unemployment among Turks (8). Periodically, workers in different cities organize demonstrations against Syrian refugees, claiming that Syrians are taking their jobs and causing unemployment (*Hürriyet* 2014).

Humanitarian agencies have been launching job-training programs for young Syrian refugees. The director of the Mavi Hilal organization summarized its program:

In İstanbul we have a youth training centre for vocational training and placing them in different jobs. Finally, now we are starting with huge project of employing Syrians for different municipalities; for example, in Kilis we have 134,000 Syrians. Two thousand two hundred Syrians will be working for the municipality in different capacities; the municipality will pay their salaries, and they will help with the municipal services. We have similar programs in Islahiye, Akçakale, Urfa, Sultanbeyli, Küçükçekmece, and Bağcılar. (İstanbul, 13 July 2016)

UN agencies, government authorities, and NGOs are now designing and implementing various livelihood projects. Generally, these encompass language and vocational training, social cohesion programs, job placement, and entrepreneurship opportunities. The UNHCR and the Turkish government are cooperating to offer employment services for Syrian refugees. For instance, the UNHCR's Livelihood program has supported more than 3,000 refugees' participation in entrepreneurship training and trained more than 300 İŞKUR (Government Employment Agency) staff in job counselling support for refugees (UNHCR 2019a, 9–14). The UN Food and Agriculture Organization (FAO) has partnered with the private sector to deliver agricultural skills training to improve livelihood opportunities for Syrian refugees; this includes the cultivation and harvesting of various crops, irrigation management, and farm management (FAO 2018).

Finally, a handful of initiatives are encouraging Syrian entrepreneurs to set up businesses in Turkey to create jobs for Syrian refugees. In Gaziantep, for example, the director of the Syrian Economic Forum – a think tank hoping to help rebuild Syria through economic opportunities and education – told us (22 June 2015) about the forum's discussions with Ankara about establishing a local tax-free economic zone to encourage Syrian investment in Turkey. He added that Syrians' cool relations with local businesses have spurred their efforts to produce a possible autonomous zone, where they could bring their equipment from Syria and create work for their compatriots. Ankara indicated that it could lift the 10 per cent quota in that zone, thus opening up job opportunities for Syrian refugees without hurting domestic workers. The director of the Syrian Economic Forum insisted: "We don't need money from them; we need them to start work. When they start work, that means our people work" (Gaziantep, 22 June 2015). He added that the potential net effect extends beyond jobs for those individuals, "because we know that each one has ten persons behind him, that'll be around half million people who will not need [a] food basket every month."

Conclusion

This chapter has outlined how government practices and policies that create irregular access to health care, housing, education, and employment help explain the diverse ways in which Syrian refugees negotiate and navigate everyday life. Another factor complicating Syrians' access to housing, employment and other social services is their uncertainty about how to access some of these services. Since the 1980s, neoliberal economic policies have been dominant in Turkey, and market-based approaches strongly shape access to health care, employment, housing, and education. Cheap labour, employer-friendly labour regulations, and relatively low payroll taxes were crucial to making Turkish exports competitive on the global market. The labour market is less flexible in Syria, which means that Syrians are more familiar with a system in which the government provides essential services, including access to food. During our interviews, many Syrians stated that they found it difficult to adapt to the market-based system's harsh realities. This unfamiliarity with the neoliberal environment has made them more vulnerable with regard to housing and employment. As noted, even when they do find jobs, they have very little room to negotiate and usually work for exploitative wages with very little protection.

Similarly, finding adequate housing is a challenge, for Turkish landlords take advantage of them and charge exorbitant rents for substandard housing. Syrians' precarious living conditions intersect with the harsh realities of neoliberal economic policies, and class and gender lines further complicate Syrians' access to social services, housing, and work. Syrians with financial and cultural capital find it easier to establish businesses and shield themselves from inadequate housing and social services. Yet most Syrians, especially women and children – who are 77 per cent of the Syrian refugees in Turkey – bear the brunt of ambiguous legal protection, exploitative job markets, and inadequate housing. Turkey's flexible labour market has created additional hazards for migrant women and children as there are minimal protections. Many of them work illegally for meagre wages, which makes it impossible for them to access whatever protections exist in the labour laws. They are vulnerable to harassment and violence (Kıvılcım 2016, 205). Syrian children are subject to similar vulnerabilities as many of them work illegally in the garment industry. It is common for employers to hire Syrian children as young as twelve and to make them work for less than minimum wage and sometimes not pay them at all (*Guardian* 2016a).

While the Turkish government provides health care and education to all Syrian refugees registered under temporary protection, lack of a housing allowance and other forms of social assistance are constant sources of instability for Syrians. As part of the European Civil Protection and Humanitarian Aid Operations (ECHO) program, the Turkish Red Crescent has been distributing monthly spending cards worth 120 Turkish lira (around $20 USD) to one million Syrian refugees living in urban centres since 2016. This initiative, which is funded by the EU and administered by the Turkish Red Crescent, is the first program to provide regular social assistance to Syrians. Prior to this program, various humanitarian organizations and charities arranged similar initiatives on an irregular basis in different cities. Similarly, the lack of regular employment opportunities and the bureaucratic hurdles involved in getting work permits have forced Syrians into the irregular job market. As noted, many Syrians work illegally and are exploited by employers seeking cheap labour. This has pitted Syrians against low-income Turkish workers, with the result that they are commonly blamed for taking jobs away from Turkish workers.

Turkey's temporary protection regime does not fully comply with international standards. Syrian refugees, with no clear path to citizenship, have to pick their way through a maze of ever-changing laws and regulations and arbitrarily dispensed social services. These precarious circumstances operate at multiple levels of space, movement, and status. This complex and continuously evolving maze renders it very difficult for Syrian refugees to establish stable lives.

CHAPTER FIVE

Resisting Precarity: Claiming Rights to Belong and to Stay

As this book has documented, Syrians in Turkey live in limbo – they are neither guests, as at the war's start, nor refugees, a status the Turkish government has denied them. Instead, they subsist legally, but under temporary protection, never to be more than temporary residents. As we saw earlier, they set about building their lives, seeking health care, housing, food, employment, and schooling, but always within this transitory process, and many of them face discrimination and harassment from those Turks who see them not as long-term settlers but as transients. Many Syrians are confronting their precarious conditions by demanding better living conditions and stronger rights to education, housing, employment, and health care. But importantly, they are also resisting their precarious living conditions in quieter ways – for example, through activities of daily life and cultural production.

Engin Isin (2017) notes that rights-claiming activities can be understood as enactments or performances of citizenship. These performances focus on what people can do to achieve membership, inclusion, and participation in the political community. Syrians can thus be seen to be engaging in a politics of citizenship, as demanding rights to belong – and to be *recognized* as belonging – in society and in their communities. But this rights-claiming does not always entail making direct political demands or protesting in the streets. As Catherine Neveu (2014) points out in her discussion of "ordinary citizenship," it is equally important to pay attention to the "'feeble signals' of 'low noise practices'" (91). She explains: "By working on 'active' (mobilized, demonstrating concern and expressing claims) citizens, social scientists would miss out on the practices, opinions and representations of the vast majority of citizens: the silent, 'ordinary' ones" (268). The following examples of how Syrians look to cultural production and practices might be seen as examples of "low noise practices." As the literature in this field has shown, individuals' and groups' participation in forms of cultural production enables them and others to understand one another better (Mistrík 2016). It also allows refugees, for example, to create more positive and more representative images of their culture (McNevin 2010; Pereira, Maiztegui-Oñate, and Mata-Codesal 2016). As Erich Mistrík (2016, 2) notes, "In the current multicultural and globalized world, [arts and arts education] play crucial roles in understanding the identities of other people. Being aware of who I am, where I stand, what I value and how I relate to other people is the core for understanding other people." Syrians can act on this premise in cultural centres, where they can create more positive images of Syrian culture and history – for example through food, music, and art – and where fellow Syrians and their Turkish neighbours can engage with and come to understand each other. Syrians understand that teaching their neighbours about their culture and history can help them grasp what it means to be Syrian and to be a refugee in Turkey. They try to challenge the common perception in Turkey that they are victims and/or a burden on society; they also try to provide alternative narratives about who they are, and through these alternatives, to make claims to be recognized as valuable new members of their communities. The next section examines how Syrians use food and the arts to build bridges between communities in urban Turkey.

Claiming Representation and Belonging through Culinary Culture

One of the most visible ways Syrians express themselves in Turkish cities is through their culinary culture. In İstanbul, Syrians began by opening small neighbourhood restaurants and fast-food joints for their own community. They have built on this success by establishing larger venues to introduce Syrian cuisine to Turks. For example, in İstanbul's heavily Syrian districts, such as Fatih and Aksaray, a number of Syrian restaurants, patisseries, and cafés serve a wide variety of food. In 2015, in Turkey, some 26 per cent of foreign-owned food businesses were Syrian or partly so (Nguyen-Okwu 2015). Some of these places

5.1 | Syrian restaurant, Tarbuş, İstanbul, Turkey, July 2015.

also serve as culinary and cultural centres. Dalia Mortada of İstanbul's Savouring Syria, notes that many of the first Syrian restaurants served hummus and falafel but that it was almost impossible to find a broader variety of Syrian food (*Hürriyet Daily News* 2017).

A legendary Syrian restaurant in İstanbul is Tarbuş (*fez*), named after the hat that both Turks and Syrians wore in Ottoman times (Topol 2016). Mohamed Bitar opened Tarbuş in 2012 on Millet Street in Aksaray. When he spoke to us in the summer of 2015, he attributed his success to his knowledge of Turkish language and culture from "working with special trading missions in Turkey between '92 and 2011," particularly in mosaic and ceramic decoration. Dismayed with the Assad government, he began writing provocative social media pieces in Syria encouraging dissent. When the government started to crack down, he feared it would target him. He fled Syria at the outbreak of the war, leaving his house and mosaic-stone factory behind in Damascus.

When he arrived in Turkey, he started cooking, which he loved to do, having learned how from his parents. "I left, I am here ... because my hobby is food, let me come to my hobby. I come to İstanbul, one thousand dollars, this is what I have. I have the knowledge about this country. So, I have one hobby. I like it so much the kitchen. Cooking, really, I have a good experience." He started by selling "some special sort of meze, some special humus." There was a market for it, as "people who live here from Syria, Palestine, from Syria, from Jordan, they miss Arabic [food] too ... So, at that time I bring from Syria some special things, some *baharat* [spice] ... [and] I start selling. Until that time there is no Syrian [food], no Arabic kitchen. No bread, [the] first Syrian bread we do" (interview, İstanbul, 2015).

Since its opening in 2012, Tarbuş has grown, and garnered Turkish and international press. It now employs more than 300 workers (Topol 2016) in nine outlets and two bakeries (Sharma 2017). His restaurant is also a community hub, a place where Syrians arriving in İstanbul can go for advice about settling in, connecting with other Syrians, and looking for work:

> Because they leave the city, they fled from the region, so they cannot go to the Embassy, so they come here. And I ask them, "How can I do? What we can do?" So, I help them: Somebody needs something? OK, I'll take them to go there. OK so this is fifty liras, so you can go. So slowly and slowly, they trust this place and they trust the knowledge ... They stay here and here, wait to just get advice, to say how and what they do. "I have a friend who has a factory. OK, you can go to this factory and work." I'll bring them and I'll make connections with all the people who want a job, who want work. I did the connections. (Interview, İstanbul, 2016)

As the restaurant succeeded and developed a reputation as a networking hub, Bitar tells us, he and fellow Syrians opened al-Tadam, a community association, and later al-Qadur, an Arabic-language elementary school, which employed nineteen Syrian teachers. By creating a successful restaurant enterprise that hires Syrians and other Middle Easterners, Bitar has challenged some Turks' negative stereotypes about Syrians, such as that they "are lazy." "OK, we leave our country, but we work. We have the work. We have the money. We pay tax here – we pay everything. We don't want you to help us by [giving us] money ... We want ... just the Turkish [people] to accept these [Syrian] people inside the work market. We want the right [to work]."

The Turkish media often hail Tarbuş as a "refugee success story" and as evidence of Turkish society's acceptance of newcomers. Even so, Bitar notes that it was a challenge to introduce Turks to Syrian food. "I tried hard to say on television, about fifty interviews, television shows, I told them: 'Your food is like our food. There are some differences in spice. Baharat.'" He says: "This is Turkey – very [hard] to change," but "you must." He adds that Turks are slowly starting to visit the restaurant and that the two cultures must move closer together to "make a middle culture."

Bitar's success is in part a result of his more privileged starting position: he came to Turkey having already established social, cultural, and economic capital as a businessman there. He already knew the Turkish culture and language, and his business connections placed him in a stronger position to open a successful venture. Tarbuş now serves as a model for others. It has encouraged many other Syrians, many of whom have less capital, to open restaurants and patisseries.

There are successful examples now of women's collective employment in the area of food production. One of the better-known Syrian initiatives is the Women's Solidarity Kitchen, also known as the Woman to Woman Refugee Kitchen. Here, Syrian women are using their knowledge of Syrian cooking to create a food business. Some fifteen Syrian women cook alongside Turkish women to produce jams and pickles. The business has provided a sustainable income for these women, besides providing them with opportunities for greater communication with their host community (Vardar 2017). Meanwhile in Gaziantep, a cultural organization called Kırkayak Kültür has been operating the Kitchen Matbakh Women's Workshop since 2016. The kitchen provides a "common space where people, especially women, come together to jointly create food, and participate in other artistic and cultural projects and, in the process, to learn about social cohesion and ways of living together" (Tarlan 2020, 257). Based on a "social initiative" model, the Kitchen Workshop brings together women to cook together, to discuss issues of food production and food culture, and to create products such as preserves, jewellery, and handicrafts. The workshop empowers women by supporting the creation of products they can then sell throughout the Middle East for a small profit (258).

In some of the cities that host large Syrian populations such as İstanbul, Gaziantep, and Kilis, restaurants and dessert cafés have opened in many neighbourhoods. In the Fatih district of İstanbul ("Little Syria"), for example, many Syrian bakers are doing especially well with Syrian baklava (a sweet pastry popular throughout the former Ottoman lands). Modern Turkish culture emphasizes food, and many Turks take strong pride in their nation's cuisine, so bridging the cultures through Syrian food may seem risky. Yet many Turks have come to appreciate and enjoy Syrian baklava, which is firmer, drier, and smaller than the Turkish version.

At one Syrian baklava store (*baklavacı*) we spoke with two young men working there. Relatives of one of the men had opened the store, which now had four branches. The men told us about the obstacles they faced: high taxes, red tape, and the scramble for funds. According to one of them, "Turkey as a country doesn't encourage that much. Everything sets you back instead of moving you forward. Check out the taxes and the laws. Until today, and it's been nine months or a year, we've only been giving money from our own pockets ... Every time you open your eyes you have something to pay. That's regarding taxes and those matters" (interview, İstanbul, 2016). They were hiring mostly Syrians, and in this way, like Tarbuş, they were supporting their compatriots and providing much-needed work for them. When we asked who frequented the *baklavacı*, one of the men explained, "Now it's more Turkish people for the main part." They had also developed an export business to North America through an uncle who had lived in the United States for thirty-five years. "We want to deliver our products to the largest number of people possible," rather than "depending on Turkish people or inside Turkey. I am open to all the world."

These are but a few examples of how Syrians negotiate their daily lives through food culture. They use restaurants and baklava shops to create work and income but also to serve as spaces for networking and

5.2 | Baklava shop, İstanbul, Turkey, July 2015.

learning about how to navigate life in Turkey. In venues like these, Syrians can proudly present different, delicious food to their neighbours and allow them to see Syrians as more than refugees – as hard workers and entrepreneurs keen to contribute to the Turkish economy and society. Moreover, in places like Tarbuş, we see a conscious effort to build bridges to Turks through their common Ottoman heritage.

5.3 | Shop with Arabic signage, İstanbul, Turkey.

Despite these positive examples of entrepreneurialism and hard work, the path toward creating a more positive image of Syrians is made more rocky by the ongoing challenges and obstacles facing Syrians. Before 2016, in urban neighbourhoods that were predominantly Syrian, such as Aksaray, many Syrian stores and restaurants displayed Arabic signage. That signage perhaps reflected Syrians' growing comfort in living in the city as well as a means to claim space and a sense of belonging. More and more Turks, though, view such signage and the growing presence of restaurants and stores as evidence that the Syrians are there to stay. Recent polls and reports have found that xenophobia toward Syrians is rising. For example, in November 2017 a survey conducted by Infakto RW found that the vast majority of Turkish people surveyed held negative attitudes toward Syrians. The results, based on interviews with 2,004 people (most of them from urban centres, and 65 per cent of whom had a secondary or higher level of education), revealed that the majority believed that "Syrians were taking jobs away from people in Turkey" (71.4 per cent), that Syrians were "raising crime rates in Turkey" (67.4 per cent), and that Syrians were threatening Turkish "moral values and traditions" (66.4 per cent) (Erdoğan and Semerci 2018). Another 2017 public opinion survey, this one undertaken by Murat Erdoğan (2017, 20), found that Turks were more likely to apply negative adjectives to Syrians, such as "lazy," "rude," "dowdy/filthy," and "untrustable/dangerous" (also noted in Makovsky 2019). Yet another CAP-commissioned poll, this one conducted in May 2018, noted that "nearly 80 percent of Turks want the Syrians to return to Syria" (Makovsky 2019).[1]

The Turkish government has responded to this anti-Syrian sentiment in various ways. One is by periodically cracking down on Arabic signage in Adana province and in the Syrian districts of various cities, including İslahiye in Gaziantep; Kırıkhan district in Hatay; and İstanbul neighbourhoods such as Fatih, Zeytinburnu, and Bayrampaşa (Stockholm Centre for Freedom 2017; *Hürriyet Daily News* 2019; Letsche 2019). According to the Turkish Standards Institute (TSE), shop signs must now be written with 75 per cent of the content in Turkish (*Hürriyet Daily News* 2019). On 15 June 2019, the Turkish Interior Minister Suleyman Soylu announced that "offending" Arabic shop signs across Turkey would be changed within six months. "There is a standard and that standard is Turkish," he said in July. "If they want to write small Arabic letters underneath, they can. Everyone will stick to the rules and the obligations, whatever they are" (Letsche 2019). The signage policy has sent a clear signal to Syrians that their visible presence is not welcome. More than this, as many have noted, this policy has fuelled further discrimination toward Syrians in Turkey. Some, like Ertugrul Kurkcu, honorary president of the pro-Kurdish Peoples' Democratic Party, criticize the government for "using the plight of Syrian refugees to garner political support," accusing it of "fanning the flames of controlled hate" (Letsche 2019). Others, like journalist Tamer Yazar in Hatay, contend that "the removal of Arabic-language shop signs is another expression of growing intolerance towards Syrians" (Letsche 2019).

Claiming Representation and Belonging through Arts Projects

Faced with this xenophobia, Syrians are harnessing their culture to challenge negative stereotypes in the media that fuel discrimination. Here the arts provide a space where Syrians can represent their identity and culture.

InEnArt in İstanbul served as a platform for launching "Searching Traces." The project "provided Syrian refugees with cameras and other film equipment to shoot short videos reflecting their new lives in Turkey with aim of shifting Turkish people's perceptions of Syrians as victims to capable individuals in control of their own lives. Focusing on themes of displacement, participants narrate their own stories through film, reflecting on their everyday experiences" (Bianet 2016). The resulting short films and documentaries were screened at local venues to counter stereotypes and encourage greater understanding of Syrian refugees in Turkey.

Other cultural spaces offer opportunities to build community. A Syrian photographer named Omar Beraktar founded the artist collective Arthere İstanbul, in 2014 in Kadıkoy, a gentrified and rather bohemian neighbourhood (Murphy and Chatzipanagiotidou 2020). Its two-storey building houses a café as well as studios for painting and photography. Beraktar operates the centre as a gathering place for Syrian artists in Turkey as well as a space for Turkish and Syrian artists to meet and work together (*T24* 2017). He could never have opened such a facility in Syria; by contrast, doing so in İstanbul was fairly easy, and it quickly became a support centre for Syrian artists in their new environment (*T24* 2017). As Burhan El-Hatib, a twenty-two-year-old musician, explained, the venue allowed him to meet other Syrian and Turkish artists and to continue to make music (*T24* 2017). Arthere can be viewed as "a space of artistic work in exile" (Murphy and Chatzipanagiotidou 2020, 2) that provides working space for artists and an opportunity to build community with both fellow exiles and Turkish artists. However, Syrian artists face tensions between their own aspirations and public perceptions about Syrian "refugee art." In conversation with one Arthere member, Murphy and Chatzipanagiotidou (2020, 2) discussed this member's objection to "how the category of 'refugee art' restricted displaced artists creatively and thematically, by valorizing predominantly artistic projects that dealt with displacement, conflict and loss." They further explain that "such categorizations and discursive constructions force artists to produce art 'on demand' to respond to particular thematic expectations or value their existing work through hierarchies of authenticity embedded in the category of 'refugee art.'" This member of Arthere explained his concerns: "The minute you call an artist a 'refugee artist' and an exhibition a 'refugee exhibition,' people think this is charity and they are not willing to pay for your art. They don't think of you as a professional" (quoted in Murphy and Chatzipanagiotidou 2020, 2).

Finding space in which to work and to build artistic community is an important first step, and a very tall one. Artists must work hard to disrupt stereotypes of Syrians as well as perceptions that Syrian art is "refugee art." Arthere provides workspace but also a community where Syrian artists can shed these labels, indeed disrupt them, while developing their individual artistic expression.

Pages is yet another important cultural space: a combination café and bookstore, designed to bring Syrians together with local Turks.[2] Pages's website describes its aim as "keeping the culture alive": "We offer a home to all cultural and artistic expressions, readings, debate and discussions. A home where Syrian culture greets and meets the world." Moreover, the website notes, "In Pages, we all believe that working to keep the culture alive is what makes this planet alive, more humane and radiant with beauty! We also believe that we all share the duty of supporting this mission and help to get to know others – without prior judgement, just the way they perceive themselves."

Pages' founder, Samer Alkadri, is a painter and graphic designer. He left Damascus with his wife and child and opened Pages in İstanbul in 2015.[3] Like Tarbuş's owner, Samer has been able to navigate the cultural scene and to open a successful business perhaps more easily than most, given the cultural and economic capital he has brought as a middle-class Syrian settling in İstanbul. Nevertheless, he encountered challenges when he chose to set up a business in İstanbul. He explains that he chose İstanbul for its thriving cultural scene, but also because it was closer to home than Germany:

> I choose İstanbul, I choose to live here ... We have visa in 2017 to Germany. I have one child. I choose to come here because I like it. But now, from three months, I really think a lot. This is I am right in this decision or I should leave. I like the city too much, I like the people, I like. But the system is very hard. Not easy, really not easy.

He cites difficulties with registration and identification cards and with costs, insurance, and work permits as a foreigner trying to open a business. In addition, new restrictions on mobility have prevented him from moving within Turkey:

> I have workshop in İzmir last month. I go there but I go to take permission to go there but they refused me because of [being a foreigner]. They told us, "You cannot travel, and we cannot give you any permission to go there." ... I cannot travel out of Turkey. I cannot travel between the cities of Turkey.

Nonetheless, he opened the business, which was not profitable at first:

> This is not business for me anyway. This is not earning money. Every month, I pay from my pocket two thousand, two thousand five hundred dollars every month to cover these costs. For us, it is a place to let the Turkish, European ... Because there is a huge European community here, to see the point of view from Syria. We talk and we know each other more and we understand each other more. This is [what is important] for us." (Interview, İstanbul 2016)

Pages serves as a community hub. Samer and his wife renovated an old building in Fatih, near the tourist site of Kariye Museum (Chora

5.4 | Pages café, İstanbul, Turkey, July 2016.

Church, a medieval Byzantine Greek Orthodox church). Their beautifully designed café, with a small garden in the back, provides an oasis of calm amid the surrounding bustle.

Pages is also an Arabic-language publishing house (a successor to the operation he opened in Damascus in 2005) and bookstore, catering to other Arabic-speakers in the area, such as Iraqis, Libyans, and Yemenis (Arango 2015). However, Pages is more than a café-bookstore. It has another dimension as well, as one member of Pages explains:

> This is community centre. We have music nights, cinema. Saturday, we have music nights, Sunday and Monday we have cinema. We have workshops for children, workshops for others. We bring professionals from outside for children, photographer, cinema

maker. We make how to write for children's books, for professional ... For all them we bring professionals from outside and give them workshop for four days or three, four, five days. And everything is free. We don't think anyone has to pay, nothing. (Interview, İstanbul 2016)

Pages brings together the Syrian community but also invites Turks to collaborate with Syrians in the arts and other cultural activities. Moreover, it informs Turkish people about Syrian music, film, literature, and art, offering them a view of Syrians as artists in their own right. Although Pages still thrives as an important Syrian cultural space in İstanbul, Samer has since chosen to leave with his family and resettle in Europe for the sake of greater stability.

As Pages demonstrates, cultural spaces and projects are important means to challenge negative perceptions of Syrians, besides providing Syrians with spaces of belonging within their communities. They are also important as spaces for bringing Syrians and Turks together as a community. In this way, art can bridge the urban social gap between Syrians and Turks, who often live quite segregated lives.

Other examples include an association named Support to Life, which used storytelling to bring together children of both peoples in Urfa (Şanlıurfa), in Anatolia, in south-eastern Turkey near the Syrian border. Almost one-quarter of Urfa's residents are Syrian, and almost half of Turkey's 3.6 million Syrians live in this border region, in centres such as Gaziantep, Hatay, Kilis, Mardin, and Şanlıurfa (*Daily Sabah* 2018). At the storytelling event (21 October 2017), Syrian refugee women recounted their childhood fairy tales. Syrian and Turkish children, along with their mothers, listened to these stories, played together, and talked about their dreams (Bianet 2017). Given the segregated lives that so many Syrian refugees lead, especially in Anatolian towns such as Urfa, this event encouraged social and emotional relations with the local population.

Similarly, a Syrian women's choir was founded with the support of the Human Resource Development Foundation (HRDF). This choir, which brought together Syrian women from various professional backgrounds – doctors, teachers, housewives, painters – has enabled Syrian refugee women to sing about their homes and their memories.

The choir performed as part of the 24th İstanbul Jazz Festival, organized by the İstanbul Foundation for Culture and Arts (IKSV) in July 2017 (*Daily Sabah* 2017). The choir provides a platform for empowering Syrian refugee women, who are able to share their music and culture with the larger Turkish society.

Cultural spaces like these enable Syrians to come together in ways that transcend their precarious urban existence. In these spaces, they may realize other dimensions of their lives as artists, creative people, and lovers of art and music. Such spaces and cultural events also challenge the stereotype that Syrians are simply refugees, people without agency let alone cultural lives and histories. They showcase Syrians as artists and as lovers of the arts through art, film, literature, and music. However, as this section has also shown, these examples of quieter forms of navigating precarity to create a sense of belonging and to make demands for recognition are themselves precarious and fraught with instability, for the greater visibility fuels xenophobia in the community.

Claiming Spaces: Syrian Refugee Participation in Community Support Initiatives

As a result of the entry of many Syrian refugees, Turkey is struggling with socio-economic strains and political conflicts, and tensions are rising between the refugees and their host communities. The AKP government established an open-door policy for Syrians in 2011, and ever since, xenophobia has been rising along with intercommunal tensions. The years since have witnessed mob violence (including lynchings) and intermittent attacks on Syrians in urban and rural Turkey, as well as online communications fomenting hatred toward Syrians (Ozduzen, Korkut, and Ozduzen 2020). According to the ICG (2018), 181 refugee-related confrontations and criminal incidents were reported in 2017, resulting in thirty-five deaths; twenty-four of the victims were Syrian. In addition to all the reported and unreported urban violence, cultural clashes have broken out in some communities (ICG 2018). Yet Syrians have also been portrayed in public and political discourse as the exemplary recipients of Turkish hospitality and humanitarianism. In this context, Kaplan (2020) notes: "Following the coup attempt in Turkey in July 2016 ... Turkish media outlets were quick to point out that many Syrian refugees were among the strongest supporters of the Turkish government" (10). Tensions and inaccurate portrayals have plagued Syrians in Turkey, in some places more than in others, and much more attention needs to be paid to how Syrians are making new lives for themselves in these circumstances. Specifically, we want to discuss how they are claiming space by promoting notions of community and belonging, and thereby opening up questions of rights, responsibilities, and agency for Syrians in urban Turkey.

This section focuses on Syrians' everyday practices of claiming space (illustrative of Neveu's [2014] "low noise practices" mentioned earlier) and examines how they claim space by organizing community support initiatives. The following analysis is informed by research on community-building and belonging (Bauder 2016; Darling 2017) and sets out to unsettle simplistic understandings of modern citizenship as a legal institution (e.g., Goldring and Landolt 2013; Isin 2017; Islar and Irgil 2018; Kılıçaslan 2016; Sigona 2015). It draws on our qualitative interviews with community support organizations in İstanbul and Gaziantep, and our observations of these urban settings, to reveal such venues as performative spaces that foster community-building and notions of belonging for Syrian refugees. By participating in these activities – as seen in the previous examples of Syrians' participation in cultural spaces, from food to art – Syrians are claiming spaces in urban Turkey to address their precarious living conditions, to make themselves visible in the public domain, to create familiar and safe spaces, and to claim these spaces as symbols of recognition and belonging. Their claims to, or appropriations of, urban space resonate with a growing body of work that explores how the politics of urban presence may offer openings for alternative forms of belonging (e.g., Darling 2017) that can involve the practice of new notions of political community (e.g., Jeffrey et al. 2018). Such claims also evoke Lefebvre's ([1974] 1996) point that such actions can challenge oppression and produce "urban space as a creative and fulfilling aesthetic experience which encompasses the full and complete usage of space by its inhabitants in their daily routines, work practices and forms of play" (141). For example, many Syrians have settled in suburban neighbourhoods in major cities such as İstanbul. In these places, as Kılıçaslan (2016) demonstrates, non-citizen Syrian Kurds are "challenging the mechanisms and processes of inclusion and exclusion" (78) by participating in the city's economic, social, and political spheres and in "right to the city" activities; these in turn help generate spaces where contestations and solidarity create new social dynamics.

Claiming Spaces in Urban Turkey

Throughout urban Turkey, self-organized centres for community support are enhancing refugees' agency and their ability to forge ties with locals. These centres are small, vary in composition and direction, and may be fragile, contested, or compromised; even so, they facilitate education, language acquisition, health, rights training, livelihood support, and community-building. Centres such as Small Projects İstanbul, Addar, Kamer Foundation, and Okuma Projesi, as well as various unlicensed medical clinics, are fostering refugees' encounters with other local members, encouraging new relationships across differences, and engendering community. Specifically, Syrians can claim space through their engagement in community support centres[4] by invoking their agency, making their voices heard, and participating in daily life. In claiming spaces, they are asserting their right to belong and to stay, and this is especially so for those who create and inhabit urban spaces through their everyday routines and thereby come to possess a right to the city (see Kılıçaslan 2016; Lefebvre [1974] 1996). Such claims also reveal that as Syrians navigate diverse sites and spaces, they also disrupt simple understandings of modern citizenship as a legal institution, one premised on the relationship between the individual and the state (see Isin 2017; Isin and Turner 2007; Staeheli 2013). In other words, their navigations of sites and spaces involve actions that are contributing to demands for citizenship and belonging and to the possibilities of social and political change. The following sections look at claiming spaces in the context of initiatives in learning and social support, women's rights, and health care.

Claiming Spaces through Learning and Social Support Initiatives

Small Projects İstanbul (SPI), in the Fatih district, emerged through the volunteer efforts of an Australian expat, Karyn Thomas, a specialist in early childhood education who moved to Syria to work with Iraqi refugees in the Yarmouk camp and then had to flee Syria due to the conflict in 2012. She relocated to İstanbul and started SPI. According to an SPI representative we interviewed, Karyn came to know some Syrian refugees, most of whom now live in and around the Çapa-Şehremini neighbourhood. At the time, she "did games in the park and this kind of thing" (interview with SPI representative, Fatih, 2015). Eventually, in mid-2014, SPI became a Turkish NGO. Its five-storey community support centre now offers quality education, fosters community-building, supports livelihoods, eases resettlement, and encourages smooth Syrian–Turkish relations.

The SPI has a network of more than 2,000 beneficiaries, including 200 families and 350 children. It operates more than forty volunteer-run programs per week for these families and children. It envisions a future in which "the Syrian community in İstanbul is socially and economically integrated, in a way that ensures their dignity and identity, enabling each person to fulfill their individual potential to live a healthy and rewarding life while contributing to their social environment."[5] To carry out its community work (Kay 2016), it relies on private donations, community ambassadors, and volunteers from Syria, Turkey, Australia, the Americas, Asia, the Middle East, and Europe. Its project partners include the Bridge to Türkiye Fund; EU Aid Volunteers: We Care, We Act; the German Federal Ministry for Economic Cooperation and Development; the German–Turkish Partnership for Vocational Skills Development; International Women of İstanbul; and Turkish Philanthropy Funds. Its operations involve many actors, decisions, and spaces that shape the involvement and participation of Syrian refugees.

Like many such centres, SPI is in the district of Fatih, which has become home to many people from Afghanistan, Iraq, Syria, and other countries over the past decade. Syrian nationals are the largest group of migrants in this area (IOM, Republic of Turkey 2019). Fatih has earned the nickname "Little Syria," a place where shops, restaurants, and markets, with their Arabic signage, cater to this new diaspora and serve as a hub for İstanbul's Syrians. As mentioned in the previous section, middle-class Syrian refugees who have started food and other businesses in Fatih (as well as Aksaray and Beyoğlu) are producing urban

5.5 | Store in Fatih neighbourhood, İstanbul, Turkey, August 2016.

space – that is, they are "re-dwelling, appropriating and place making" (Turner 2018). Syrians here can locate spices from Aleppo, coffee from Damascus, and a wide variety of other goods such as clothes from Syria. However, Fatih is also known as a conservative district and a place where there have been tensions between Syrians and local Turks. Some of these tensions can be linked to concerns about the financial support and incentive policies that Syrians are provided that are not available to Turks. Other tensions have surfaced at times since Turkey closed its border with Syria in 2016 (see also *Al Jazeera* 2018), such as when police conducted security sweeps in the area, and throughout the 2019 local elections. During that election, Ilay Aksoy, the nationalist İYİ (Good) Party candidate for the district of Fatih, set out to escalate xenophobia in the neighbourhood. Running under the slogan "I won't surrender Fatih to Syrians," she launched a vigorous campaign that featured videos discussing the problems with Syrians living in the district and highlighting the need to replace Arabic with Turkish signs.

Despite all this, SPI has brought together displaced Syrian families in the Çapa-Şehremini neighbourhood – a place where many Syrians are struggling – by engaging them in community support initiatives (interview with SPI representative, Fatih, 2015). SPI's programs engage in community-building through shared spaces of learning and being together that foster Syrians' agency and ability to claim space, to belong and to stay, and to generate urban space. Its formal initiatives include teaching pre-school children and promoting social and language skills through song, crafts, storytelling, and "group cohesion" activities; a "homework club" in maths and sciences for elementary and middle-grade students; a "teens' club"; classes in women's computer literacy and Web development for young adults led by Syrian volunteers working in the field; Arabic literacy sessions; "conversation exchange" to facilitate daily interactions with Turks; and efforts to encourage Turkish and Syrian neighbours to meet, because "these kinds of ideas ... start with the kids" and with "getting different groups together" (interview with SPI representative, Fatih, 2015). Less formally, the SPI distributes food weekly to Syrian families and sponsors movie nights and other social gatherings where community members and volunteers share a meal (interview with SPI representative, Fatih, 2015). SPI informs Syrian refugees about how to become active agents in urban life and to claim spaces in Fatih by demonstrating their long-term residence and contribution to urban spaces, including through work, participating in cultural and recreational activities, and enhancing children's educational skills and know-how. These everyday activities, which some scholars refer to as "acts of citizenship" (e.g., Isin

2017, 2008; Nyers 2008), enable Syrian refugees to share practices of learning, exchanging information, and transforming aspects of their precarious conditions; they also demonstrate how urban spaces are learned though ordinary activities and how that knowledge can help articulate political claims (see, for example, Darling 2017) and forge new social relationships and communal bonds (see, for example, Staeheli 2008). In other words, this knowledge is not separated from the politics of citizenship but rather is, as Nyers (2015, 32) emphasizes, "immanent to ... citizenship."

Since 2015, SPI has been developing an initiative called Women's Social Enterprise that provides opportunities for women in the community to earn a small income through handicraft production and sales (https://www.smallprojectsistanbul.org). Women's handicraft collectives are helping women develop skills and support themselves and their families. One teaches women to make and design earrings as part of Drop Earrings Not Bombs, an SPI jewellery-making social enterprise founded in March 2016 by Paolo Thiago, a Brazilian, Alp Gürbüs, a Turk, and Syrian refugee women. Lodi, a leader of the initiative, observes: "It feels like living as a family being part of the [SPI] community centre; it feels like we are all working for our families, inside and outside. We are able to meet people from other communities and we can learn from each other. In Syria, I studied Physics in depth, now I continue to study. These days I study languages, both English and Turkish" (see SPI). Drop Earrings provides these women with a small income and space to produce their creations. These women are shifting their precarious situation to their advantage and making themselves more visible as they participate in and help transform İstanbul's workspaces (see Kılıçaslan 2016 on Syrian Kurds in İstanbul). In 2017, SPI launched "Muhra" – an Arabic word meaning female foal, representing growth and strength – featuring their Drop Earrings Not Bombs collection, as a socially conscious and empowering brand.

SPI offers instruction in the arts. Its *capoeira* program combines dance and movement as a form of dialogue between participants. Its video production workshops teach young students technical skills to shoot and edit their own short films; one facilitator described the dynamics of producing films and videos:

5.6 | Jewellery made by Syrian women working with Small Projects, İstanbul, Turkey, August 2016.

I've always wanted these [young adults with] promising talents to find a direct link with the outside world by sharing their own point of view, and to express themselves in the way they want the world to see them and breaking down stereotypes. I believe we're achieving that through our modest means – film and video making. We're encouraging them to take notice of how we give meaning to the people and things around us; the progression of feelings. They are discovering what's behind their emotions in order to create a meaning. What's incredibly beautiful is that they're willing to succeed – they have patience, passion, and perseverance in a huge frame of perspectives. (See SPI)

These and similar programs aim to build confidence, teamwork, communication, responsibility, and respect among participants, and to foster their everyday relations and notions of belonging to urban spaces.

Through SPI and other such centres, many Syrians can live and work in Fatih and gather together regularly for social, cultural, and other events. In our visits to SPI, we learned that Fatih's Syrian population is diverse, has many voices, and reflects class, gender, and religious lines in its day-to-day affairs. We also identified parks, churches, and other public spaces as locales that help create and reflect Syrian identities through practices that foster community within a diverse cultural landscape. These spaces can change or disappear, but overall, Syrians have claimed a range of urban spaces by working, opening businesses, making homes, and connecting themselves to local practices and communities, thus establishing their right to belong and to stay. These acts of claiming space can activate the contingent possibility of including the excluded in existing social and political relations; they can also make possible new subject identities and support strategies for claiming the right to have rights.

Other community support centres provide social assistance to marginal populations, such as Syrian refugees, and organize community events in which they can experience their cultural heritage and engage in İstanbul's social life. In the diverse district of Beyoğlu, which has many migrants and refugees, a multitude of centres offer instruction and social support. When Turkey began to urbanize in the 1950s, Beyoğlu offered cheap homes for new migrants, and by the 1980s it was a slum. In the 1990s, the intelligentsia and artists began to purchase and renovate many old apartments, which led to new shops, bookstores, art galleries, and living quarters. Since 2011, displaced middle-income Syrians have been opening food and retail businesses there, and social services and support centres have emerged to assist Syrians throughout the city. Some observers view the Syrian settlement in Beyoğlu, and similar ones elsewhere in İstanbul, as creeping ghettoization.

A number of community support centres in Beyoğlu encourage belonging and solidarity-building for Syrians. Addar ("home" in Arabic), founded in 2014 for young Syrian and Palestinian-Syrians, is a volunteer operation, secular and non-political. It is open to everyone, including local Turks. Its activities include English and Turkish classes for Syrian youth, book clubs, concerts, salsa and yoga courses, and theatre workshops for adults. The centre aims to provide cultural and social support to young refugees, who may lack access to cultural events and who struggle daily to overcome their precarious living conditions. It encourages Turkish volunteers to work with them to introduce Turkish culture to Syrians and to familiarize them with daily life in their new land. Addar receives support from organizations such as the Rights Now Foundation and the Asfari Foundation.[6] For example, Rights Now in Sweden funds efforts that aim to provide "humans with more power, agency, more influence and more choices" and encourages human empowerment and social mobilization (http://rightsnow. se/about).

One of Addar's many initiatives helps Syrian children and their families adjust to a new environment, a new language, and new neighbourhoods and classrooms. One initiative connects children to neighbourhood schools. Volunteer Turkish tutors help these youngsters with homework and Turkish language and mediate between their families and the schools. This helps the children feel comfortable in the school and participate actively. In 2017, Addar received Asfari backing for a project to help young Syrians (between the ages of twelve and thirty-five) rebuild their lives through education and skills training. As many as thirty-five of them will take certified English courses and exams, as many as fifteen will do baccalaureates, and as many as 150 will study the Turkish and English languages. The project employs three Syrian women to oversee a centre in Beyoğlu, its classes, and its students (see https://www.asfarifoundation.org.uk/ad-dar-centre).

More and more Syrians are enrolling in Turkish universities. In 2017–18, 20,701 Syrians were enrolled in Turkish higher education institutions; by 2018–19, the figure was 27,606 (Komşuoğlu 2019). The greatest number of these students were in İstanbul, the next greatest in Gaziantep (Dereli 2018). Many universities in these and other cities have developed programs for Syrian community-building and to help Syrians claim spaces through learning. These programs include music and cultural activities as well as Syrian student clubs and organizations. For Syrian students, making local friends and contacts can help them build community, reduce their social isolation in university settings (Dereli 2018), and foster their claims to the right to belong and stay in learning environments and in the city.

Universities with large Syrian student populations have launched special welcoming projects to promote refugee students' access to higher education. For example, İstanbul University offers a program called Welcoming Syrian Refugees to İstanbul University. The participants in this project aim to increase awareness of the presence of Syrians among the university's student body and administration. They also work to identify barriers to higher education through interviews, focus groups, and workshops (Komşuoğlu 2019). Similarly, as part of their efforts to claim the right to belong in spaces of learning, Syrian students are devoting time to community services and migrant health polyclinics as interpreters for recent arrivals from Syria (interview with UNHCR official, İstanbul, 1 August 2019).

Creating spaces and sites of learning can promote social cohesion (see ICG 2018) and help newcomers build community supports. Syrians' rights-claiming activities emphasize daily acts of claiming rights to belong and rights to stay. Overall, community and social support initiatives and centres allow Syrian children and their families to belong to multiple spaces (schools, neighbourhoods) and to make them their own by participating in organized and daily activities, contributing to them, and putting down roots in many other ways. These Syrian participants are making urban spaces part of their lives and identities, and this is creating new social dynamics that are challenging normative views of "place" and Syrian identity in urban İstanbul. Such local-level space-making practices offer Syrians a degree of visibility and political subjectivity, besides serving as a basis for starting the process of gaining recognition as social and political actors. These processes connect to the social and political terrain on which rights, entitlements, and obligations are reshaped and activated through the everyday practices of claiming space and through various acts of citizenship (see, for example, Goldring and Landolt 2013 on negotiating non-citizenship; Isin 2017 on "performative citizenship"; Islar and Irgil 2018 on the politicization of citizens; Sigona 2015 on "campzenship"). For example, Islar and Irgil (2018) describe the politicization of citizens after Spain's Indignados movement, which emerged in 2011 and consisted of protests against the erosion of social welfare and the political mismanagement of Spain's socio-economic challenges. The right to a city is about much more than the right to access urban amenities. The Indignados movement claimed the right to participate in the transformation of Barcelona, and involved itself in initiatives to create spaces of cooperation and new platforms for politics. It positioned these rights as "collective rights" in the broader context of citizenship. In Turkey, such collective rights are now operating in the spaces that Syrians are occupying and claiming on their own and with others.

Claiming Spaces through Women's Rights Initiatives

A number of community support centres in Turkey focus on women's issues. Some emphasize women's health, well-being, skills development, and employment; others are more attentive to women's rights specifically. Many of these centres are in İstanbul, such as KADAV – the Women's Solidarity Foundation (KADAV 2016) and the International Migrant Women's Solidarity Association (see IMWSA). Both these groups provide legal, psychosocial, and community support to refugee women. They establish women's solidarity groups in community centres, where refugees and hosts can gather to share their experiences. The Kamer Foundation is another NGO that works on refugee women's rights. Located in Gaziantep, Kamer instructs female refugees about their rights and offers training and awareness-raising vis-à-vis women's rights.

Kamer started by conducting research on how to educate women about their rights. According to one representative, it began "a six-month project last July [2016]. We conducted a needs assessment study to see what the need out there is and what we can do about it. Now we are expanding on this work" (interview, Gaziantep, 2017). Kamer offers various services to local women, especially Syrians, such as an emergency support line for victims of domestic violence; awareness-raising about women's legal rights; women's craft programs; and a five-week program on gender equality for parents and children. "Participants do not need to be the mother; they can be any caregiver whether it is an aunt or a grandmother" (interview, Gaziantep, 2017).

Kamer's staff introduce themselves to Syrian women, provide them with UN hygiene kits, and inform them about a range of services, such as workshops on asylum law and reproductive health. The centre organizes its services at a grassroots level: it finds out what women in the community need and want, then tries to provide it. Kamer approaches refugee women not as victims but as subjects with agency. Through its contacts with more than 400 Syrian women in Gaziantep and Kilis, Kamer learned more about their everyday challenges. One Kamer spokesperson emphasized their difficult experiences: "Harassment on the streets. [People] not renting homes to Syrians. Syrians talk very loudly in parks … Some people tell them, 'You speak louder than Turkish women' … Many of them understand Turkish but cannot speak it, because they haven't been here for a long time. On buses, on the dolmuş, they hear people say, 'These people are everywhere'" (interview, Gaziantep, 2017). The Kamer representative also discussed the challenges children face:

> Many experience problems involving their children as people in the neighbourhood react to them. A lot of children are working anyway. They don't go to school. They are on the streets. There are a lot of instances in hospitals that we hear of. People can tell right away if someone is Syrian or not from the way they are dressed, their mannerism. I think that there are two reasons for this. First is a problem internal to Syrians … they feel insecure due to their asylum-seeker status. They are worried about the future, very worried. But that does not refrain them from accessing services. (Interview, Gaziantep, 2017)

Kamer's human rights programs increase Syrian women's awareness of their rights and help them to engage in ways that reduce their social exclusion and create new spaces for participation. Challenging exclusion requires sustained projects and programs: "Long term. This is what our programs are based on. We have never been an emergency response organization, neither do we want to be that in the future. Our goal is women's empowerment and survival ... If they have emergency needs, we refer them to those organizations" (Kamer representative, Gaziantep, 2017). Kamer's community initiatives and spaces have allowed many Syrian women in Gaziantep to experience a greater sense of belonging and cope with the struggles of daily life.

Claiming Spaces through Health Care Initiatives

As noted in earlier chapters, Syrian refugees under temporary protection in Turkey have limited rights to health, education, social assistance, and work. Many face obstacles to health care because they do not speak Turkish, encounter discrimination, and face bureaucratic barriers. In particular, Syrian women struggle to access services related to mental health, work-related injuries, and birth complications (see Cloeters and Osseiran 2019). Furthermore, Syrian-trained doctors find it hard to obtain accreditation, so many of them cannot work legally. In response to these obstacles, more than 100 unlicensed charitable medical clinics in cities such as Gaziantep, İstanbul, and Mersin employ Syrian doctors and cater to their compatriots (T24 2016b). A Syrian physician who works in one of these clinics says he has been trying for more than four years to gain accreditation from the Turkish Health Ministry. This requires an electronic confirmation from his medical school in Damascus, which, as Syria and Turkey have no diplomatic relations, never arrives (*Gazete Duvar* 2016). Nevertheless, these clinics[7] exemplify practical solutions to everyday challenges. According to Abdullah, the manager of one clinic, Syrians "come here because Turkish hospitals don't treat Syrians fairly, and because we speak their language" (*Newsweek*, 19 June 2016). These centres allow Syrian doctors to offer, and Syrian patients to receive, care in a supportive environment. These new spaces allow Syrians to "live" their right to medical services; here, they can feel secure about that care and feel a sense of belonging. Because these clinics often have no legal status, municipal authorities can close them down. An eye surgeon who fled Deir Ezzor in eastern Syria in 2012 and who operates an illegal clinic in İstanbul noted that "we are unlicensed. At any moment, the municipality can come and close us down. If this happens, I will either return to Syria or take the boat to Europe" (*Newsweek*, 19 June 2016). The manager of another clinic points out that these endeavours relieve some of the burden on Turkey's medical services, so the government ignores them: "They [government] turn a blind eye because we only treat Syrians. Refugees treating refugees" (*Newsweek*, 19 June 2016).

There are also "legitimate" clinics for Syrians in Turkey, operated by accredited Syrian doctors, nurses, pharmacists, and lab technicians. For example, the Nour Clinic in Fathi sees more than 10,000 Syrian patients a month. It receives public and private donations and charges patients who can afford it a small, fixed fee. It occupies three floors, employs twenty-nine doctors and support staff, boasts several specialist departments, and offers blood analysis and a pharmacy. According to its director, Dr Mehdi Davut, "as time went by, and the number of Syrians in İstanbul increased, we found that we needed to open a dental department, an internal medicine department and a pediatrics department. Now we have all kinds of specialities" (see *Al Jazeera*, n.d.). In these Syrian-run facilities, refugees can feel at home with medical compatriots, which encourages them to participate in their own health care. This is very unlike the precarious access they often experience in state hospitals, where they often feel inarticulate and politically estranged. These Syrian-run spaces have emerged through the daily interactions of Syrian refugees. Like other community-based support initiatives, they foster refugees' agency and establish their right to stay and belong; they also provide openings for creating dynamics of social inclusion and community-building. The Turkish Health Ministry has recently opened Migrant Health Centres (MHCs) in some provinces for Syrians with temporary protection status (UNHCR n.d., "Help"). These MHCs often employ Arabic-speaking staff, including Syrian doctors, and serve as primary health clinics; since 2016 they have employed "more than 380 Syrian doctors" and trained some "360 nurses and midwives ... for serving the refugees across Turkey" (*Daily Sabah* 2018).

The negotiations associated with Syrians' claims to the right to belong and to stay provide lessons not only about the content of rights struggles but also about the implications of making claims for particular rights, which so commonly enact the frictions integral to citizenship. Isin writes that citizenship is deeply "performative": in "struggling for their rights, the rights of others, and the rights to come, under certain conditions, people constitute themselves as citizens" (2017, 507). Through such processes, people, including "citizens and non-citizens, with or without rights," undertake responsibilities toward one another; this in turn can transform them as a group. In this regard, Syrians' rights-making claims, authorized or not, are reshaping them and their ties to others, thus enabling them to act as political subjects.

Conclusion

In this chapter, we have emphasized that rights-claiming is an act of citizenship that remains part of counter-precarity activities and that these acts are being carried out in a context in which many people are struggling to survive and to make a decent living. Syrians' ongoing rights-claiming and community-building initiatives in Turkey are working to transform and improve their daily lives; they are also shaping the various groups and communities with which they share a common vision of the future. These rights-claiming activities offer us ways to better understand migrant populations: they are more than simply displaced people in need of protection and humanitarian assistance; they are also political agents who can challenge exclusionary practices, negotiate access to rights and resources, and seek alternative forms and spaces of protection. Initiatives to claim rights through community-building activities can lead to greater solidarity, even if on a small scale, as well as foster dialogue and mechanisms for migrant participation and inclusion at many levels. Whatever their form, size, intensity, and scope, acts of rights-claiming have the potential to open up new political spaces with the ability to reshape the social geographies of urban places and thereby generate inclusive movements, be they long-term or temporary. In any case, acts of rights-claiming are important to examine so as to better understand their possibility to disrupt precarious relations and living conditions and reform migration and integration regimes.

This chapter has explored how Syrians develop creative strategies to address, and even resist, their precarious living conditions in Turkey's cities. But for many Syrians, daily life becomes simply too difficult, with little hope of a better future. Europe may beckon, for they can hope to be recognized as Convention refugees, with all the rights that accompany that legal status. In the next chapter, precarious resistance takes the form of what may be a risky journey to Europe. Demands for the right to settle are at times accompanied by demands for the right to movement, including "the right to escape" (Mezzadra 2004). The next chapter focuses on the right to escape and highlights the many ways in which Syrians have departed from Turkey, including the many journeys they have taken on their own and with the support of intermediaries, and on all the challenges they face in this type of migration.

CHAPTER SIX

Precarious Resistances and Claiming the Right to Leave

MAISSAA ALMUSTAFA

After escaping war in Syria, refugees who have failed to find sufficient protection in neighbouring countries find themselves trapped within borders and by border controls that emphasize deterrence and the prevention of access to asylum rather than refugee protection (Crawley et al. 2018; Squire 2011; Mainwaring 2016; Mountz 2010; Johnson 2014). As described in chapter 2, refugees from Syria often face sharply restricted movement, and this forces them to embark on dangerous and often illegal journeys in search of safety. As De Vries and Guild (2018, 7) explain, "In brief, rather than a movement from insecurity to safety, migration trajectories are often characterised by recurring of continued displacement."

This chapter explores refugees' journeys as they were recounted to us in interviews. It offers three representative narratives culled from some forty interviews conducted and recorded in the spring of 2016.[1] The three journeys involved individuals who had escaped the Syrian war only to find themselves living in deteriorating conditions in Turkey and who chose to try to reach Europe from there. Arad was interviewed in Kitchener, Ontario, in March 2016, after the Canadian government had resettled him and his family after their journey of displacement via Turkey. Ammar and Khaled, who live in Germany, were interviewed through Skype in April 2016. All three of these narratives reflect the intense precarity and unpredictability of their journeys. They also demonstrate that Syrian refugees are not victims who are powerless to exercise agency and make decisions. Forced to flee war and hardship, all three left Syria and wound up in Turkey. Their precarious living conditions there (see, for example, Danış 2019a; Erdoğan 2015; İçduygu 2015a; İneli-Ciğer 2015; Kirişçi 2016), as illustrated in chapters 3 and 4, made them desperate enough to try for a third country. These movements were expressions of their own decision and agency – they were practising their "right to escape" (Mezzadra 2004). Mezzadra proposes the term "right to escape" in order to "highlight the elements of subjectivity which permeate the migratory movements and which must be kept in mind if one wants to produce an image of these movements as social movements in the full sense" (270). In this sense, a refugee journey is a social transformation and a life-changing experience – a form of "escape" or refusal to participate in or accept a social order (Papadopoulos, Stephenson, and Tsianos 2008). Exercising this right to escape entails agency. Escape is, as Mezzadra puts it, "a road to freedom and independence" (2004, 297). It is a form of migration that requires "an individual motion (made by a concrete woman or man, embedded in family and social networks but nonetheless capable of agency) of desertion from the field where those objective causes operate, a reclaiming precisely of a 'right to escape'" (270). During their journeys, refugees often encounter restrictive border controls and dehumanizing experiences of detention, both of which reveal how freedom and coercion intertwine in migratory movements (Mezzadra 2015) and produce subjectivities and differentiations at borders (Andrijasevic 2009; Bendixen 2016).

The rest of this chapter describes the journeys of three individuals – Arad, Ammar, and Khaled – revealing their reasons for fleeing Syria as well as how they arrived in and later escaped from Turkey. As noted earlier, temporary protection generates a variety of forms of precarity that can make living in Turkey untenable. When Syrians are unable to negotiate living with this precarity in ways that enable them to settle into their communities, they exercise the right to escape in the hope that they will be able to demand protection and create a more stable future elsewhere for themselves and their families.

Arad's Journey

Arad worked in an auto repair shop in Aleppo in northwestern Syria. He and his family left that city for Turkey but found the situation there so difficult that they quickly decided to go to Europe. While this is but one story among many, it is representative. Its horrifying details demonstrate the extreme precarity and risk facing Syrians but also their strength and resolve.

Arad described his journey in detail. He and his wife and children fled Aleppo for Turkey through a Syrian military zone scattered with land mines, guided by a smuggler who ran in front of them. There was a dam on the Turkish side near their border crossing. When the Turkish authorities open the dam gates, the river becomes too deep and dangerous to cross. On the day that Arad and his family decided to cross, the water reached above Arad's knees. He worried about falling as he jumped over the rocks with his son and his suitcase:

It was very difficult at the borders. We waited for about two hours and were then ordered to run without looking back. We had to run through a rocky river. I carried a suitcase on one side and my son on the other, running and jumping from one rock to another. My kids were too young to keep up the pace, and my wife was hardly able to manage her way. It took about half an hour to reach the borderline, which was a razor-wired fence with holes in it made purposely by smugglers to allow people to cross through to the other side.

The image of Arad and his family crossing mine fields and a river captures the plight of refugees who, to escape a brutal civil war, found themselves crossing the border illegally. During the interview, Arad's voice reflected the shame he felt about this illegal crossing, and his wife wept when she recalled the mud that covered them when they reached Turkey.

Turkey has a reputation for treating Syrian refugees tolerably well. However, as this book has shown, refugees there more often face highly precarious living conditions and experience exclusion. These challenges, which Arad described in detail, were the main reasons he decided that his family would seek refugee status outside Turkey.

Arad first told us about his family's experience of discrimination. They are Kurdish Syrians, which affected the support they received from charities in Turkey: "They preferred to support Arabs over Kurds and more favourably Muslims … It wasn't hard to tell that they were affiliated with the Syrian opposition coalition, like most charities in Turkey." Another type of discrimination flowed from the geopolitics of the Syrian conflict and Turkish policies toward Syrians:

> We moved to Avcılar [in İstanbul], which is a municipality managed by Alevis.[2] Syrian refugees were badly treated by the officials at that area. They prejudged all Syrian refugees as traitors for escaping their country; instead, they thought we should have stayed in Syria to fight the extremists. Some locals even refused to rent houses to Syrians and kept questioning us about reasons for leaving Syria. They persistently asked us to return, but how is that possible? There is war there, our house was destroyed, how can we go back? Municipalities managed by Erdoğan's party treated Syrians a little bit more humanely and provided some assistance.

As Arad's story illustrates, Syrian refugees often face stigma, rejection, and humiliation as they struggle to establish new lives in Turkey. Such barriers also impact whatever work they can find. Arad's employer refused to pay him for five months and forced him to work for many hours without a break. Arad found another job but was again at his new boss's mercy, and like many Syrians, he could not complain to the authorities: "In Turkey, they do not recognize us at all; our existence is simply not acknowledged … My employer was generous with me but expected me to work very long hours; he would wake me up early in the morning and kept asking for more working hours. He was nice, but the working conditions were pretty tough. Many people could not continue working in such circumstances." Such extremely precarious work (e.g., Banki 2013) is a consequence of Syrians' temporary protection in Turkey (see, for example, Kaya 2016; Korkut 2016; Şenses 2015; Yıldız and Uzgören 2016), which also makes it much more difficult for them to find health care.

> The hospitals refused to accept us because we are Syrians. When my daughter broke her arm, I took her from one hospital to the

other (three hospitals in total), only to be denied by all three. I was desperate and contacted my employer, who drove us to a hospital near Aksaray [a district in İstanbul], but when they found out she is Syrian, they referred us to another place and a third place ... It was a public hospital, and if you are not registered within the system, they won't let you in.

As we saw in chapter 4, the government introduced identity cards (*kimlik*) for Syrians to improve their access to health care. But for Arad and his family, "there was no *kimlik* when we arrived in Turkey. We were among the first people who had the *kimlik*. But it did not help much and did not make any difference. We were still denied access to health care even after we received it." The *kimlik* also did not help him secure education for his children, who could not attend Turkish schools. They could learn Arabic (Syria's official language) only in a private school, which he could not afford, so for two years they were not in school. For Arad, this was a reason to leave Turkey and resettle elsewhere. "I wanted to move to another country just to secure education for them. I wanted them to go to school. I was ready to go back to Syria. I did not care about the war there. I wanted to see my kids attending schools. They have been out of school for more than three years. I could not see them roaming the streets without any education."

Arad was one of the lucky few Syrians in Turkey to register with the UNHCR in İstanbul in 2013. He did so after an Iraqi neighbour suggested he do so. The UNHCR interviewed him in İstanbul and in Ankara. For Arad, acceptance in the UNHCR's resettlement program launched his family on a long process of applications, interviews, and protracted waiting to seek possible protection (see Khosravi 2021 on waiting). A few months later, the Canadian embassy in Ankara accepted his resettlement application. In the year until he and his family resettled in Canada as refugees, they remained in legal limbo, without social assistance and schooling and with limited access to health care and other public services. When they arrived in Canada, they received their permanent residency status at the airport, which gave them full access to social rights, including to education, employment, health care, and social welfare. His wife's tears while watching her children enter their Canadian school for the first time said a lot. Arad was the kind of refugee whose movement the system accredited and regulated, providing him with legal safe passage (Johnson 2014).

Ammar's Journey

Ammar told of similar difficulties in Turkey. However, he was unable to register with the UNHCR to leave Turkey legally and safely, so – like far too many Syrians – he sought help from smugglers. He explained to us that İstanbul offered smuggling openly in certain hubs, so he went to Aksaray, which had a network consisting of members who did not know one another but who reported to the same Turkish boss. "Everyone knew what was going on in those gathering places. Migrants, who were about to embark on their journey to Greece, gathered in big numbers. There are shops filled with life jackets … I mean it was so obvious. It is ironic that some Turkish locals started waving goodbye to us while policemen ignored us totally." Because of official indifference, refugees are at the mercy of the smugglers and unable to complain about any violations or ill treatment.

The smuggling networks' "deposit offices" accepted payment from the refugees for their travel – from 2,000 to 5,000 euros per person. The offices kept these payments in trust, issuing secret codes for refugees to pass to the smugglers once they arrived at their Greek island destination. Most refugees know that smugglers and deposit offices are part of the same network, which offers them no guarantees. After making their deposits, refugees often encounter delays and false promises, and this makes them more willing to accept poorer conditions once the actual journey starts.

Ammar told us about the many dangers that smugglers pose to Syrians. For example, he tried to cross the Aegean with their help. On the night of his departure, the Turkish coast guard appeared at the gathering point and started shooting in the air, but the armed smugglers shot back, forcing the police to withdraw. Ammar spent the night in the woods near the shore with hundreds of other refugees. It was still dark when another bus arrived. The smugglers started to gather people into groups of forty to fifty, ordering them onto rubber boats (*balams*). The smugglers threatened them with their guns and prevented them from taking any belongings, which they had to throw into the water.

They attacked anyone who complained and even beat some men. The Turkish coastal patrol intercepted the first *balam*, but the smugglers continued to send one *balam* after another. They gave instructions to the refugees who were navigating:

> The situation was horrifying. The *balam* behind us capsized, and the fate of the people in it became unknown. As we reached international waters, another *balam* capsized too. It was terrifying in the true sense. The loud cries of the women and the children filled the air. We threw our life jackets to the people who were struggling in the water. Happily, they were then rescued by Greek coast guards … A group of six young men on our boat, including myself, decided to jump into the water and swim next to our boat in order to make it lighter and faster. We held the ropes on the sides of the boat and swam. The plan worked, and we made it to the shore in one hour. Unfortunately, only thirteen of the eighteen *balams* that departed that night reached Mytilene Island.

Ammar's narrative tells of a nightmare common to many refugees – watching others drown nearby yet having to carry on (see also Almustafa 2019; Crawley et al. 2018; De Genova 2018; Stierl 2016b; Squire 2020).

Khaled's Journey

Another Syrian refugee, Khaled, described similar dangers. When he and his family tried to leave Turkey, the smugglers changed their plans and routes many times without informing them: "Why would they consult with us? They treated us like sheep." Refugees have no other way to reach Greece. Moreover, the sea trip takes place in the dark. "The smugglers started loading us in closed trucks. The truck was overloaded, and one of my nephews was almost crushed underneath other people. My sister started to scream and refused to continue. The smugglers brought a small car for her and her family, whereas thirty people including myself were crowded inside the closed truck for about five hours" (Khaled, Berlin, Germany, April 2016).

Eventually Khaled and his family reached the coast, where hundreds of refugees, many of them women and children, had been waiting on shore for several days, under the control of armed men and with no idea when and how they would leave. Some refugees had to help prepare the *balams*, which took hours and required unloading them and carrying them a few kilometres.

We were about to board the *balam* when a helicopter appeared above our heads. We tried to escape and took the *balam* under the trees, but soon realized that we were surrounded by the police and the smugglers just disappeared ... The police took all of us in seven buses to a police station that overlooked the shore and all of the smuggling operation. It was clear that the Turkish police were aware of the whole process. They only intervene when they receive an alert about a particular smuggling activity.

Despite these initial difficulties, Khaled and his group made a second attempt a few days later. Under the supervision of armed men, they made it again to the shore and departed in two *balams*:

The smugglers forced fifty-five people to board in each of the two *balams*, which exceeded the normal loading capacity. Before boarding, my brother-in-law volunteered to be the driver. He was briefly tested for his sailing abilities by the Turkish smuggler and then agreed. People rushed to the *balam* chaotically, but I was the last person to board, as I was concerned for the safety of my sister and her kids while her husband became responsible for the whole *balam*. My friend, who was still travelling with me, carried one of the kids with a suitcase, while I took the other two kids with me.

Khaled recalled the trauma and hostility the refugees on his *balam* endured:

The water reached our necks ... We had twelve children and twenty women with us, and they were really scared. In fact, everyone was terrified. People prayed and recited the Quran loudly … At one point, the engine stopped because someone stepped on the cable. We silently sat holding our hearts in our hands, until my brother-in-law managed to fix the problem. Yet hostility started to increase between refugees as they shouted and fought with each other. This is when my brother-in-law purposely stopped the engine and refused to move ahead until everyone calms down and listen to him. He even threatened to kill anyone who does not listen and reminded everybody that he was in charge, and he would not accept any complaints or resistance. Everyone complied until we reached the island [Samos].

Those refugees who survive the often harrowing water crossings face new forms of vulnerability on the Greek islands. On arrival, they must register with the police in order to qualify for six months' legal residence. Ammar arrived in Mytilene, the main city on Lesvos:

Thousands of Syrians, Africans, and Afghans were waiting there. People waited in long queues to register their names. Then they had to wait at the camp for their names to be called so they can obtain the passing papers. The camp was an olive-tree orchard outside the town, where people had to spend about a week to obtain their papers. There were no services, no NGOs, and no humanitarian agencies. Hostility between refugees started to increase as people were frustrated and tired. The Greek police intervened on many occasions and used violence against refugees.

Unlike Ammar, Khaled reached Samos, which had no registration camps. He and his group arrived at the main town (also Samos) after a long and exhausting walk:

The hotels refused to receive us, since we had no legal papers yet. So, we had to spend the night on the streets, sleeping on carton boards, surrounded by thousands of refugees like us. We had to wait for three days until we managed to obtain the permissions from the police and get on the ferry towards Athens. During those days, we had no access to facilities. We slept in the streets with no blankets, no showers, and four thousand of us shared three washrooms ... It was very humiliating. The hot days and cold nights added to our misery.

When they reached Athens, they found smuggling services on public offer by the harbour. During the summer of 2015, thousands of refugees boarded buses heading toward the Macedonian border. The Greek police stopped their bus in order to verify that each refugee held permission documents from Lesvos, but Ammar felt that they were not serious, because in the end they allowed everyone to depart, with or without the permission.

At the border, arbitrary changes created ambiguity and unpredictability as well as different conditions for Ammar and Khaled. Khaled, who had arrived at the border a few days before Ammar, had a startling experience. The border was open, and refugees were crossing under the aegis of several NGOs and charities, which provided food and water generously. The presence of a Greek minister supervising the situation after several days of border closure had led to this "five-star treatment," as Khaled called it. The Macedonian police then organized the refugees into groups and helped them book train tickets for Serbia.

Yet when Ammar reached this same border a few days later, in August 2015, he encountered an entirely different, more militarized situation. Thousands of refugees had arrived at the fence running along the border. But the Macedonian army blocked them, while Greek police prevented their return to Greece. They had to wait to find out what would happen:

The Macedonian army were heavily present at the border, which was a razor-wired fence. The army used violence and tear gas to deter refugees from approaching the fence ... Clashes between refugees and the Macedonia[n] army increased in frequency and violence. The Red Cross teams who were initially trying to assist pregnant women, the sick, and the elderly, started to focus on those who were injured by the army ... Many families and groups were separated because of this situation, and I lost the group that I hanged out with.

Such violence rarely deters migrants and refugees; but it does transform them into illegal subjects, and it penalizes them for crossing borders clandestinely. Despite the incidents of violence at the Greek–Macedonian border during the summer and autumn of 2015, the many illegal crossings showed refugees' resistance. Ammar, for example, watched as masses of desperate refugees challenged the Macedonian army in order to keep moving north in Europe. He was able to cross the border only because the Macedonian army rewarded him and several other young men for assisting the Red Cross teams in translating for and moving injured people. He boarded the train to Serbia only to join thousands of refugees in securitized registration centres close to the Macedonian–Serbian border, without water and food – a powerful example of "biopolitical bordering practices" (Vaughan-Williams 2015, 81). Ammar continued on his way:

> In Serbia we were gathered in an old, abandoned factory building surrounded by heavy security. We were left with no food or water. The movement was strictly restricted until authorities collected personal information. This process took two days to complete, during which basic needs and services were non-existent. It was a miserable situation … Add to that the frequent and harsh attacks by Serbian police. On one occasion, violence broke out between Syrian and Afghani refugees due to accumulated sensitivities between the two groups. The Serbian army intervened and detained young men from both sides. I was detained with the Syrian group. We were released after two days and continued our journey towards Belgrade.

This particular case of hostility revealed the border as a "social space," where multiple actors shape the dynamics within asymmetrical power relations that often cause violence against refugees and migrants.

The Hungarian border with Serbia proved even more precarious and violent. Refugees heading for central and northern Europe were keen to cross Hungary without having to provide their fingerprints or apply for asylum, which would have halted their journey. The EU's Dublin Regulation (1990, rev. 2003 and 2013) determines which member-state examines asylum claims – usually it is the nation of first entry

(European Council 2016). Those who apply in another member-state face deportation to the initial country. Although most refugees were aware of this rule, the majority did not know about recent changes. Germany had just suspended the regulation vis-à-vis Syrian refugees and had instructed its immigration officers not to deport them to their initial EU country (Holehouse 2015). National asylum policies in Europe were changing quickly in 2015 as masses of refugees landed onto its shores, and even the savviest migrants, with connections to strong networks of family and friends, could not keep track of everything. Their harsh journeys brought occasional breaks in communication for some, adding to their uncertainty. Their resulting handling of border encounters exposed them at times to further official harshness and violence.

In June 2015, Hungary closed its border with Serbia as part of its harsh policy against illegal migrants and refugees (*Guardian* 2015). Ammar recalled: "The border fence between Serbia and Hungary was three metres high, with police forces all over the place. It was impossible to get through without being caught. The police made accessible one exit through the fence for refugees to cross, in order to take them to gathering camps. Refugees were forced to provide fingerprints to the Hungarian police, which meant that they cannot seek asylum in Germany." Ammar also recalled the difficulties in crossing borders illegally.

Stranded, refugees had to make crucial decisions. Ammar, unaware of Germany's new policy on Syrian refugees, was desperate to avoid Hungarian border controls and attempted to cross the border illegally. Serbian armed gangs attacked him near the border, and human smugglers made him false promises. He tried to cross through the fence with a group of Afghani refugees but failed:

I decided to join a group of Afghani refugees whom I communicated with in Persian. Our plan was to cut through the fence and escape. At five a.m. we entered a swamp close to the borderline accompanied with women and children. The Afghani group had special scissors, which they used to cut the fence, but only a few seconds after crossing through the hole in the fence we were attacked by the Hungarian army forces with a helicopter above our heads. They captured the guy who made the hole while we escaped through the swamp and hid in the waters for close to five hours. They released the guy who was captured, and he soon joined us. Signs of torture marked his body as he limped towards us. His money was stolen as well. While in the water I saw a snake passing by me and felt hopeless that we are not going to make it through. I convinced the group to return to the forest and decided to try again at night. We were certain that we will be caught but we had to try.

Ammar's words convey a combination of powerlessness and determination. He and his group were desperate to avoid border controls. After many unsuccessful attempts, and with the assistance of the GPS of his smart phone, Ammar reached a Hungarian gas station well-known to refugees. Taxi drivers there take refugees to Budapest for 100 euros per person. Ammar paid. In Budapest, however, train services were stopped, trapping thousands of refugees for days.

Khaled had decided on the Netherlands as his destination after learning while on the move that it was faster than its neighbours at processing applications for family reunion – a crucial factor for him. Yet he and his group decided to cross the Serbian border into Hungary under Hungarian police supervision; they could not risk an illegal crossing, concerned as they were about the safety of Khaled's sister and her children. But with Germany's policy changes and Hungary's tightening of its borders except toward Germany, the group's decision to cross under police supervision made Germany, rather than the Netherlands, Khaled's ultimate destination. He could not afford to continue by himself, so he followed his group heading for Germany.

Though they had crossed legally into Hungary, Khaled's group ended up in a detention centre there:

The borders were heavily militarized, with drones and helicopters. Those who tried to escape and cross the borders through the corn fields were captured and brutally treated … We crossed the borders under heavy police supervision. The borders were at an extreme security alert … After, we walked for about 500 metres and found thousands of people sitting on the floor. We sat there for about ten hours through the night. At 6 a.m. in the morning

Precarious Resistances 195

we boarded one of the buses, and it drove ten minutes and dropped us at a prison ... Yes. It was a real prison.

In the detention centre, they again faced "biopolitical abandonment" (Vaughan-Williams 2015, 83). Khaled explained:

A policeman placed coloured bracelets around our arms and took us through another fence to an area that was full of military tents ... Thousands of people were there; some have been waiting for days and others for weeks. We thought that we will have our fingerprints taken and we then continue our journey, but soon discovered that we were actually detained. We were in a prison with our children, with no food and no water for days. The police refused to give water even for kids, and they treated us extremely bad.

Such practices represent "sovereignty's retakings" (Nyers 2003, 1087). The treatment of refugees at those camps reflected the violence of European bordering practices against irregular migrants and refugees (Vaughan-Williams 2015). Yet refugees can resist and contest such treatment and create new forms of politics even under exclusion (see, for example, Johnson 2013; Jacobsen, Karlsen, and Khosravi 2021). According to Khaled, some refugees set their tents on fire in protest, while others, including Khaled, also acted:

The situation in Hungary was the worst. We were hungry, humiliated, and imprisoned ... We were getting very frustrated as they shouted and threatened with sticks at anyone who complains. My brother-in-law found a carton board and wrote in English that we needed to drink water. He went around tents trying to get as many people as possible to join in carrying the board in front of the media who were standing outside the fence. We immediately managed to attract the media's attention, and they started asking us questions about the situation inside. But police surrounded us while cameras where recording. We were asked to calm down and wait until they arranged for an Arabic-speaking translator ... The police promised to let us out without taking fingerprints, and people started to cheer for Hungary. After one hour, they brought us water and ham sandwiches. The quantity was not enough, and many refugees refused to eat, even though they were starving.[3]

After two days, we were taken to a hall near the detention centre and informed us [*sic*] that we will be leaving. We boarded buses with windows totally covered, accompanied by two policemen. We arrived at a police station and went through a strict inspection process. Then we were switched from one room to another, spending four to five hours in each, with no food or water. We were so hungry and thirsty we begged them to give at least [to] the children, but they simply refused.

They started taking our fingerprints, and I reminded them of their promise not to take fingerprints, they told me that they were lying ... My friend who resisted to give his fingerprints was approached by a policeman who forcibly tried to take his fingerprints until he changed his mind and agreed to comply only to avoid their brutality. We were ordered to sign documents that were not in English, and, when we asked about the content, we were told that those documents confirm that the Hungarian authorities were cooperative and provided us with both food and water, respecting human-rights agreements. Later, we were offered some food and water and were handed official documents which stated that we were asylum-seekers in Hungary.

Khaled's description here highlights the ongoing contestations between refugees and Hungarian authorities during a humiliating registration process that lasted for days. They even had to give their fingerprints in exchange for food and water and thus became asylum-seekers in Hungary against their will.

Khaled and his group made their way to Budapest, where they saw thousands of people who had been trapped there for more than ten days. Smugglers were charging 700 euros per person to take people to Germany, a fee that many refugees could not afford. Khaled contacted his cousin in Germany, who reached out to a group of activists, who were assisting stranded refugees in Hungary to reach Germany. They were part of a large solidarity network.

Khaled finally reached Germany at the end of August. He was making his way through Austria on the day that a truck full of refugees' bodies was discovered on an Austrian highway (BBC 2015). As a consequence of this tragic incident, smuggling stopped briefly in Hungary, and Ammar, who reached Budapest a few days later, was stranded at the train station. Hungarian authorities were stopping trains, and smugglers were refusing to take refugees through restrictive security. Ammar watched in disbelief as twenty buses arrived from Austria and started loading refugees without asking for documents or fees. He and hundreds of other refugees travelled to Vienna, where they boarded trains to Munich, where groups of Germans at the station welcomed them with cheers. Ammar moved on to Hanover, where he currently lives. He has since received a three-year renewal of temporary protection in Germany.

Khaled is now in Berlin. He has obtained temporary protection for one year, subject to annual renewals. This status does not allow him to apply for family reunification, which is his ultimate goal. His journey has not ended, for he is desperate to bring his family to Germany. His wants to offer his family a new life and to save his boys from the horrors he witnessed during the war in Syria and his long journey of displacement and statelessness.

Conclusion

This chapter has offered insights into the complex and shifting nature of the journeys made by Syrian refugees. It has emphasized the ways in which these journeys connect to the "refugee crisis" and are differentially experienced and entangled in protracted waiting, frustration, disappointment, violence, and trauma. In the course of their journeys, people on the move have challenged processes depicting them as victims instead of political agents and decision-makers; they have also resisted migrant and bordering policies and practices and their resulting precarities. The telling of these journeys has complicated and opened up the critical role of journey narratives in producing knowledge about migrant struggles, smuggling, the ever-changing terrain of restrictive migration policies to reduce the movements of people seeking protection, and the hope and imagination for a stable life.

CONCLUSION

The conflict in Syria that began in March 2011 with anti-government demonstrations has become part of an internationalized armed conflict in which as many as 511,000 people have lost their lives (HRW 2019d) and more than 12.7 million people have been forced to leave the country and live without adequate protection, social assistance, and legal employment. They are now struggling to access residency, social rights, and citizenship. Hundreds of Syrians and other migrants are arriving daily on European shores after walking great distances, climbing barbed wire fences, passing through internal and external border controls, enduring police brutality, humiliation, and mistreatment, and undertaking precarious journeys across the Aegean and Mediterranean in search of greater protection and security. The scale of displacement of Syrians has led to increasing demands for international and national humanitarian aid for those seeking food, shelter, health care, and accommodation in Syria's neighbouring countries and in other host states. This scale of displacement has been so noteworthy that, as Loyd, Ehrkamp, and Secor (2017) remind us, it has partly overshadowed concerns over prevailing refugee dislocation in the region and elsewhere in Asia and East Africa, where most of the world's refugees are found today.[1]

A photograph drew international attention to the displacement of Syrians and to their precarious migrant journeys: that of the body of a three-year-old Syrian child, Alan Kurdi, that washed up on a Turkish beach near Bodrum on 2 September 2015. His family had been attempting to reach Greece by sea. The photo and the accompanying story of a father's loss, which appeared on the front pages of newspapers across Europe and North America, brought to the forefront the devastating impact of the Syrian war and the increasing numbers of people fleeing Syria in search of international protection. It led to strong expressions of international responsibility and a tremendous increase in charitable donations for migrant and refugee aid organizations. Secor (2018) reminds us that the photo also stimulated editorial criticism of Western authorities for their indecisiveness in the face of the soaring numbers of refugees and asylum-seekers arriving in Europe and in cities across the global North, which some writers have referred to as the "migration crisis."[2] In the background of this "crisis," President Erdoğan of Turkey has emphasized that European states have failed to address the conflict in Syria, which has been dislodging millions of Syrians, with Turkey bearing the brunt of economic responsibility for hosting them, meanwhile receiving insufficient aid from other countries.

There have been various reactions to this so-called crisis, which has politicized these forced migrants to the point that their movements are now closely governed. Reactionary policy responses have proliferated: greater resources have been invested in border enforcement (Mountz 2020), European countries have fortified their borders (Crawley et al. 2018; Hyndman and Reynolds 2020), and spaces of containment, control, abandonment, and violence have been established (Tazzioli 2020). In tandem with all this, a neocolonial image of refugees has developed, so that at times they are depicted as dangerous, threatening, and intrusive (Ozduzen, Korkut, and Ozduzen 2020). That image often presents refugees as a mass of bodies, including in state policy-making practices, such as those in Turkey, but also in the United States, the EU states, Australia, Saudi Arabia, and elsewhere (Hakli and Kallio 2020). More critically, the crisis has been presented as a "problem" having to do with so many people crossing international borders, reaching Europe to seek safety and protection, and becoming a "threat" to host societies. Hyndman and Reynolds (2020) remind us that the crisis "was constructed largely by states in the Global North about the uninvited asylum seekers arriving on their shores, often ignoring the violence and displacement in Syria, but also South Sudan and Eritrea" (66). Similarly, Syria's neighbours, including Jordan and Lebanon, have securitized their discourses and border control practices, the result being precarity for Syrian refugees. Various policies and practices have focused on reducing or ending the entry of Syrian refugees and restricting access to employment and health care for them (e.g.,

AI 2016c; Içduygu and Nimer 2019). These and other related responses have resulted in unequal distributions of security, safety, protection, and hope for Syrian refugees around the world, including in Turkey.

Since 2011, Turkey has taken in around 3.6 million Syrian refugees, the largest number of any country. Though that country has also taken in Iraqis, Afghanis, Iranians, Pakistanis, Somalis, and others, it is Syrian refugees who are increasingly at the nexus of Turkey's domestic, regional, and international discussions and policies. Some critics have noted that they are serving as a useful "bargaining chip" for the current AKP government against the EU (Tuğal 2016).[3] Many Syrians who have arrived in Turkey since 2013 have been given temporary protection status and access to humanitarian aid, and a rare few – those with greater economic and social capital – have been granted national citizenship by the Turkish government. Around 1 million Syrians are employed in Turkey's informal sector with minimal pay, no social security (*New York Times* 2018),[4] and no access to permanent residency or formal citizenship. The rights and entitlements of permanent residency and national citizenship for Syrian refugees in Turkey have served to divide Syrian populations within the country and to codify their presence through market logics and sentiments that function in tandem with state and humanitarian agendas and thereby contribute to Syrians' struggles.

In this book, we have focused on the impact of humanitarian emergency responses to forced migrant populations, the resulting precarity and ambiguity faced by those whom the responses are meant to help, and how the recipients experience these responses in their daily lives, with particular attention given to Syrian refugees in Turkey today. Much of our analysis has been directed toward understanding the precarious conditions that are shaping the lives of Syrian refugees in Turkey. We have paid particular attention to how precarity is produced through governing practices, primarily through Turkey's regime of temporary protection, which provides Syrians with certain rights, such as the right to stay, and free public health care and education, but nevertheless restricts their ability to access national citizenship, regular employment, permanent residency status, and free movement within Turkey. Language barriers, accreditation challenges, identity-based discrimination, and lack of information about their rights

CONCLUSION

further complicate their lives. This book's description of the precarity they face does not represent an extreme case. Indeed, it reflects what too many refugees and other migrants are increasingly experiencing around the world, processes that Tsing (2015) would describe as an "earthwide condition."

Our analysis has drawn on wide-ranging policy and media materials, fieldwork in Turkish cities, and in-depth, qualitative interviews with Syrian refugees and representatives of NGOs and community groups. Based on this research, we have argued that an architecture of precarity strongly shapes many Syrian refugees' daily lives (and those of other migrants) in Turkey. The term "precarity" neatly encapsulates both vulnerability and ambiguity, simultaneous inclusion and exclusion. Our research has also paid careful attention to Syrians' own thoughts and feelings about their lot, in their own languages and in their own terms. This book has allowed them to be their own knowledge-makers and the narrators of their own experiences. At the same time, we recognize that their experiences can be, like those of other migrants elsewhere (see, e.g., Basok and Candiz 2020; Cabot 2016; Murphy and Chatzipanagiotidou 2020; Ramsay 2019; Sigona 2017), linked to bordering practices, differential inclusion processes, gender, race, and class dynamics, and other relations of power. Our book offers a lens through which to better explore and understand Syrian refugees' daily lives and how they confront and navigate an ever-spinning web of legal relations, social and political environments, and migration and movement challenges in and beyond the Turkish context. We have also drawn attention to their complicated daily struggles by highlighting the more subtle forms of their political agency and the transformative potential of their performative acts of citizenship. Here we have focused on their rights-claiming activities, be it the right to leave Turkey for Europe or to stay in Turkey and find ways to belong there. We have seen such rights-claiming in their community-building endeavours, which are sometimes obscured by their precarious living conditions.

The defining features of precarity are encountered in the legal, political, and social domains; they can be international, regional, national, or local in scale; and they are found in distinct spaces such as markets, neighbourhoods, and cities. These together form part of the "architecture of precarity." Under this rubric, we have identified three dimensions of precarity that foster both vulnerability and ambiguity: status, space, and movement. *Precarious status* refers to insecure conditions that arise when governing authorities assign refugees a certain socio-legal status, such as the temporary protection status that has been granted to many Syrian refugees in Turkey. Compared to other status terms such as "irregular migrants," this one is more malleable and inclusive (see Goldring et al. 2009): it can determine specific and at times limited rights to residence, health care, welfare, and work; be further intensified by restricted access to citizenship and labour rights; and create uncertainty about the future. It can also foster ways for migrants to negotiate the constraints of their status and engage with an alternative future. *Precarious space* refers to those spaces that receive meaning through the precarious experiences and daily lives of marginal groups. These socio-spatial domains include squalid accommodations, marginalized neighbourhoods, and sites of struggles and negotiations in daily life. *Precarious movement* refers to those governing practices that deny migrant subjects rights in transit, detain them, or compel them to relocate. Such mobility control practices transform migrants' social status as well as their place of residence; they also bring to the fore how migrants address the challenges of accessing limited resources in urban spaces.

Our analysis has addressed three related questions: How do responses to forced migration develop? How do they generate precarious situations for forced migrants? And in what ways do migrants then engage in counter-responses? We have paid particular attention to the governance dimensions of forced migration since the League of Nations was founded after First World War. That era institutionalized refugee camps and massive urban refugee spaces and saw the earliest development of policies for controlling mobile populations. Then, after the horrors of the Second World War, vast numbers of new refugees entered their homelands. This led to the founding of the UNHCR in 1950 as an international organization for protecting refugees; the adoption of the 1951 Refugee Convention, which, until the 1967 Protocol, only applied to refugees fleeing the aftermath of the Second World War (and to European refugees in particular); and the emergence of international and national schemes to control refugee movements with respect to borders, residency, and citizenship. Linked to these

CONCLUSION

humanitarian and international policy developments was a particular kind of humanitarian emergency response that we conceptualized as involving both care and control (see also, for example, Agier 2011; Hyndman 2000; Ilcan and Rygiel 2015; Pallister-Wilkins 2015). This approach allows for an in-depth understanding of the social and political dimensions of refugee resettlement and demonstrates the close links between humanitarian emergency responses and precarity. This form of governance encompasses diverse groups of people on the move who are experiencing the precarious effects of migrant policies, practices, types of protection, and constructions of migrant identities; it is today part of the architecture of precarity. Our conceptual orientation for understanding precarious status, movement, and space, as well as counter-precarity activities, has focused on Syrian refugees arriving in, living in, and departing from Turkey during the Syrian conflict.

Since the Syrian war broke out, governing responses to the displacement of Syrians have not been uniform. Instead, they have been profuse and complex, and have included: the creation of barriers along borders to prevent Syrians and other migrants from entering nearby countries and the EU (e.g., Austria, Bulgaria, Hungary, Turkey); provision of temporary protection status (e.g., Germany, Sweden, Turkey) rather than full protection under the 1951 Refugee Convention; and the signing of the 2016 EU–Turkey Statement (see, for example, Bulley 2017a; European Council 2016; Karadağ 2019), which has attempted to create stronger border control of coastal waters, curb refugees' movement into the EU, and establish the Turkish government as the EU's *de facto* border security agency. Alongside all this, in April 2019, Russian and Syrian government forces launched a major military offensive to recapture Idlib governate and neighbouring areas in northwestern Syria (HRW 2020). Syrians who tried to escape a slaughter (which killed at least 1,600 civilians before the fighting halted in March 2020 [HRW 2020]) found the border to Turkey had closed. In terms of bordering practices, which are often gendered and racialized, there has been an increase in checkpoints, as well as raids around and beyond Turkey's territorial border sites, and in the arrests of Syrians without documents or permits to travel outside the cities where they registered. Moreover, Turkish provincial authorities have effectively halted registrations for new arrivals,[5] which means that recent Syrian arrivals cannot receive health care through hospital visits, or work legally, and that they are vulnerable to arrest.[6]

Since then, many Syrian refugees have been stopped by police officers in train stations and other public places and asked to show their *kimlik*, and there have been mass arrests of Syrian refugees in İstanbul and illegal deportations of them back to Syria. It is illegal to deport them to Syria because of the risk they will be subjected to human rights violations; even so, some refugees have been asked to sign documents that Turkish authorities have told them are registrations, receipts, or even forms stating that they wish to remain in Turkey (AI 2019; DW 2019b). In fact, those forms are "voluntary return" statements written in Turkish. Many Syrians who unwittingly signed them have found themselves being deported back to Syria. The Turkish government has claimed that these Syrians *chose* to return to Syria in the midst of the conflict there; yet according to Amnesty International, "dozens of refugees told the organization that the Turkish police beat and threatened them into signing documents saying they were willingly returning to Syria" (DW 2019a). Indeed, several recent reports (e.g., AI 2019, 2020; DW 2019a; *Guardian* 2019b) have stressed that hundreds of Syrian refugees from Turkey have been sent back to Syria unlawfully and against their will in recent years, which has been deeply traumatic for them (see Khosravi 2021).

In light of all this, it is disconcerting that according to the agreement between Turkey and Russia of 22 October 2019, those two countries will jointly patrol most of the Syrian–Turkish border formerly held by Kurdish-led forces (HRW 2019c) so that there can be the "'safe and voluntary return' of refugees to a yet-to-be-established 'safe zone'" (DW 2019b), a safe zone that, according to President Erdoğan, will resettle 2 million Syrian refugees currently living in Turkey. Safe zones, however, are geopolitically motivated in that their creation is about, according to Hyndman (2003), the geopolitical interests of authoritarian states rather than about the lessening of civilian suffering. She points out that safe zones within conflict territories are rarely safe. But they can serve as an instrument of refugee *containment*, which in turn can draw attention to the politics of precarity embedded in safety and protection discourses. Furthermore, the deportation of Syrian refugees from Turkey to safe zones in Syria may not mean a termination

CONCLUSION

of the migration cycle; instead it could foster, as Khosravi emphasizes, "another phase of recirculation, and consequently of further waiting," which in turn can involve "different geographies, other people and different phases of life" (2021, 203).

Refugees and asylum-seekers from Syria and elsewhere have been attempting to seek safety, international protection, or a better life in Europe by engaging in sea and land journeys, such as the well-reported but dangerous sea journeys between Turkey and Greece, and Libya and Italy. Many of these people on the move have been reaching their destinations "safely," but others have drowned or been seriously harmed during these journeys (e.g., Almustafa 2019; Crawley et al. 2018; see also UNHCR 2015a, b). This is part of what Andersson (2014) might describe as a multimillion-dollar "illegality industry." More than this, though, it reflects the collective criminality of the state, and the "global fault lines" between Europe, Africa, and the Middle East and between military and humanitarian governance (Albahari 2016), as well as indirect and geographically "distant" forms of violence within European liberal democracies (Isakjee et al. 2020). An Amnesty International report titled *A Perfect Storm: The Failure of European Politics in the Central Mediterranean* links the high rates of deaths in the Mediterranean to failing EU policies and emphasizes that by giving NGOs the main responsibility for search and rescue operations, Europe's governments have failed to prevent drownings and the horrendous abuses many refugees and other migrants face. This kind of border regime not only makes migrant deaths more likely but also, De Genova reminds us, "compels us to reckon with the brute fact that the lives of migrants and refugees, required to arrive to European soil by 'irregular' [illegalized] means, have been systematically exposed to lethal risks" (2018, 1767).

The EU's failing policies have been relevant to our study of Syrian refugees in Turkey and the social and political relations shaping their precarious legal status, precarious space, and precarious movements. Countries in Europe and elsewhere are closing their borders rather than upholding their international legal obligations to protect refugees. This study has emphasized the limitations and failures of Turkey's temporary protection of Syrians, the precarious living conditions they face, and the broader context of the EU's arrangements with Turkey vis-à-vis Syrian refugees. Most asylum-seekers who arrive in

Turkey, including Syrians, are from outside Europe and thus ineligible for refugee status there. Until 9 September 2018, they were required to apply to the international refugee agency, UNHCR, for refugee status while in Turkey. However, very few Syrians have received refugee status from the UNHCR.

There has been a lack of information about the details of temporary protection for Syrian refugees in Turkey, and moreover, the UNHCR has not been giving priority to registering Syrians who have temporary protection for settlement in third countries, even if they may be eligible. It has been registering Syrians in Turkey only in cases of emergency or family unification, for it considers them otherwise safe with temporary protection. Adding to this precarious status for Syrians, some humanitarian organizations that have been aiding Syrian refugees in Turkey are not fully aware of the legal intricacies of the temporary protection regime, which has resulted in unwarranted confusion and hardship for Syrians. On 10 September 2018, the UNHCR terminated its registration of international protection seekers in Turkey as part of the process of transferring responsibilities for determining refugee status to Turkish authorities, namely the Turkish General Directorate of Migration Management, which was established to address migration flows, register asylum-seekers, and supervise the humanitarian aspects of Syrian refugee settlement. Currently, all applications for international protection are directly registered with the Provincial Directorate for Migration Management; this is the case for Syrian refugees registering under Turkey's temporary protection regime (UNHCR 2018c). In these most recent registrations, for example, applicants have been issued an ID card with a Foreigner's ID number, which provides applicants with certain "rights and services as per the Turkish legislation" (UNHCR 2018c). However, while the registration of applications for international protection is conducted by the Provincial Directorate for Migration Management across all eighty-one of Turkey's provinces, applicants are only allowed to reside in "satellite cities." And according to the UNHCR, nineteen provinces – including İstanbul, İzmir, and Ankara – are now excluded from the "satellite city" system (UNHCR 2018c).[7]

Temporary protection status has made Syrians' movements in Turkey much more precarious, for they are required to obtain an exit permit from the Directorate General of Migration Management through the Provincial Directorate of Migration Management of the city in which they registered. Thus, though many Syrians have had to remain in Turkey under temporary protection and live in precarious spaces and living conditions, their movement into and outside the country has become increasingly more perilous as a consequence of the border politics between Turkey and the EU, particularly the EU–Turkey Statement. There have been many criticisms of the Statement,[8] which is a recent example of a broader trend in migration and asylum management through security measures and border controls. It aims to block asylum-seekers and refugees, particularly Syrians, from EU territories, where they might register asylum claims and seek refugee status with a better standard of living than is available in Turkey. As emphasized in this book, the EU–Turkey Statement represents a failure by the international community and the EU, especially those who signed the European Convention on Human Rights, to recognize Syrians as refugees, which has contributed to their precarity. And given the current economic downturn in Turkey related to international trade tensions, the global pandemic, the devaluation of the Turkish lira against the US dollar, and the subsequent increase in commodity prices such as for food, countless people, including Syrians, are particularly hindered. Many Syrians who are working without legal documentation are especially affected; some are losing their jobs and being forced to engage in various kinds of precarious work in the informal economy, and others are unable to make a stable life and are contemplating leaving the country with the help of intermediaries. Their indeterminate status in Turkey has objectified them as lacking the normative authority of citizenship; it has also presented them as particular *kinds* of people in need of care, thus highlighting what Barnett (2011) would call the present system's "humanitarian paternalism." Yet their precarious legal status has also fostered ways for some Syrians to make rights claims, such as claiming the right to leave, thereby challenging the assumption that they are victims (i.e., voiceless, defenceless, and helpless). Indeed, they are now breaking down barriers and finding ways to negotiate their precarity (see Isin 2017). In so doing, many of them are making what are often perilous journeys to Europe in search of refugee status and a more stable future.

Still, many Syrians have decided to stay in Turkey, gained the support of local community and solidarity initiatives, developed their own social and economic networks, and made lives for themselves, just like other migrants living elsewhere (see, e.g., Basok et al. 2015; Barbero 2012; Murphy and Chatzipanagioutidou 2020; Darling 2014; Goldring and Landholt 2021; Cabot 2018). In doing so, they are reinscribing and reconfiguring the relations between new arrivals and local citizens as well as challenging their own precarity (e.g., Butler 2009, 2004; Jonsson 2020; Şahin Mencütek 2019) through a diverse array of socially and politically inspired collectivities, such as community-building initiatives. In recognizing that Syrian refugees and other migrants in Turkey are not simply victims of precarious situations and governing efforts, we have emphasized their resistance as a form of political activism that counters precarity and the exclusionary policies of temporary protection. In this regard, many Syrians have proclaimed their visibility and dignity and invested in their lives through community-building initiatives through which they carve out spaces in an effort to claim the right to stay and to belong. Rights-claiming is an act of citizenship and is part of counter-precarity activities; both occur in the context of multitudes of people struggling to survive and make a decent living. As such, they help us understand migrant populations not simply as those who are displaced, without adequate economic infrastructure, or in need of protection and humanitarian assistance, but as agents who can engage in everyday political activities, challenge practices of exclusion, negotiate ways to access rights and resources, and seek alternative forms and spaces of protection.

Rights-claiming through community-building initiatives has been materializing in many parts of the world. Such initiatives are contesting states' dominant framings and imaginings of migrant populations, calling into question the criminalization and securitization of migrants, countering xenophobic views of them (see for e.g., Kallius, Monterescu, and Kumar Rajaram 2016; McNevin 2006; Muller 2016), and fostering safer and friendlier urban environments for those who are claiming rights. For example, cities of welcome, cities of sanctuary, safe cities, and human rights cities have been one development to emerge in some urban environments; these offer migrants (both regular and irregular) access to labour markets and basic human and social

CONCLUSION

services without discrimination and regardless of national policies. These cities are developing policies and practices aimed at migrant inclusion, so that precarity can be lessened and thereby give rise to migrant struggles with the potential to disrupt precarious conditions, reduce refugee seclusion, consolidate social and political groupings, and create new community-based and political possibilities.

In this book, our analysis has built on and contributed to a substantial body of academic literature that has demonstrated the impact of humanitarian emergency responses on forced migrant populations[9] and the resulting precarity and ambiguity they face (Goldring and Landholt 2011, 2013; Wall, Campbell, and Janbek 2015). Such precarity has been orchestrated through governing actors that have transnational scope (Ticktin 2014). It is cultivated by national policy approaches based on temporary protection initiatives (e.g., Baban, Ilcan, and Rygiel 2017b; Bastaki 2018; Durieux 2015; Hallett 2014; İçduygu 2015b; Kaya 2016; Korkut 2016; Orchard and Miller 2014; Şenses 2015; Yıldız and Uzgören 2016). These initiatives, which are not functioning as an extraordinary response to safeguard the lives of refugees, have permeated the 1951 Refugee Convention, especially given that many people on the move over the past several decades have received temporary protection status. That status is eroding the need for refugee protection and clear pathways toward accessing legal employment, residency, and citizenship; it is also cultivating precarious and insecure living. The result has been expanding grey zones of exclusion around the world, which Yuval-Davis, Wemyss, and Cassidy (2019) refer to as "borderscapes," as well as classification regimes that amount at times to "slow violence" against migrants (Mayblin, Wake, and Kazemi 2019). Yet temporary protection initiatives are also intersecting with refugees' daily lives of vulnerability in ways that are inspiring political responses to their own plight.[10]

In our analysis, we have emphasized Syrian refugees' lack of adequate protection at the legal, economic, and social levels and their precarious living conditions in the country, as well as the ability of the Turkish government, as a member-state signatory to the 1951 Refugee Convention, to be able to ignore the associated rights that are supposed to be granted to refugees under that Convention. Such an approach permits Turkey, and other countries in the Middle East, Europe, and elsewhere, following similar paths and temporary protection regimes, to generate precarious status, space, and movement for refugees and asylum-seekers. In this regard, it is crucial to identify national and regional refugee policies, such as the 2013 Law on Foreigners and International Protection and the EU–Turkey Statement, as important sites for agenda setting, normative pronouncements, and the undermining of protection rights for refugees.

It is also critical to pay attention to how such policies and related practices can fail refugees, who are often unable to actualize the protection rights they are supposed to enjoy. If the goal is to alleviate human suffering, the status quo is simply not sustainable. Landau and Amit (2014)[11] remind us that "legal failures cannot effectively be addressed solely through legal means." There needs to be a wider focus on refugee protection rights that involves acknowledging the need for humane and secure spaces of living and working and for sustainable and socially just refugee policies and practices. The latter can encompass a range of social and policy fields so that formal assurances to refugee protection can be rendered as concrete forms of protection (legal, economic, cultural) and practical ways of accessing rights (citizenship, employment, housing, education, mobility, safety) at local, national, regional, and international levels. These forms of protection and access to rights are neither uniform nor stable, and they need to be recognized across diverse social lines, including those of gender, ethnicity, social class, sexuality, age, and location. Hyndman and Reynolds emphasize their concern regarding responses to human mobility on an international scale, including decision-making processes that dismiss the lived realities of people most affected by displacement and the privileging of state sovereignty over human beings (2020). They are asking "scholars of migration, asylum, and displacement to engage more critically with protection at different scales and in spaces not governed by international law" (2020, 66), which we regard as an indispensably important undertaking.

Encouraging a broader and more critical focus on refugee protection rights frameworks will involve, among other things, a commitment to understanding and appreciating that refugees and other migrants are the first to recognize and experience different forms of precarity in migrant management laws and policies, including those at the regional

CONCLUSION

and international levels. This would do much to improve and shape the political subjectivity and mobilization of refugees. Refugees are political agents who are initiating and participating in community-building initiatives and fostering their own and others' everyday negotiations for change, rights, and belonging, which often exceed migrant-centric orientations and processes. The agents in these kinds of initiatives have the potential to create new spaces for collective mobilization and to contribute to social and economic transformations. Research on such community-building (and other related initiatives) and on refugees' ability to challenge exclusionary policies and practices, and influence local government, public bureaucracies, urban policy, and everyday social and political relations, is worthy of scholarly attention, for it has the potential to contribute to the lives of people on the move in ways that are collective, transformative, and sustainable.

NOTES

Introduction

1 World Population Review (2019) puts the European population at about 728 million as of 2016.

2 This includes the League in Italy, the Fidesz party in Hungary, and the Law and Justice Party in Poland. Far-right parties have also made important gains in entering parliaments, with the Alternative for Germany entering the German parliament for the first time in 2017, the Sweden Democrats' increasing popularity in Sweden's 2018 election, and the Freedom Party now playing a role in Austria's coalition government (Calamur 2018). Immigration and refugee issues have become a key electoral issue in many European countries with the potential to threaten the European integration project altogether.

3 Of course, these numbers must also be treated with some scepticism since as the IOM itself notes on its Missing Migrants Project webpage, "the data are estimates from IOM, national authorities and media sources." As Weber and Pickering's (2011) work details, the reporting of numbers is highly political, with some national governments likely to over-report and others to underreport based on the ways numbers are mobilized to justify policy responses. As the authors note, "Being able to measure deaths at the border implies a need for action. It is also increasingly used by government agencies in crafting and re-crafting migration and security policies" (Weber and Pickering 2011, 36). More forcefully, Heller and Pécoud (2020, 480) have argued that "while media, activists, and policy makers often mention precise figures regarding the number of deaths, little is known about the production of statistical data on this topic." Moreover, the same authors (ibid.) argue that the IOM's counting of migrant deaths has proved to be ultimately counter-productive: "In producing statistics on border deaths, IOM depoliticizes this data and challenges the critical framework that was central to earlier civil society initiatives."

Chapter One

1 In this regard, Barnett (2013, 387) reminds us that more new providers of humanitarian emergency assistance are working in countries where Western-based agencies cannot. They include new donors (e.g., Brazil, China, the Gulf states, and India), new South-based NGOs (e.g., the Bangladesh Rural Advancement Committee and Mercy Malaysia), and Turkey's İnsani Yardım Vakfı (Foundation for Human Rights and Freedoms and Humanitarian Relief [İHH]), which gained international recognition when it sponsored the Turkish relief fleet to Gaza in 2010 and is increasingly active in the Horn of Africa, which is a prime site of humanitarian responses to emergency. In any case, only some actors partaking in emergency practices, such as grassroots and social justice–oriented organizations, attempt to provide long-term support and seek to explore and ameliorate the relations of power, economic inequities, gender, class, and ethnic inequalities, as well as precarious conditions of living that underlie the lives of many forced migrants.

2 The government interventions that emerge in response to migration emergencies range from short-term policy initiatives to address migrants' movements, and tighter border controls and policing, to new asylum and citizenship policies. In this context, authorities may create "safe zones" for containing and controlling migrant populations, detention centres and refugee camps, "offshore processing" areas, and other similar spaces to deliver emergency relief and services (e.g., food, shelter, and medical aid; education and skills training; trauma counselling) to mobile groups such as refugees, internally displaced persons (IDPs), and asylum-seekers.

3 In the 1930s a number of relief organizations formed, such as the American Relief Administration and Save the Children; they focused their efforts on various groups opposing Nazi Germany and its allies (Barnett and Weiss 2011, 41–2).

4 At this time, some displaced persons and political refugees were located in these territories. This was for various reasons, for example, they had been slave labourers for the Nazi regime, they were fleeing the movements of armies and the bombing of urban centres during the war, or they were fleeing persecution and the threat of enslavement.

5 The formation of a single international body (soon termed the International Relief Organization [IRO]) intended to "handle adequately all phases of the problem presented by refugees and displaced persons." A special committee, comprised of twenty representatives of the United

NOTES TO PAGES 31–3

Nations, was formed by the Economic and Social Council on 8 April 1946 to offer recommendations regarding the founding of the IRO, which took place on 20 April 1946 (Office of Public Affairs 1946, 4). The IRO assumed most of the functions of the UNRRA. The latter was heavily engaged in liberal practices of interwar and postwar planning. It relied on expert forms of knowledge, the establishment of new spaces for caring for and managing populations, and strategies for governing the lives of these populations (Ilcan and Aitken 2012). The IRO was replaced by the UNHCR on 14 December 1950.

6 Such naming practices, according to Feldman (2008, 157), helped delimit "a discursive space of claim-making" that in turn would shape humanitarian emergency efforts. In this postwar context, Feldman (2007) emphasizes that "the aid regimes that were emerging" at this time "both the international refugee regime and the Palestine-specific assistance program – depended on making distinctions among people in terms that were patently inadequate to capture" their required levels of assistance. In her words, "Although identifying people as 'refugees' (displaced and dispossessed) or 'natives/citizens' (the 'merely' dispossessed) did not say anything about their level of need, these were the terms that governed relief" (2007, 130).

7 In October 2014, Lebanon's Council of Ministers adopted the first comprehensive policy on Syrian displacement. One key goal of this policy is to decrease the number of Syrians living in Lebanon by reducing access to territory and encouraging them to return to their home country. See Janmyr (2016) for more on the legal status of Syrian refugees in Lebanon.

8 See UNHCR (2014b).

9 The proliferation of camps coincided with governments switching "from integration and resettlement to repatriation and 'preventative protection'" (Johnson 2011, 1016).

10 For example, Europe's response to the refugee emergency flowing from the war in the former Yugoslavia (1991–2001) was far more restrictive. Political and sociocultural conditions no longer favoured refugees' reception in Western Europe, and the United States no longer accepted large groups of refugees from Europe. Since the crisis was on the European Union (EU's) doorstep, the international community preferred solutions in the region of origin, in the name of human security and the "right to remain." Safe zones emerged in 1992–95 in Bosnia, with the UNHCR supporting IDPs through its good offices (see Biondi 2016, 210).

11 For example, in May 2013 the Australian Parliament approved a controversial law expunging certain areas of Australia (namely, Christmas

Island, the Ashmore and Cartier Islands, and the Cocos Islands) from the country's migration zone. Non-citizens arriving on those islands to seek asylum would not be able to make valid applications for any form of visa (including protection visas) without the minister's approval. Even if they reached mainland Australia, the authorities could still send them to offshore processing centres, such as Nauru and Manus Island in Papua New Guinea (PNG). Kevin Rudd's Labor government later consolidated this policy – the first of its kind in the world – with its Regional Resettlement Arrangement with PNG in July 2013. Australia thereafter sent all asylum-seekers arriving by boat to PNG for processing and, ultimately, resettlement (see ASRC 2013). In February 2016, Australia's High Court upheld the country's right to detain asylum-seekers offshore for as long as it helped processing of refugee claims (see Hurst and Doherty 2016). Article 31 of the 1951 Refugee Convention prohibits state parties from penalizing asylum-seekers on account of their "unlawful" entry into a country from a territory where their life or freedom was in danger.

12 Refugee camps today vary in size, composition, management, and provision of state and humanitarian services. As they come to house people over a long period of time – or become "temporally stretched" (Bulley 2015) – refugees often face precarious conditions of living, including minimal rights to citizenship and legal employment and inadequate housing, land, food, health care, and education. Refugees living in urban spaces can face other kinds of challenges.

13 For more on these and other similar detention conditions and treatment, see https://www.echr.coe.int/Documents/FS_Detention_ conditions_ENG.pdf.

14 Some researchers, such as Wall, Campbell, and Janbek (2015, 2–3), have found that in the Zaatari refugee camp, Syrian refugees' uncertain access to news and personal information – "information precarity" – can threaten their well-being.

15 For example, the United Kingdom can grant "humanitarian protection" to people who do not qualify as refugees but are at risk of torture or other serious abuse in their home country. The protection is usually for three years, renewable, with rights to work, education, health care, and other benefits (Orchard and Miller 2014, 5). The United States offers temporary protected status (TPS) to forced migrants, a designation that Hallett (2014, 621) asserts is rife with ambiguity and contradiction. Under TPS, migrant guest-worker programs may provide benefits to certain employers while denying TPS migrants other rights and benefits.

NOTES TO PAGES 38–42

16 Status-holders are sometimes able to claim asylum and receive individual assessment of their claims (Orchard and Miller 2014, 5).

17 More recently, as part of efforts to combat COVID-19, various states have implemented border closures that prevent the entry of non-citizens to their territories, thus ultimately eroding the non-refoulement principle. In this regard, Canada temporarily suspended its refugee resettlement program in May 2020, Italy closed it ports to migrant vessels in early 2020, and the US has halted its asylum processing (Jonsson 2020). Although international border closures, travel bans, and refugee program deferments are often emphasized as temporary under the current pandemic situation, they can worsen the precarious conditions facing many people who have escaped or are trying to escape from war zones in countries such as Syria (Ilcan 2020). Such conditions can place these people in limbo situations – they are unable to gain protection from their home country but simultaneously have been immobilized and prevented from relocating and exercising the right to seek asylum.

18 By the end of 2019, "the number of people forcibly displaced due to war, conflict, persecution, human rights violations and events seriously disturbing public order had grown to 79.5 million, the highest number on record according to available data" (UNHCR 2019c, n.p.). An estimated 30 to 34 million of these displaced people are children under eighteen. Forced-migrant populations, such as refugees, live in the South in refugee camps in Africa, Asia, and the Middle East and in cities and towns. Eighty-five per cent of the world's refugees are hosted in developing countries (UNHCR 2019b).

19 Some scholars emphasize that while actors differ in their responses to emergencies, they seek to govern, if indirectly (e.g., Agier 2011; Ticktin 2011b). For example, Ilcan and Rygiel (2015) perceive a humanitarian field with international and national governing actors and strategies of care, resilience, and responsibility that operate in routine spaces where refugees reside. Importantly, for Ticktin, humanitarian actors in such spaces act on the everyday, "prioritizing emergency or crisis situations" (2011b, 152).

20 Precarious experiences can displace people – for example, as public discourses aim to shape their identity in ways that create social and cultural barriers for them. Yet such experiences can also spur them to collective action. For example, Barchiesi (2011) introduces the notion of "precarious liberation" to demonstrate how the labour process connects to the liberation struggle and the social imaginaries and subjectivities of

NOTES TO PAGES 43–63

workers in South Africa, and how such struggles nurture the growing precariat movement, which demands certain rights for workers as well as a universal, basic, "citizenship income" (Banki 2013, 451).

21 As discussed later in the book, the Temporary Protection Regulation (dated 22 October 2014) regulates the right to work for the beneficiaries of temporary protection. Founded on this legal basis, a Council of Ministers introduced a new regulation on 15 January 2016 that determines the principles and procedures for issuing work permits. Under this new regulation, the beneficiaries of temporary protection are permitted to apply for work permits six months after their registration. For more on these and other related issues, see http://www.unhcr.org/tr/en/livelihoods.

22 In this context, Strauss (2018) emphasizes that "points-based systems" in countries like Canada are increasingly being adopted elsewhere to establish channels of entry for skilled workers. At the same time, temporary migration (guest-worker) programs often link "highly restrictive conditions to 'low-skilled' workers who are granted visas to work in areas such as domestic service, agriculture, hospitality, and food services" (2018, 6). She adds that even though migration can make work/life balance possible for many people living in the Global North, "migrants and racialized workers are employed in the most flexible and low-paid jobs of the postindustrial economy." For Strauss, such precarious employment conditions create a tenuous "work-life balance for many migrants, especially those who leave families behind to migrate with no route to settlement and family reunion in the host country" (2018, 6).

Chapter Two

1 Tima Kurdi, their aunt in Canada, had tried unsuccessfully to sponsor her brother Mohammad (the boy's uncle), because she had only enough money to sponsor one brother at a time. However, Canada rejected her application because the uncle was not formally a refugee, so she could not make a "G5" application to be a private sponsor.

2 Although Turkey is a signatory to the 1951 Refugee Convention and the 1967 Protocol, it has always maintained a geographical limitation following Article 1b of this Convention (Zeldin 2016), recognizing only "persons who have become refugees as a result of events occurring in Europe" (UNHCR 2017d; see also Soykan 2010 for a discussion of this).

3 For example, the 1951 Refugee Convention guarantees refugees a number of rights, all of which could be said under some circumstances to be at

NOTES TO PAGES 64-7

risk for people living under temporary protection in Turkey, as we see in this chapter and in chapters 3 and 4. These rights include the right to access the courts (Article 16); the right to work (Article 17); the right to choose place of residence and to move freely within the territory (Article 26), which includes travel documents permitting travel abroad (Article 28); prohibition of expulsion or return *(refoulement)* (Article 33); and the right to naturalization (Article 34).

4 The recent changes specify that "international protection applications are received by 81 provinces while permanent stay in some cities is not allowed under the legislation. If you apply to one of the provinces where residence is not allowed, you will be referred to a province where longer-term residence is regulated" (UNHCR 2018c).

5 The EU has been working to create a Common European Asylum System (CEAS) since 1999 to harmonize minimum standards around asylum between EU countries. However, according to Kale and colleagues (2018, 3-4), this initiative to date "has not been easy" and has come with "challenges," including "preserving the right to asylum" while preventing so-called asylum-shopping. Moreover, as Lehner (2019, 179) notes, "The general principle of EU asylum law is that national authorities are competent for the application of the EU asylum laws." Thus there are significant differences in asylum rates and practices among the EU member-states. Along these lines, Burmann and Valeyatheepillay (2017) have noted that "the recognition rate for citizens of the same country of origin varies substantially between different European destination countries even though all EU countries abide by the Geneva Convention and the Common European Asylum System when it comes to determining who gets refugee status. While the majority of Syrian asylum seekers (97%) were deemed refugees according to the Geneva Convention in Germany in 2015, the refugee recognition rates for Syrians in Sweden and Hungary was only 10% and 6% respectively." In addition, the experiences of resettlement, rights, and integration vary enormously *within* European countries, as illustrated in earlier work by Bauböck (1994) and more recently Bauböck and colleagues' project "Access to citizenship and its impact on immigrant integration (ACIT)," which examined citizenship laws and their impact on integration, with results published on the EUDO CITIZENSHIP observatory at www.eudo-citizenship.eu.

6 This number has steadily decreased, from as many as 5,096 in 2016, to 3,139 in 2017, to 2,277 in 2018 (UNHCR, n.d., "Operation Portal ... Mediterranean situation").

7 Williams and Mountz (2018, 74) review empirical research to date on numbers of deaths at borders and correlate this to externalization policies, arguing that "although discourse about interception and externalization has shifted to humanitarian rescue narratives, offshore enforcement by any other name continues to be highly correlated with migrant deaths."

8 The legally binding nature of the deal – really a statement – is a subject of debate among scholars. "Apparently, the EU's procedure for negotiating and concluding treaties with third countries, laid down in Art. 218 TFEU, has not been followed," yet "both the text and context of the EU–Turkey Statement support the view that it is a treaty" (Den Heijer and Spijkerboer 2016). For details on the deal, see European Commission (2015, 2016b). Lehner (2019, 177) argues that the "'deal' between Turkey and the EU is a political agreement which lacks the political qualifications to be considered either as a former legal act or as a binding agreement within the scope of international law." Most recently, the General Court of European Union (CJEU) ruling declaring that "the EU–Turkey statement, as published by means of a Press Release No 144/16, cannot be regarded as a measure adopted by the European Council, or, moreover by any other institution, body, office or agency of the European Union, or as revealing the existence of such a measure that corresponds to the contested measure" became final in September 2018 (Kostantinou and Georgopoulou 2018, 14).

9 Scholars argue that the agreement risks violating the principle of non-refoulement and the right to seek asylum under the 1951 Refugee Convention but also related to Articles 3 and 13 of the European Convention on Human Rights (ECHR), since Turkey's asylum system has systematic problems and returnees are at the risk of being deported. Additionally, Greek authorities may send irregular migrants, who are under threat in Turkey, back to Turkey without an effective evaluation. There is also the risk of violation of Article 4 of Protocol No. 4 of the ECHR. When Turkey is accepted as a safe third country and asylum applications are found inadmissible because they come from Turkey, individual assessments are avoided. This runs counter to the prohibition of collective deportation. Finally, because of the deal, Greek islands are overcrowded and detention conditions are inhumane, in violation of Articles 3 and 5 of the ECHR (for a full discussion of this, see Ulusoy and Battjes 2017).

10 This is based on Rygiel's earlier field research and visit to İzmir in the summer of 2013 as part of a grant, "Geographies of Exclusion: Rethinking Citizenship from the Margins," funded by the Social Sciences and Humanities Research Council of Canada.

NOTES TO PAGES 86–115

11 This information was based on an interview with a rescue worker in Mytilene, 3 August 2013, as part of Rygiel's earlier field research and visit to İzmir in the summer of 2013.

12 This includes some 17,081 refugees at Lesvos; 4,950 at Chios; 6,896 at Samos, 4,5,26, at Kos, and 2,875 at Leros (UNHCR, n.d., "Operational Portal ... Greece").

13 Ibid.

14 The International Organization for Migration (IOM) runs the AVRR, which offers "reintegration assistance," which can include financial and employment opportunities as incentives to return. The IOM describes the program as "an indispensable part of a comprehensive approach to migration management aiming at orderly and humane return and reintegration of migrants who are unable or unwilling to remain in host or transit countries and wish to return voluntarily to their countries of origin." See https://www.iom.int/assisted-voluntary-return-and-reintegration.

Chapter Three

1 Turkey signed the 1951 Refugee Convention on 24 August 1951 and ratified it on 30 March 1962. Status as at 22 February 2016, *Convention Relating to the Status of Refugees*, UN Treaty Collection (UNTC), https://treaties.un.org/pages/ViewDetailsII.aspx?src=TREATY&mtdsg_no=V-2&chapter=5&Temp=mtdsg2&lang=en. It acceded to the protocol on 31 July 1968. Status as at 22 February 2016, *Protocol Relating to the Status of Refugees*, UNTC, https://treaties.un.org/ pages/ViewDetails.aspx ?src=TREATY&mtdsg_no=V-5&chapter=5&lang=en, archived at https://perma.cc/26SR-5SLA.

2 The Arabic term is Ansar-I Muhacir. In the text, the Turkish usage of Ensar is used.

3 The Disaster and Emergency Management Agency (Turkish: Afet ve Acil Durum Yönetimi Başkanlığı, AFAD) was established in 2009 to provide emergency management and civil protection and reports to the prime minister.

4 The Provincial Directorate of Migration Management (PDMM) is the provincial representative of the national Directorate General for Migration Management.

5 In 2016, Turkey was still governed by a parliamentary system that was headed by a prime minister. The 2017 Constitutional Referendum changed the Turkish government system to a presidential one. Binali Yildirim was the last prime minister under the parliamentary system.

NOTES TO PAGES 116–74

6 For more on attacks or xenophobic sentiments against Syrian refugees in Turkey, see Saraçoğlu and Belanger (2019a).

Chapter Four

1 In urban centres, the *muhtar* is an elected local administrator responsible for issuing registrations and other relevant official documents.

Chapter Five

1 Makovsky (2019, n87) explains the poll as follows: "These figures are from a CAP-commissioned and designed nationwide poll of Turkey conducted by the Turkish polling firm Metropoll. The survey is based on 2,534 face-to-face interviews with Turks using stratified sampling and weighting methods in 28 provinces. Seventy percent of in-person respondents were then called by phone to verify the data. The survey was conducted May 24 to June 4, 2018."

2 As of 2019, *Pages* is under new ownership. The founder, Samer Alkadri, has resettled with his family in Europe.

3 *Pages*, http://pagesbookstorecafe.com/istanbul.

4 In Turkish cities, municipal support for refugees reflects policies and practices, as we saw in earlier chapters. For example, in İstanbul, which has more than 400,000 registered Syrians and an estimated 100,000 unregistered (see Woods and Kayalı 2017), there is little support for Syrians in Tarlabaşı, in Beyoğlu district, or Okmeydanı, between Kağıthane and Şişli districts, where land use and property redevelopment vex relations between residents and government. In contrast, Esenyurt, Fatih, and Zeytinburnu provide more support, both financial and in opening spaces for Syrian civic initiatives (Mackreath and Sağnıç 2017).

5 Small Projects İstanbul (SPI), https://www.smallprojectsistanbul.org.

6 Ayman Asfari, a London-based British oil magnate born in Syria, and his wife, Sawsan, set up the Asfari Foundation in England in 2006 to support education and civil society. It supports more than fifty partner organizations in Turkey and abroad, which operate on diverse issues, including the crisis in Syria, youth education and employment, and development of citizenship and a resilient civil society. With their partners, they identify, develop, and fund transformative ideas for many young people from Syria, Lebanon, Palestine, and Britain. For more information, see https://www.asfarifoundation.org.uk.

NOTES TO PAGES 178–203

7 The EU funds health centres – it plans up to 178 of them – across Turkey to treat and employ Syrian refugees. For example, in Ankara, Altındağ Bab-i-Sifa (Door to Health) offers free primary health services to approximately two hundred refugees daily. The EU has granted 300 million euros to Turkey's Ministry of Health, and these clinics will employ 1,500 Syrian medical professionals, who qualify through apprenticeship-style programs, where they work side-by-side with Turkish doctors. These facilities aim to provide not emergency relief but long-term services (*DW* 2017).

Chapter Six

1 These stories derive from original field research by Dr Maissaa Almustafa (Balsillie School of International Affairs, Wilfrid Laurier University) as part of her doctoral thesis (2019), "A Journey towards Protection: Syrian Refugees Caught between War and Walls of Security." These provide the basis for chapter 6, which she has authored. She conducted these interviews with the financial support of the authors' SSHRC-funded project (2015–19, and extended to 2020) on "Humanitarian Aid, Citizenship Politics, and the Governance of Syrian Refugees in Turkey."

2 A branch of Shi'a Islam among ethnic Turks and Kurds in Turkey and the Balkans, related to – though distinct from – Alawism in Syria. Alevis make up 20 per cent of Turkey's Muslims and comprise its largest religious minority (Harvard Divinity School).

3 Devout Muslims will not eat pork.

Conclusion

1 For an extended discussion on the displacement and resettlement of refugees and the geopolitics of trauma, see Loyd, Ehrkamp, and Secor (2017).

2 For a provocative analysis of the war in Syria, its images, and its affective politics on diverse levels, see Secor (2018).

3 For more on this issue, see Tuğal (2016).

4 For more on these matters, see *New York Times* (2018).

5 For example, the Turkish border authorities in the border province of Hatay have been involved in pressuring some Syrians arriving at the border to sign "voluntary return" documents. These in effect either waive their right to seek protection or place them in indefinite detention. Human rights organizations have documented cases of arbitrary

224   NOTES TO PAGES 204–10

detention and deportation of Syrians from Hatay, as well as Iraqis from Van and Afghans from Erzurum and Osmaniye, in recent years (ECRE 2018). In 2018, Hatay province suspended the registration of temporary protection beneficiaries due to the high number of persons registered, challenges in the provision of humanitarian and social services, and other conditions. A similar suspension has been implemented and then reversed in İstanbul. Furthermore, there have been reported violations along the Turkey–Syria border (*Washington Post* 2019b). For example, around 250,000 Syrian refugees were apprehended and returned to Syria by Turkish authorities in the first few months of 2017. In these border situations, incidents of mistreatment have been reported, including push-backs and shootings by border guards (HRW 2018c). For more on border controls and issues of detention in Turkey, see ECRE (2018).

6 For an elaboration of these and other related issues, see *The Guardian* (2018); HRW (2018d).

7 For more on the UNHCR's ending of its registration of asylum-seekers in Turkey, see UNHCR (2018c). See also Informigrants (2018).

8 One key question has been whether Turkey can be considered a safe third country. According to the EU Asylum Procedures Directive, the return of irregular migrants to a third country depends on that country being safe under the following definition: "offering no risk of serious harm or threat on account of race, religion, nationality, social group, or political opinion; respecting the principle of non-refoulement; refraining from the use of torture and degrading treatment; and allowing the possibility for migrants to request refugee status" (Bulley 2017a, 66).

9 On this issue, see for example Agier 2011; Barnett and Weiss 2011; Bulley 2017a; Chimni 2009; Fassin 2007; Johnson 2014; Hyndman 2000; Hyndman and Giles 2017; Nyers 2006; Ramadan 2012; Ticktin 2014; and Türk 2015.

10 See for example Banki 2013; Bilecen and Yurtseven 2018; Lecadet 2016; Isin 2017; Johnson 2016; Kallius, Monterescu, and Kumar Rajaram 2015; Saraçoğlu and Belanger 2019b; Sigona 2012, 2015; Stierl 2016a; and Trimikliniotis, Parsanoglou, and Tsianos 2015.

11 For more on this issue in the southern African context, see Landau and Amit (2014).

REFERENCES

AFAD. 2016. "Current status in AFAD temporary protection centres." https://www.afad.gov.tr/EN/IcerikDetay1.aspx?ID=16&IcerikID=848.

Agier, M. 2007. "From Refugee Camps to the Invention of Cities." In *Cities of the South: Citizenship and Exclusion in the 21st Century*, ed. B. Drieskens, F. Mermier, and H. Wimmen, 169–76. London: Saqi Books.

– 2008. *Gérer les indésirables: Des camps de réfugiés au gouvernement humanitaire*. Paris: Flammarion.

– 2011. *Managing the Undesirables: Refugee Camps and Humanitarian Government*. Cambridge: Polity Press.

– 2012. "From Refuge the Ghetto Is Born: Contemporary Figures of Heterotopias." In *The Ghetto: Contemporary Global Issues and Controversies*, ed. Ray Hutchison and Bruce Haynes, 265–92. Boulder: Westview Press.

Ahval. 2019a. "25,000 refugees return to Turkey following Eid holiday in Syria." https://ahvalnews.com/syrian-refugees/25000-refugees-return-turkey-following-eid-holiday-syria.

– 2019b. "İstanbul governor uses dozens of buses, charters planes to ship out undocumented migrants." 2 August. https://ahvalnews.com/refugees/istanbul-governor-uses-dozens-buses-charters-planes-ship-out-undocumented-migrants.

AI (Amnesty International). n.d. "Syria's refugee crisis in numbers," https://www.amnesty.org/en/latest/news/2016/02/syrias-refugee-crisis-in-numbers/.

– 2014. "Struggling to survive: Refugees from Syria in Turkey." 20 November. https://www.amnesty.org/en/documents/EUR44/017/2014/en/.

– 2016a. "EU-Turkey refugee deal a historic blow to rights." 16 March. https://www.amnesty.org/en/latest/news/2016/03/eu-turkey-refugee-deal-a-historic-blow-to-rights.

– 2016b. "No safe refuge: Asylum-seekers and refugees denied effective protection in Turkey." https://www.amnesty.org/download/Documents/EUR4438252016ENGLISH.pdf.

– 2016c. "Syria–Jordan border: 75,000 refugees trapped in desert no man's land in dire conditions." 15 September. https://www.amnesty.org/en/latest/

news/2016/09/syria-jordan-border-75000-refugees-trapped-in-desert-no-mans-land-in-dire-conditions.

– 2017a. "A blueprint for despair: Human rights impact of the EU–Turkey deal." https://www.amnesty.org/en/documents/eur25/5664/2017/en.

– 2017b. "Greece: Court decisions pave way for first forcible returns of asylum-seekers under EU-Turkey deal." 22 September. https://www.amnesty.org/en/latest/news/2017/09/greece-court-decisions-pave-way-for-first-forcible-returns-of-asylum-seekers-under-eu-turkey-deal.

– 2019. "Turkey: Syrians illegally deported into war ahead of anticipated 'safe zone.'" 25 October. https://www.amnesty.org/en/latest/news/2019/10/turkey-syrians-illegally-deported-into-war-ahead-of-anticipated-safe-zone.

AIDA (Asylum Information Database). n.d. "Registration under temporary protection." https://www.asylumineurope.org/reports/country/turkey/registration-under-temporary-protection.

Akyüz, S., and B. Coşkun. 2014. "Gendered (In)Securities: Refugee Camps in Southeastern Turkey." *Journal of Conflict Transformation and Security* 4(1–2): 7–22.

Al Jazeera. n.d. "The Syrian doctors: Treating refugees in Turkey." https://interactive.aljazeera.com/aje/shorts/syrian-doctors-turkey/index.html.

– 2016. "Syria death toll: UN envoy estimates 400,000 killed. Staffan de Mistura's estimate, which far exceeds those given by UN in the past, is not an official number." 23 April. http://www.aljazeera.com/news/2016/04/staffan-de-mistura-400000-killed-syria-civil-war-160423055735629.html.

– 2018. "Life goes on the Syrian way in Istanbul's 'Damascus Bazaar.'" Umut Uras. 27 July.

Albahari, M. 2015. *Crimes of Peace: Mediterranean Migrations at the World's Deadliest Border.* Pennsylvania Studies in Human Rights. Philadelphia: University of Pennsylvania Press.

– 2016. "After the Shipwreck: Mourning and Citizenship in the Mediterranean, Our Sea." *Social Research: An International Quarterly* 83(2): 275–94.

Aliverti, A. 2012. "Making People Criminal: The Role of Criminal Law in Immigration Enforcement." *Theoretical Criminology* 16(4): 417–34.

Almustafa, M. 2018. "Relived Vulnerabilities of Palestinian Refugees: Governing through Exclusion." *Social and Legal Studies* 27(2): 164–79.

– 2019. "Refugees from Syria Caught between War and Borders: A Journey towards Protection." PhD diss. in Global Governance, Balsillie School of International Affairs, Waterloo. https://scholars.wlu.ca/etd/2151/.

REFERENCES

Anderson, B. 2007. "Battles in Time: The Relation between Global and Labour Mobilities." University of Oxford, Centre on Migration, Policy, and Society, Working Paper No. 55.

– 2013. *Us and Them? The Dangerous Politics of Immigration Control.* Oxford: Oxford University Press.

Andersson, R. 2014. *Illegality, Inc.: Clandestine Migration and the Business of Bordering Europe.* Berkeley: University of California Press.

Andrijasevic, R. 2009. "Sex on the Move: Gender, Subjectivity, and Differential Inclusion." *Subjectivity.* Special issue: *Conflicts of Mobility: Migration, Labour, and Political Subjectivities.*

Arango, T. 2015. "Syrian migrants in Istanbul confront choice: Stay or move on." *New York Times.* 23 December. https://www.nytimes.com/2015/12/24/world/europe/syrian-migrants-in-istanbul-confront-choice-stay-or-move-on.html.

Aras, B., and Y. Duman. 2018. "I/NGOs' Assistance to Syrian Refugees in Turkey: Opportunities and Challenges." *Journal of Balkan and Near Eastern Studies.* https://doi.org/10.1080/19448953.2018.1530382.

Aras, B., and S. Yasun. 2016. "The educational opportunities and challenges of Syrian refugee students in Turkey: Temporary education centers and beyond." İstanbul: İstanbul Policy Center. https://www.dropbox.com/sh/yıtprereliwagtk/AABfB1woytKDlN8uUVRXFTAaa?dl=0&preview=237.+The+Educational+Opportunities+and+Challenges+Of+Syrian+Refugee+Students+In+Turkey+Temporary+Education+Centers+and+Beyond+%2CTemmuz+2016%2C+IPC.pdf.

Arnold, D., and J.R. Bongiovi. 2013. "Precarious, Informalizing, and Flexible Work: Transforming Concepts and Understandings." *American Behavioral Scientist* 57(3): 289–308.

Arriola, E. 2007. "Accountability for Murder in the Maquiladoras: Linking Corporate Indifference to Gender Violence at the US–Mexico Border." *Seattle Journal for Social Justice* 5(2): 1–57.

Arslan, R. 2016. "Suriyelilere vatandaşlık: AKP seçmeni ne diyor?" BBC Turkish Service, 13 July. https://www.bbc.com/turkce/haberler-turkiye-36780544.

ASRC (Asylum Seeker Resource Centre) 2013. "Offshore Processing Myth Buster." http://www.asrc.org.au/wp-content/uploads/2013/07/Offshore-Processing-Mythbuster_August-2013.pdf.

Ataç, C. 2018. "Pax Ottomanica No More! The 'Peace' Discourse in Turkish Foreign Policy in the Post-Davudoglu Era and the Prolonged Syrian Crisis." *Digest of the Middle East Studies* 28(1): 48–69.

Ataç, I., G. Heck, S. Hess, Z. Kaşlı, P. Ratfisch, C. Soykan, and B. Yılmaz. 2017. "Contested B/Orders: Turkey's Changing Migration Regime." *Movements: Journal for Critical Migration and Border Regime Studies* 3(2): 9–22.

Ataç, I., K. Rygiel, and M. Stierl. 2016. "Introduction: The Contentious Politics of Refugee and Migrant Protest and Solidarity Movements: Remaking Citizenship from the Margins." *Citizenship Studies* 20(10): 1–18.

Baban, F., S. Ilcan, and K. Rygiel. 2017a. "Playing Border Politics with Urban Syrian Refugees: Legal Ambiguities, Insecurities, and Humanitarian Assistance." *Movements: Journal for Critical Migration and Border Regime Studies* 3(2). http://movements-journal.org/issues/05.turkey/06.baban,ilcan, rygiel--playing-border-politics-with-urban-syrian-refugees.html.

– 2017b. "Syrian Refugees in Turkey: Pathways to Precarity, Differential Inclusion, and Negotiated Citizenship Rights." *Journal of Ethnic and Migration Studies* 43(1): 41–57.

Baban, F., and K. Rygiel. 2017. "Living with Others: Fostering Radical Cosmopolitanism through Citizenship Politics in Berlin." *Ethics and Global Politics* 10(1): 98–116.

Balibar, E. 2013. "Europe: An 'Unimagined' Frontier of Democracy." *Diacritics* 33(3–4): 36–44.

Balkan, B., et al. 2018. "Immigration, Housing Rents, and Residential Segregation: Evidence from Syrian Refugees in Turkey." Discussion Paper, Iza Institute of Labour Economics. June.

Banki, S. 2013. "Precarity of Place: A Complement to the Growing Precariat Literature." *Global Discourse* 3(3–4): 450–63.

Barbero, I. 2012. "Expanding Acts of Citizenship: The Struggles of Sinpapeles Migrants." *Social and Legal Studies* 21(4): 529–47.

Barchiesi, F. 2011. *Precarious Liberation: Workers, the State, and Contested Social Citizenship in Postapartheid South Africa*. Scottsville: University of KwaZulu-Natal Press.

– 2012. "Precarious Liberation: A Rejoinder." *South African Review of Sociology* 43(1): 98–105.

Barnett, M. 2001. "Humanitarianism with a Sovereign Face: UNHCR in the Global Undertow." *International Migration Review* 35(1): 244–77.

– 2011. *Empire of Humanity: A History of Humanitarianism*. Ithaca: Cornell University Press.

– 2013. "Humanitarian Governance." *Annual Review of Political Science* 16: 379–98.

Barnett, M., and T. Weiss. 2011. *Humanitarianism Contested: Where Angels Fear to Tread*. London: Routledge.

REFERENCES

Basok, T., D. Belanger, M. Wiesner, and G. Candiz. 2015. *Rethinking Transit Migration: Precarity, Mobility, and Self-Making in Mexico*. New York: Palgrave Macmillan.

Basok, T., and G. Candiz. 2020. "Containing Mobile Citizenship: Changing Geopolitics and Its Impacts on Solidarity Activism in Mexico." *Citizenship Studies*. https://doi:org/10.1080/13621025.2020.1755160.

Bastaki, J. 2018. "Temporary Protection Regimes and Refugees: What Works? Comparing the Kuwaiti, Bosnian, and Syrian Refugee Protection Regimes." *Refuge: Canada's Journal on Refugees* 34(2): 73–84.

Batalla, L., and J. Tolay. 2018. "Toward Long-Term Solidarity with Syrian Refugees? Turkey's Policy Response and Challenges." Washington, DC: Atlantic Council, 20 September.

Bates-Eamer, N. 2019. "Border and Migration Controls and Migrant Precarity in the Context of Climate Change." *Social Sciences* 8(7): 1–17.

Bauböck, R., ed. 1994. *From Aliens to Citizens*. Aldershot: Avebury.

Bauböck, R., I. Honohan, T. Huddleston, D. Hutcheson, J. Shaw, and M. Vink. n.d. "Access to citizenship and its impact on immigrant integration: European summary and standards." European University Institute, Robert Schuman Centre for Advanced Studies and European Union Democracy Observatory. https://cadmus.eui.eu/bitstream/handle/1814/29828/AccesstoCitizenshipanditsImpactonImmigrantIntegration.pdf.

Bauder, H. 2014. "Why We Should Use the Term 'Illegalized' Refugee or Immigrant: A Commentary." *International Journal of Refugee Law* 26(3): 327–32.

– 2016. "Sanctuary Cities: Policies and Practices in International Perspective." *International Migration* 55(2): 174–87.

BBC. 2015. "Europe: Migrant crisis: Grim find of bodies in Austria lorry." 27 August. http://www.bbc.com/news/world-europe-34073534.

– 2016. "Turks hit back at Erdogan plan to give Syrians citizenship." https://www.bbc.com/news/world-europe-36704791.

– 2020. "Moria migrants: Fire destroys Greek camp leaving 13,000 without shelter." https://www.bbc.com/news/world-europe-54082201.

Behrman, S. 2014. "Legal Subjectivity and the Refugee," *International Journal of Refugee Law* 26(1): 1–21.

Berg, M.L., and N. Sigona. 2013. "Ethnography, Diversity, and Urban Space." *Identities: Global Studies in Culture and Power* 20(4): 347–60.

BETAM (Bahcesehir University Ekonomik ve Toplumsal Araştırmalar Merkezi). 2018. "Opportunities for Syrian youth in Istanbul: A labour market assessment." January. https://betam.bahcesehir.edu.tr/wp-content/uploads/2019/07/OPPORTUNITIES-FOR-SYRIAN-YOUTH-IN-ISTANBUL.pdf.

Betts, A., L. Bloom, J. Kaplan, and N. Omata. 2017. *Refugee Economies: Forced Displacement and Development.* Oxford: Oxford University Press.

Bezmialem. 2015. "İstanbul'da Yaşayan Geçici Koruma Altındaki Suriyeliler." İstanbul: Bezmialem Üniversitesi.

Bianet. 2014. "Solidarity Demonstration with Syrians in Antep." 29 August. https://bianet.org/english/world/158198-solidarity-demonstration-with-syrians-in-antep.

– 2016. "Mülteci kadınlar Çocuklara Masallar anlatacak." 19 October. https://bianet.org/bianet/cocuk/179763-multeci-kadinlar-cocuklara-masallar-anlatacak.

– 2019. "Turkey rounded up 153 thousand illegal migrants, deported 43 thousand in 2019." https://bianet.org/english/migration/210817-turkey-rounded-up-153-thousand-illegal-migrants-deported-43-thousand-in-2019.

Biehl, K. 2015. "Governing through Uncertainty: Experiences of Being a Refugee in Turkey as a Country for Temporary Asylum." *Social Analysis* 59(1): 57–75.

Bigo, D. 2002. "Security and Immigration: Towards a Critique of the Governmentality of Unease." *Alternatives* 27(1) (supplement): 63–92.

Bilecen, B., and D. Yurtseven. 2018. "Temporarily Protected Syrians' Access to the Healthcare System in Turkey: Changing Policies and Remaining Challenges." *Migration Letters* 1: 113–24.

Biondi, P. 2016. "Human Security and External Burden-Sharing: The European Approach to Refugee Protection between Past and Present." *International Journal of Human Rights* 20(2): 208–22.

Bleby, M., C. Fitzsimmons, and N. Khadem. 2013. "'We came by boat': How Refugees Changed Australian Business." *Business Review Weekly* (Melbourne). 29 August. http://www.brw.com.au/p/business/we_came_by_boat_how_refugees_changed_pHm96uKvMaQT2B2NFCdcRJ.

Boswell, C. 2003. "The 'External Dimension' of EU Immigration and Asylum Policy." *International Affairs* 79(3): 619–38.

Branch, E.H., and C. Hanley. 2011. "Regional Convergence in Low-Wage Work and Earnings, 1970–2000." *Sociological Perspectives* 54(4): 569–92.

Brian, T., and F. Laczko, eds. 2014. *Fatal Journeys: Tracking Lives Lost during Migration.* Geneva: International Organization of Migration.

Bulley, D. 2015. "Ethics, Power, and Space: International Hospitality beyond Derrida." *Hospitality and Society* 5(2–3): 185–201.

– 2016. "Occupy Differently: Space, Community, and Urban Counter-Conduct." *Global Society* 30(2): 1–21.

REFERENCES

- 2017a. *Migration, Ethics, and Power.* London: Sage.
- 2017b. "Shame on EU? Europe, RtoP, and the Politics of Refugee Protection." *Ethics and International Affairs* 31(1): 51–70.

Burmann, M., and M. Valeyatheepillay. 2017. "Asylum Recognition Rates in the Top 5 EU Countries." IFO DICE report, 15 (2 June): 48–50. https://www.ifo.de/DocDL/dice-report-2017-2-burmann-valeyatheepillay-june.pdf.

Butler, J. 2004. *Precarious Life: The Powers of Mourning and Violence.* New York: Verso.

- 2009. *Frames of War: When Is Life Grievable?* New York: Verso.
- 2012. "Precarious Life, Vulnerability, and the Ethics of Cohabitation." *The Journal of Speculative Philosophy* 26(2): 134–51. (Special issue with the Society for Phenomenology and Existential Philosophy.)

Cabot, H. 2016. "'Contagious' Solidarity: Reconfiguring Care and Citizenship in Greece's Social Clinics." *Social Anthropology* 24(2): 152–66.

- 2018. "The European Refugee Crisis and Humanitarian Citizenship in Greece." *Ethnos.* https://doi.org/10.1080/00141844.2018.1529693.

Calamur, K. 2018. "A Surprising Finding about Refugees in Europe amidst a Political Reckoning." *The Atlantic.* 19 September. https://www.theatlantic.com/international/archive/2018/09/eu-refugees/570628.

- 2019. "The Nativists Won in Europe." *The Atlantic.* 16 March. https://www.theatlantic.com/international/archive/2019/03/europe-refugees-syria-borders/585097.

Calhoun, C. 2004. "A World of Emergencies: Fear, Intervention, and the Limits of Cosmopolitan Order." *Canadian Review of Sociology/Revue canadienne de sociologie* 41(4): 373–95.

- 2008. "The Imperative to Reduce Suffering: Charity, Progress, and Emergencies in the Field of Humanitarian Action." In *Humanitarianism in Question: Politics, Power, Ethics*, ed. M. Barnett and T. Weiss, 73–98. Ithaca: Cornell University Press.
- 2010. "The Idea of Emergency: Humanitarian Action and Global (Dis)Order." In *Contemporary States of Emergency: The Politics of Military and Humanitarian Interventions*, ed. D. Fassin and M. Pandolfi, 29–58. New York: Zone Books.

Canefe, N. 2016. "Management of Irregular Migration: Syrians in Turkey as Paradigm Shifters for Forced Migration Studies." *New Perspectives on Turkey* 54(2): 9–32.

- 2018. "Invisible Lives: Gender, Dispossession, and Precarity amongst Syrian Refugee Women in the Middle East." *Refuge* 34(1): 39–49.

Carpi, E., and P. Şenoğuz. 2019. "Refugee Hospitality in Lebanon and Turkey: On Making 'The Other.'" *International Migration* 57(2): 126–42.

Casas-Cortes, M. 2019. "Care-tizenship: Precarity, Social Movements, and the Deleting/Re-Writing of Citizenship." *Citizenship Studies* 21(1): 19–42. https://doi.org/10.1080/13621025.2018.1556248.

Cassarino, J.P. 2007. "Informalising Readmission Agreements in the EU Neighborhood." *International Spectator* 42(2): 179–96.

Çelik, C., and A. İçduygu. 2019. "Schools and Refugee Children: The Case of Syrians in Turkey." *International Migration* 57(2): 253–67.

Changia, F. 2019. "'Switzerland doesn't want me': Work, Precarity, and Emotions for Mobile Professional Partners." *Migration Letters* 16(2): 207–17.

Chalaux, M. 2018. "Conditions in Moria – Europe Should Be Ashamed!" Oxfam International. January 31. https://oxfam.medium.com/conditions-in-moria-europe-should-be-ashamed-6ccdad3d1cb.

Chimni, B. 1998. "The Geopolitics of Refugee Studies: A View from the South." *Journal of Refugee Studies* 11(4): 350–74.

– 2009. "The Birth of a 'Discipline': From Refugee to Forced Migration Studies." *Journal of Refugee Studies* 22(1): 11–29.

Cloeters, G., and S. Osseiran. 2019. "Healthcare Access for Syrian Refugees in Istanbul: A Gender-Sensitive Perspective." İstanbul Policy Centre, Sabanci University.

Collyer, M. 2006. "Migrants, Migration, and the Security Paradigm: Constraints and Opportunities." *Mediterranean Politics* 11(2): 255–70.

Çorabatır, M. 2016. "The Evolving Approach to Refugee Protection in Turkey: Assessing the Practical and Political Needs." Migration Policy Institute. September. https://www.migrationpolicy.org/research/evolving-approach-refugee-protection-turkey-assessing-practical-and-political-needs.

Council of the European Union 2001. "Council Directive 2001/55/EC of 20 July 2001 on minimum standards for giving temporary protection in the event of a mass influx of displaced persons and on measures promoting a balance of efforts between Member States in receiving such persons and bearing the consequences thereof." *Official Journal L 212, 07/08/2001.*

Coutin Bibler, S. 2000. *Legalizing Moves: Salvadoran Immigrants' Struggle for US Residency.* Ann Arbor: University of Michigan Press.

Crawley, H., F. Düvell, K. Jones, S. McMahon, and N. Sigona. 2018. *Unravelling Europe's "Migration Crisis": Journeys over Land and Sea.* Bristol: Polity Press.

Crawley, H., and K. Jones. 2020. "Beyond Here and There: (Re)Conceptualizing Migrant Journeys and the 'In-Between.'" *Journal of Ethnic and Migration Studies.* https://doi:org/10.1080/1369183X.2020.1804190.

REFERENCES

Crawley, H., and D. Skleparis. 2018. "Refugees, Migrants, Neither, Both: Categorical Fetishism and the Politics of Bounding in Europe's 'Migration Crisis.'" *Journal of Ethnic and Migration Studies* 44(1): 48–64.

Crépeau, F. 2013. "Report of the Special Rapporteur on the Human Rights of Migrants, François Crépeau: Regional Study: Management of the External Borders of the European Union and Its Impact on the Human Rights of Migrants." Human Rights Council, twenty-third session. Agenda item 3: "Promotion and Protection of All Human Rights, Civil, Political, Economic, Social and Cultural Rights, including the Right to Development." United Nations General Assembly, A/HRC/23/46. 24 April. http://www.ohchr.org/Documents/HRBodies/HRCouncil/RegularSession/Session23/A.HRC.23.46_en.pdf.

Cumhuriyet Daily. 2018. "Hangi Erdogan 'Ilanihaye saklayacak halimiz yok' diyen Erdogan vatandasliksozu vermisti." 8 February. https://www.cumhuriyet.com.tr/haber/hangi-erdogan-ilanihaye-saklayacak-halimiz-yok-diyen-erdogan-vatandaslik-sozu-vermisti-922330.

Dağtaş, S. 2017. "Whose Misafirs?: Negotiating Difference along the Turkish–Syrian Border." *International Journal of Middle East Studies* 49(4): 661–79.

Daily Sabah. 2017. "Special project from 24th İstanbul Jazz festival." 20 July. https://www.dailysabah.com/music/2017/07/21/special-project-from-24th-istanbul-jazz-festival.

– 2018. "Turkish border cities host almost half of Syrian refugees." 8 January. https://www.dailysabah.com/turkey/2018/01/09/turkish-border-cities-host-almost-half-of-syrian-refugees.

Danış. D. 2019a. "Kutuplasan Toplumun Tutkali Suriye Dusmanligi." 6 August. *Gazete Karinca.* https://gazetekarinca.com/2019/08/didem-danis-kutuplasan-toplumun-tutkali-suriyeli-dusmanligi.

Danış, D., and D. Nazlı. 2019. "A Faithful Alliance between the Civil Society and the State: Actors and Mechanisms of Accommodating Syrian Refugees in Istanbul." *International Migration* 57(2): 143–57.

Darling, J. 2009. "A City of Sanctuary: The Relational Reimagining of Sheffield's Asylum Politics." *Transactions of the Institute of British Geographers* 35(1): 125–40.

– 2014. "Asylum and the Post-Political: Domopolitics, Depoliticisation, and Acts of Citizenship." *Antipode* 46(1): 72–91.

– 2017. "Forced Migration and the City: Irregularity, Informality, and the Politics of Presence." *Progress in Human Geography* 4(2): 178–98.

Davudoğlu, A. 2013. "Zero Problems in a New Era." *Foreign Policy.* 21 March. https://foreignpolicy.com/2013/03/21/zero-problems-in-a-new-era.

De Genova, N. 2010. "The Deportation Regime: Sovereignty, Space, and the Freedom of Movement." In *The Deportation Regime: Sovereignty, Space, and the Freedom of Movement*, ed. N. De Genova and N. Peutz, 33–65. Durham: Duke University Press.

– 2018. "The 'Migrant Crisis' as Racial Crisis: Do Black Lives Matter in Europe?" *Ethnic and Racial Studies* 41(10): 1765–82.

De Vries, L.A., and E. Guild. 2018. "Seeking Refuge in Europe: Spaces of Transit and the Violence of Migration Management." *Journal of Ethnic and Migration Studies* 45(12): 2156–66.

Delegation of the EU to Turkey. 2017. "EU and Turkish Ministry of National Education launch €300 million project to improve Syrian children's access to education." 10 June. https://www.avrupa.info.tr/en/pr/eu-and-turkish-ministry-national-education-launch-eu300-million-project-improve-syrian-childrens.

Den Heijer, M., and T. Spijkerboer. 2016. "Is the EU-Turkey Refugee and Migration Deal a Treaty?" *EU Law Analysis* of 07.04.2016. http://eulawanalysis.blogspot.ca.

Dereli, B. 2018. "Refugee integration through higher education: Syrian refugees in Turkey," United Nations University. https://i.unu.edu/media/gcm.unu.edu/publication/4405/Final_Begu%CC%88m-Dereli_Policy-Report.pdf.

Diken. 2016. "Suriye Kökenli Yurttaşlara Doğru." http://www.diken.com.tr/suriye-kokenli-yurttaslara-dogru.

Doerr, N. 2010. "Politicizing Precarity, Producing Visual Dialogues on Migration: Transnational Public Spaces in Social Movements." *Forum: Qualitative Social Research* 11(2).

Duffield, M. 2018. *Post-Humanitarianism: Governing Precarity in the Digital World.* London: Wiley.

– 2019. "Post-Humanitarianism: Governing Precarity through Adaptive Design." *Journal of Humanitarian Affairs* 1(1): 15–27.

Durieux, J.-F. 2015. "Temporary Protection: Hovering at the Edges of Refugee Law." In *Netherlands Yearbook of International Law 2014*, vol. 45, ed. M. Ambrus and R.A. Wessel, 221–53. Cambridge: Cambridge University Press.

Düvell, F. 2012. "Transit Migration: A Blurred and Politicised Concept." *Population, Space, and Place* 18(4): 415–27.

DW (*Deutsch Welle*). 2016. "Erdogan threatens to open borders after European Parliament vote." 25 November. https://www.dw.com/en/erdogan-threatens-to-open-borders-after-european-parliament-vote/a-36518509.

REFERENCES

- 2017. "EU funds Turkish health centres to help Syrian refugees." Diego Cupolo. 14 November. http://www.dw.com/en/eu-funds-turkish-health-centers-to-help-syrian-refugees/a-41362710.
- 2019a. "Amnesty: Turkey forced Syrian refugees back into war zone." 25 October. https://www.dw.com/en/amnesty-turkey-forced-syrian-refugees-back-into-war-zone/a-50978424.
- 2019b. "Can the EU–Turkey deal be fixed?" https://www.dw.com/en/can-the-eu-turkey-deal-be-fixed/a-50680789.

EC (European Commission). n.d. "The hotspot approach to managing exceptional migratory flows." https://ec.europa.eu/home-affairs/sites/homeaffairs/files/what-we-do/policies/european-agenda-migration/background-information/docs/2_hotspots_en.pdf.

- 2015. "EU–Turkey joint action plan factsheet." 15 October. https://europa.eu/rapid/press-release_MEMO-15-5860_en.htm.
- 2016a. Fourth Report on the Progress Made in the Implementation of the EU–Turkey Statement. Communication from the Commission to the European Playing Border Politics with Urban Syrian Refugees. 101st Parliament, European Council and the Council. COM (2016) 792 final. ec.europa.eu.
- 2016b. "Implementing the EU–Turkey Statement – Questions and Answers." 15 June. https://europa.eu/rapid/press-release_MEMO-16-1664_en.htm.
- 2016c. Press release: "Relocation and resettlement: EU member states urgently need to deliver European Commission." Strasbourg, 12 April. http://europa.eu/rapid/press-release_IP-16-1343_en.
- 2017. "Report from the Commission to the European Parliament, The European Council and the Council: Seventh Report on the Progress made in the Implementation of the EU–Turkey Statement. 6 September. COM (2017) 470 final. https://ec.europa.eu/neighbourhood-enlargement/sites/near/files/20170906_seventh_report_on_the_progress_in_the_implementation_of_the_eu-turkey_statement_en.pdf.
- 2018. Press release: "EU Facility for Refugees in Turkey: The Commission Proposes to Mobilise Additional Funds for Syrian Refugees." 14 March. https://ec.europa.eu/commission/presscorner/detail/en/IP_18_1723.
- 2019. "Legislative Train Schedule Towards a New Policy on Migration: EU–Turkey Statement and Action Plan." http://www.europarl.europa.eu/legislative-train/theme-towards-a-new-policy-on-migration/file-eu-turkey-statement-action-plan.
- 2020. "The EU Facility for Refugees in Turkey." October. https://ec.europa.eu/neighbourhood-enlargement/sites/near/files/frit_factsheet.pdf.

REFERENCES

ECRE (European Council on Refugees and Exiles). 2018. "Turkey: Refugees at the border faced with choice between detention and return, report finds." https://www.ecre.org/turkey-refugees-at-the-border-faced-with-choice-between-detention-and-return-report-finds.

European Council. 2016. Press release: "EU–Turkey statement." 18 March. 144/16 http://www.consilium.europa.eu/en/press/press-releases/2016/03/18-eu-turkey-statement.

European Court of Human Rights. 2018. Fact sheet: "Detention conditions and treatment of prisoners."

Ege Postası 2015. "Basmane Esnafının Suriyeli Rahatsızlığı." http://www.egepostasi.com/haber/basmane-esnafinin-suriyeli-rahatsizligi/106342.

Eğici, M.T. 2019. "Migrant Health Care Services Provided by Public Sector in Turkey." *Anatolian Journal of Family Medicine* 2(1): 7–12.

Erdoğan, E., and P.U. Semerci. 2018. "Attitudes towards Syrians in Turkey-2017." German Marshall Fund Discussion on Turkish Perceptions of Syrian Refugees. Presentation slides from İstanbul Bilgi University Center for Migration Research. 12 March 2018. https://goc.bilgi.edu.tr/media/uploads/2018/03/12/turkish-perceptions-of-syrian-refugees-20180312.pdf.

Erdoğan, M. 2015. *Türkiye'deki Suriyeliler: Toplumsal Kabul ve Uyum.* İstanbul: Bilgi University Press.

– 2017. "Syrians-Barometer-2017: A Framework for Achieving Social Cohesion with Syrians in Turkey." Ankara: Hacettepe University and others.

Esterling, K. 2014. *Extrastatecraft: The Power of Infrastructure Space.* London and New York: Verso.

Estukyan, V. 2016. "Suriyelilere linç planı." *Agos.* 15 July 2016. from http://www.agos.com.tr/tr/yazi/15901/suriyelilere-linc-plani.

Ettlinger, N. 2007. "Precarity Unbound." *Alternatives: Global, Local, Political* 32(3): 319–40.

EU (European Union). 2016. "Turkey: Labour market integration and social inclusion of refugees." https://www.dropbox.com/sh/yıtprereliwagtk/AABfB1woytKDlN8uUVRXFTAaa?dl=0&preview=233.+Turkey+Labour+Market+Integration+and+Social+Inclusion+of+Refugees+2016.pdf.

Eurostat. 2019. "News release: 'Asylum in the EU member states.'" 46/2019-14 March 2019. https://ec.europa.eu/eurostat/documents/2995521/9665546/3-14032019-AP-EN.pdf/eca81dc5-89c7-4a9d-97ad-444b6bd32790.

Faist, T., and A. Ette, eds. 2007. *The Europeanization of National Policies and Politics of Immigration: Between Autonomy and the European Union.* London: Palgrave Macmillan.

REFERENCES

Fakhoury, T. 2019. "Multi-Level Governance and Migration Politics in the Arab World: The Case of Syria's Displacement." *Journal of Ethnic and Migration Studies* 45(8): 1310–26. https://doi.org/10.1080/1369183X.2018.1441609.

Fantone, L. 2007. "Precarious Changes: Gender and Generational Politics in Contemporary Italy." *Feminist Review* 87: 5–20.

FAO (UN Food and Agricultural Organization). 2018. "Agricultural skills training to address the impact of the Syrian refugee crisis in Turkey." http://www.fao.org/3/I8479EN/i8479en.pdf.

Fassin, D. 2007. "Humanitarianism: A Nongovernmental Government." In *Nongovernmental Politics*, ed. M. Feher, 149–60. New York: Zone Books.

– 2011. *Humanitarian Reason: A Moral History of the Present*. Berkeley: University of California Press.

Fassin, D., and M. Pandolfi, eds. 2010. *Contemporary States of Emergency: The Politics of Military and Humanitarian Interventions*. New York: Zone Books.

Feldman, I. 2007. "The Quaker Way: Ethical Labor and Humanitarian Relief." *American Ethnologist* 34(4): 689–705.

– 2008. "Refusing Invisibility: Documentation and Memorialization in Palestinian Refugee Claims." *Journal of Refugee Studies* 21(4): 498–516.

Ferris, E., and K. Kirişçi, 2016. "Syrian Refugees: Challenges to Host Countries and the International Community." In *The Consequences of Chaos: Syria's Humanitarian Crisis and the Failure to Protect*, 33–79. Washington, DC: Brookings Institution Press. http://www.jstor.org/stable/10.7864/j.cc1cqws.7.

Fleming, M. 2016. "UNHCR chief pledges more support for Turkey refugee response." UNHCR News. 1 September. https://www.unhcr.org/news/latest/2016/9/57c856484/unhcr-chief-pledges-support-turkey-refugee-response.html.

France24. 2019. "Attacks against Syrians in Turkey raise fears of escalation." 12 July. https://www.france24.com/en/20190712-attacks-against-syrians-turkey-raise-fears-escalation.

– 2020. "Erdogan warns Europe to expect 'millions' of migrants after Turkey opens borders." 3 March. https://www.france24.com/en/20200303-erdogan-warns-europe-to-expect-millions-of-migrants-after-turkey-opens-borders.

Frederiksen, A. 2012. "Making Humanitarian Spaces Global: Coordinating Crisis Response through the Cluster Approach." PhD diss., Columbia University.

Frelick, B., I.M. Kysel, and J. Podkul. 2016. "The Impact of Externalization of Migration Controls on the Rights of Asylum Seekers and Other Migrants."

Journal on Migration and Human Security 4(4): 190–220.
https://www.hrw.org/sites/default/files/supporting_resources/jmhs.pdf.

Frenzen, N. 2012. "UN Special Rapporteur on HR of migrants expresses concern over plight of irregular migrants in Greece; calls for EU assistance; Frontex patrolling Greece-Italy sea border." 5 December. https://migrantsatsea.org/2012/12/05/un-special-rapporteur-on-hr-of-migrants-expresses-concern-over-plight-of-irregular-migrants-in-greece-calls-for-eu-assistance-frontex-patrolling-greece-italy-sea-border.

Fresia, M. 2014. "Performing Repatriation? The Role of Refugee Aid in Shaping New Beginnings in Mauritania." *Development and Change* 45(3): 434–57.

Fresia, M., and A. Von Kanel. 2015. "Beyond Space of Exception? Reflections on the Camp through the Prism of Refugee Schools." *Journal of Refugee Studies* 29(2): 250–72.

FRONTEX. 2011. *FRONTEX Annual Risk Analysis.* Warsaw: European Agency for the Management of Operational Cooperation at the External Borders of the Member States of the European Union (FRONTEX). http://www.frontex.europa.eu/news/annual-risk-analysis-2011-IsVGtW.

Fullerton, M. 2001. "Failing the Test: Germany Leads Europe in Dismantling Refugee Protection." *Texas International Law Journal* 36: 231–76.

Garelli, G., and M. Tazzioli. 2016. "The EU hotspot approach at Lampedusa." *Open Democracy.* 26 February. https://www.opendemocracy.net/en/can-europe-make-it/eu-hotspot-approach-at-lampedusa.

Gavanas, A., and I. Calzada. 2016. "Multiplex Migration and Aspects of Precarization: Swedish Retirement Migrants to Spain and Their Service Providers." *Critical Sociology*, 1–14. https://doi.org/10.1177/0896920516628306.

Gazete Duvar. 2016. "İstanbul'da Suriye Hastanesi." https://www.gazeteduvar. com.tr/saglik/2016/08/16/istanbulda-suriye-hastanesi.

Geiger, M. 2016. "Policy Outsourcing and Remote Management: The Present and Future of Border Migration Politics." In *Externalizing Migration Management: Europe, North America, and the Spread of "Remote Control" Practices*, ed. Martin Geiger and Antoine Pecoud, 15–40. Basingstoke: Palgrave Macmillan.

Glasman, J. 2017. "Seeing Like a Refugee Agency: A Short History of UNHCR Classifications in Central Africa (1961–2015)." *Journal of Refugee Studies* 30(2): 337–62.

Gökay, B. 2015. "Reflections on Turkish Foreign Policy under Davudoglu: From Status Quo to a 'New' Grand Strategy?" *Journal of Global Faultlines* 2(2): 44–9.

Goldring, L., C. Bernstein, and J. Bernhard. 2009. "Institutionalizing Precarious Status in Canada." *Citizenship Studies* 13(3): 239–65.

REFERENCES

Goldring, L., and P. Landolt. 2011. "Caught in the Work–Citizenship Matrix: The Lasting Effects of Precarious Legal Status on Work for Toronto Immigrants." *Globalizations* 8(3): 325–41.

– 2013. "The Conditionality of Legal Rights and Status: Conceptualizing Precarious Non-Citizenship." In *Producing and Negotiating Non-Citizenship: Precarious Legal Status in Canada*, ed. L. Goldring and P. Landolt, 3–27. Toronto: University of Toronto Press.

– 2021. "From Illegalised Migrant toward Permanent Resident: Assembling Precarious Legal Status Trajectories and Differential Inclusion in Canada." *Journal of Ethnic and Migration Studies.* https://doi.org/10.1080/1369183X.2020.1866978.

Gökalp Aras, N.E. 2019. "Coercive Engineered Syrian Mass Migration in the EU–Turkey Relations: A Case Analysis for Future Reference." *International Migration* 57(2): 186–99.

Government of Turkey. n.d. DGMM – Directorate General of Migration Management. n.d. "Temporary Protection." http://www.goc.gov.tr/icerik6/gecici-koruma_363_378_4713_icerik.

– 2014. "Temporary Protection Regulation." Law No. 6458 of 2013 on Foreigners and International Protection. http://www.refworld.org/docid/56572fd74.html.

– 2019. Ministry of Interior. Directorate General of Migration Management. Statistics. "International Protection." https://en.goc.gov.tr/international-protection17.

– 2020. Ministry of Interior. Directorate General of Migration Management. Statistics. "Temporary Protection." https://en.goc.gov.tr/temporary-protection27.

Guardian. 2015. "Hungary: Hungary may use army to secure border against migrants." 26 August. https://www.theguardian.com/world/2015/aug/26/hungary-army-border-migrants-serbia.

– 2016a. "EU-Turkey refugee plan could be illegal, says UN official." https://www.theguardian.com/world/2016/apr/02/eu-turkey-refugee-plan-could-be-illegal-says-un-official.

– 2016b. "Hidden child labour: How Syrian refugees in Turkey are supplying Europe with fast fashion." 29 January. https://www.theguardian.com/sustainable-business/2016/jan/29/hidden-child-labour-syrian-refugees-turkey-supplying-europe-fast-fashion.

– 2016c. "Syrian refugee wins appeal against forced return to Turkey." 20 May. https://www.theguardian.com/world/2016/may/20/syrian-refugee-wins-appeal-against-forced-return-to-turkey.

- 2018. "'It's against the law': Syrian refugees deported from Turkey back to war." 16 October. https://www.theguardian.com/global-development/2018/oct/16/syrian-refugees-deported-from-turkey-back-to-war.
- 2019a. "'It's not legal': UN stands by as Turkey deports vulnerable Syrians." 23 August. https://www.theguardian.com/global-development/2019/aug/23/its-not-legal-un-stands-by-as-turkey-deports-vulnerable-syrians.
- 2019b. "Turkey accused of using threats and deception to deport Syrian refugees." 25 October. https://www.theguardian.com/global-development/2019/oct/25/turkey-accused-of-using-threats-and-deception-to-deport-syrian-refugees.

Guild, E. 2009. *Security and Migration in the 21st Century*. Cambridge and Malden: Polity Press.

Gunewardena, N., and M. Schuller. 2008. *Capitalizing on Catastrophe: Neoliberal Strategies in Disaster Reconstruction*. Plymouth, UK: AltaMira Press.

Haber 7. 2014. "Cumhurbaşkanı Erdoğan: Bizler Ensar Sizler Mülteci." http://www.haber7.com/ic-politika/haber/1208342-cumhurbaskani-erdogan-bizler-ensar-sizler-muhacir.

Haddad, E. 2008. "The External Dimension of EU Refugee Policy: A New Approach to Asylum?" *Government and Opposition* 43(190). https://doi.org/10.1111/j.1477-7053.2007.00250.x.

Hakli, J., and K. Kallio. 2020. "Bodies and Persons: The Politics of Embodied Encounters in Asylum Seeking." *Progress in Human Geography*. https://doi.org/10.1177/0309132520938449.

Hallett, M. 2014. "Temporary Protection, Enduring Contradictions: The Contests and Contradictory Meanings of Temporary Immigration Status." *Law and Social Inquiry* 39(3): 621–42.

Harvey, D. 2012. *Rebel Cities: From the Right to the City to the Urban Revolution*. London and New York: Verso.

Hathaway, J.C. 2005. *The Rights of Refugees under International Law*. Cambridge and New York: Cambridge University Press.

- 2007. "Forced Migration Studies: Could We Agree Just to 'Date'?" *Journal of Refugees Studies* 20(3): 349–69.

Hathaway, J.C., and T. Gammeltoft-Hansen. 2015. "Non-Refoulement in a World of Cooperative Deterrence." *Columbia Journal of Transnational Law* 53(2): 235–84.

Hauge, H.L. 2017. "FEUTURE: The future of EU–Turkey relations: Mapping dynamics and testing scenarios." EU 28 Country Report: Germany. March. https://feuture.uni-koeln.de.

Heck, G., and S. Hess. 2016. "European restabilization of the border regime: A report from the contested borders in the Aegean region." https://harekact.bordermonitoring.eu.

REFERENCES

- 2017. "Tracing the Effects of the EU-Turkey Deal: The Momentum of the Multi-Layered Turkish Border Regime." *Movements: Journal for Critical Migration and Border Regime Studies* 3(2). Special issue: *Turkey's Changing Migration Regime and Its Global and Regional Dynamics.* http://movements-journal.org/issues/05.turkey/04.heck,hess--tracing-the-effects-of-the-eu-turkey-deal.html.

Heller, C., and A. Pécoud. 2020. "Counting Migrants' Deaths at the Border: From Civil Society Counterstatistics to (Inter)Governmental Recuperation." *American Behavioral Scientist* 64(4): 480–500.

Hersh, N. 2017. "Refugee Claims and Criminalization of Same-Sex Intimacy: The Case of Sebastiao." *Canadian Journal of Women and the Law* 29(2): 227–58.

Hess, S. 2012. "De-Naturalizing Transit Migration: Theory and Methods of an Ethnographic Regime Analysis." *Population, Space, and Place* 18(4): 428–40.

Hilhorst, D., and B. Jansen. 2010. "Humanitarian Space as Arena: A Perspective on the Everyday Politics of Aid." *Development and Change* 41(6): 1117–39.

- 2012. "Constructing Rights and Wrongs in Humanitarian Action: Contributions from a Sociology of Praxis." *Sociology* 46(5): 891–905.

Hilhorst, D., I. Desportes, and C. de Milliano. 2019. "Humanitarian Governance and Resilience Building: Ethiopia in Comparative Perspective." *Disasters.* https://onlinelibrary.wiley.com/doi/epdf/10.1111/disa.12332.

Hodge, E. 2019. "Making Precarious: The Construction of Precarity in Refugee and Migrant Discourse." *Borders in Globalization Review* 1(1): 83–90.

Hodge, P. 2015. "A Grievable Life? The Criminalisation and Securing of Asylum Seeker Bodies in the 'Violent Frames' of Australia's Operation Sovereign Borders." *Geoforum* 58:122–131.

Holehouse, M. 2015. "Germany drops EU rules to allow in Syrian refugees. *Telegraph.* 24 August. https://www.telegraph.co.uk/news/worldnews/europe/germany/11821822/Germany-drops-EU-rules-to-allow-in-Syrian-refugees.html.

HRW (Human Rights Watch). 2002. "'By invitation only': Australian asylum policy." December 14(10): 62–5. https://www.hrw.org/reports/2002/australia.

- 2014a. *Australia: Pacific Solution Redux: Still Discriminatory, Arbitrary, Unfair, Inhumane.* New York: HRW. https://www.hrw.org/news/2012/08/17/australia-pacific-solution-redux.

- 2014b. "Jordan: Palestinians escaping Syria turned away." 7 August. http://www.hrw.org/news/2014/08/07/jordan-palestinians-escaping-syria-turned-away.

REFERENCES

- 2015. "Geleceğimi Hayal Etmeye Çalıştığımda Hiç Bir Şey Göremiyorum." New York: HRW. https://www.hrw.org/sites/default/files/report_pdf/ turkey1115tu_web.pdf.
- 2016. "EU: Don't send Syrians back to Turkey." 20 June. https://www.hrw. org/news/2016/06/20/eu-dont-send-syrians-back-turkey.
- 2017. "I have no idea why they sent us back: Jordanian deportations and expulsions of Syrian refugees." https://www.hrw.org/report/2017/10/02/ i-have-no-idea-why-they-sent-us-back/jordanian-deportations-and-expulsions-syrian.
- 2018a. "Jordan: Step forward, step back for urban refugees: They get legal status but lose health subsidies." 25 March. https://www.hrw.org/news/ 2018/03/25/jordan-step-forward-step-back-urban-refugees.
- 2018b. "Turkey stops registering Syrian asylum seekers: New arrivals deported, coerced back to Syria." 16 July. https://www.hrw.org/news/2018/ 07/16/turkey-stops-registering-syrian-asylum-seekers.
- 2018c. "Turkey/Syria: Border guards shoot, block fleeing Syrians." 3 February. https://www.hrw.org/news/2018/02/03/turkey/syria-border-guards-shoot-block-fleeing-syrians.
- 2019a. "Greece: Events of 2018 – part of the EU chapter." https://www.hrw. org/world-report/2019/country-chapters/greece.
- 2019b. "Turkey forcibly returning Syrians to danger." 26 July. https://www.hrw.org/news/2019/07/26/turkey-forcibly-returning-syrians-danger.
- 2019c. "Turkey: Syrians being deported to danger." 24 October. https://www.hrw.org/news/2019/10/24/turkey-syrians-being-deported-danger.
- 2019d. "World Report 2019: Syria – Events of 2018." https://www.hrw.org/ world-report/2019/country-chapters/syria.

Huddleston, T., O. Bilgili, A.L. Joki, and Z. Vankova. 2015. *Migrant Integration Policy Index 2015*. Barcelona/Brussels: CIDOB and MPG. http://mipex.eu/ sites/default/files/downloads/files/mipex-2015-book-a5.pdf.

Hürriyet. 2014. "Ayakkabıcılar sitesinde Suriyeliler isyanı." 14 August. http://www.hurriyet.com.tr/ekonomi/ayakkabicilar-sitesinde-suriyeli-isci-isyani-27005301.

- 2018. "600 Binden Fazla Suriyeli Öğrenci Ders Başı Yaptı." 26 September. http://www.hurriyet.com.tr/egitim/600-binde-fazla-suriyeli-ogrenci-ders-basi-yapti-40968290.

Hürriyet Daily News. 2016. "Suriyeli Mültecilere Çalışma İzni Yürürlüğe Girdi." http://www.hurriyet.com.tr/suriyeli-multecilere-calisma-izni-yururluge-girdi-40053841.

REFERENCES

- 2017. "Suriye Füzyonu." 1 March. http://www.hurriyet.com.tr/ekonomi/suriye-fuzyonu-40435365.
- 2019. "Governor's office orders Syrians to leave Istanbul for their registered cities." 22 July. http://www.hurriyetdailynews.com/governors-office-orders-syrians-to-leave-istanbul-for-their-registered-cities-145168.

Hurst, D., and B. Doherty. 2016. "High Court upholds Australia's right to detain asylum seekers offshore." *The Guardian* 2 February https://www.theguardian.com/australia-news/2016/feb/03/high-court-upholds-australias-right-to-detain-asylum-seekers-offshore.

Huysmans, J. 2000. "The European Union and the Securitization of Migration." *JCMS: Journal of Common Market Studies* 38(5): 751–77.

- 2006. *The Politics of Insecurity: Fear, Migration, and Asylum in the EU.* London: Routledge.

Hyndman, J. 2000. *Managing Displacement: Refugees and the Politics of Humanitarianism.* Minneapolis: University of Minnesota Press.

- 2003. "Beyond Either/Or: A Feminist Analysis of September 11th." *ACME: An International E-Journal for Critical Geographies* 2(1): 1–13.

Hyndman, J., and W. Giles. 2011. "Waiting for What? The Feminization of Asylum in Protracted Situations." *Gender, Place, and Culture* 18(3): 361–79.

- 2017. *Living on the Edge: Refugees in Extended Exile.* London: Routledge.

Hyndman, J., and A. Mountz. 2007. "Refuge or Refusal: The Geography of Exclusion." In *Violent Geographies: Fear, Terror, and Political Violence,* ed. Derek Gregory and Allan Pred, 77–92. New York: Routledge.

- 2014. "Another Brick in the Wall? Neo-Refoulement and the Externalization of Asylum by Australia and Europe." *Government and Opposition* 43(249). https://doi.org/10.1111/j.1477-7053.2007.00251.x.

Hyndman, J., and J. Reynolds. 2020. "Beyond the Global Compacts: Reimagining Protection." *Refuge* 36(1): 66–74.

İçduygu, A. 2015a. "Syrian Refugees in Turkey: The Long Road Ahead." *MPI Reports.* Washington, DC: Migration Policy Institute.

- 2015b. "Turkey's Evolving Migration Policies: A Mediterranean Transit Stop at the Doors of the EU." *Instituto Affari Internazionali Working Papers* 15(31). http://www.iai.it/sites/default/files/iaiwp1531.pdf.

İçduygu, A., and M. Nimer. 2019. "The Politics of Return: Exploring the Future of Syrian Refugees in Jordan, Lebanon, and Turkey." *Third World Quarterly,* 1–36.

İçduygu, A., and D. Yükseker. 2012. "Rethinking Transit Migration in Turkey: Reality and Representation in the Creation of a Migratory Phenomenon." *Population, Space and Place* 18: 441–56.

244 REFERENCES

ICG (International Crisis Group). 2014. "The rising costs of Turkey's quagmire." 30 April. https://d2071andvipowj.cloudfront.net/the-rising-costs-of-turkey-s-syrian-quagmire.pdf.

– 2016. "Turkey's Refugee Crisis: The Politics of Permanence." 30 November. Europe Report No. 241. Brussels. http://www.iai.it/sites/default/files/iaiwp1531.pdf.

– 2018. "Turkey's Syrian refugees: Defusing metropolitan tensions." Brussels. 29 January. https://www.crisisgroup.org/europe-central-asia/western-europemediterranean/turkey/248-turkeys-syrian-refugees-defusing-metropolitan-tensions.

IFRC (International Federation of Red Cross and Red Crescent Societies). 2015. "Statement on the Valletta Summit on Migration."

İGAM (İltica Ve Göç Araştırmaları Merkezi). 2013. "Sivil Toplum Örgütlerinin Türkiye'deki Suriyeli Mülteciler İçin Yaptıkları Çalışmalar İle İlgili Rapor." Ankara. https://igamder.org/uploads/belgeler/IGAMSuriyeSTK2013.pdf.

Ilcan, S. 2013. "Paradoxes of Humanitarian Aid: Mobile Populations, Biopolitical Knowledge, and Acts of Social Justice in Osire Refugee Camp." In *Mobilities, Knowledge, and Social Justice*, ed. S. Ilcan, 177–206. Montreal and Kingston: McGill-Queen's University Press.

– 2014. "Activist Citizenship and the Politics of Mobility in Osire Refugee Camp." In *Routledge Handbook of Global Citizenship Studies*, ed. E. Isin and P. Nyers, 186–95. London: Routledge.

– 2018. "Fleeing Syria – Border-Crossing and Struggles for Migrant Justice." In *Mobilities, Mobility Justice, and Social Justice*, ed. D. Butz and N. Cook, 54–66. London: Routledge.

– 2020. "The Borderization of Waiting: Negotiating Borders and Migration in the 2011 Syrian Civil Conflict." *Environment and Planning C: Politics and Space*. https://doi.org/10.1177%2F2399654420943593.

Ilcan, S., and R. Aitken. 2012. "Postwar World Order, Displaced Persons, and Biopolitical Management." *Globalizations* 9(5): 623–36.

Ilcan, S., M. Oliver, and L. Connoy. 2017. "Humanitarian Assistance, Refugee Management, and Self-Reliance Schemes: Nakivale Refugee Settlement." In *Transnational Social Policy – Social Support in a World on the Move*, ed. Luann Good-Gingrich and Stefan Kongeter, 152–77. London and New York: Routledge.

Ilcan, S., and K. Rygiel. 2015. "'Resiliency Humanitarianism': Responsibilizing Refugees through Humanitarian Emergency Governance in the Camp." *International Political Sociology* 9: 333–51.

Ilcan, S., K. Rygiel, and F. Baban. 2018. "The Ambiguous Architecture of Precarity: Temporary Protection, Everyday Living, and Migrant Journeys of

REFERENCES

Syrian Refugees." *International Journal of Migration and Borders* 4(1–2): 51–70.

ILO (International Labour Organization). 2016. "Refugees – social inclusion and integration in the labour market." European Parliament Employment Committee Hearing. 18 February. Geneva.

Informigrants. 2018. "The UN Refugee Agency UNHCR ends asylum seeker registration in Turkey." September. http://www.infomigrants.net/en/post/12025/unhcr-ends-asylum-seeker-registration-in-turkey.

İngev. 2019. "Suriyeli Algı Araştırması ve Ötekileştirme." 4 August. http://ingev.org/wp-content/uploads/2019/08/ingev-den-suriyeli-algi-arastirmasi.pdf.

İneli-Ciğer, M. 2015. "Implications of the New Turkish Law on Foreigners and International Protection and Regulation No. 29153 on Temporary Protection for Syrians Seeking Protection in Turkey." *Oxford Monitor of Forced Migration* 4(2): 28–36.

IMWSA (International Migrant Women's Solidarity Association). https://www.facebook.com/miwosa.gkdd.

IOM (International Organization for Migration). n.d. *Missing Migrants Project.* https://missingmigrants.iom.int.

– 2014. "Fatal journeys: Tracking lives lost during migration." Geneva. http://publications.iom.int/system/files/pdf/fataljourneys_counting theuncounted.pdf.

Isakjee, A., T. Davies, J. Obradovic-Wochnik, and K. Augustova. 2020. "Liberal Violence and the Racial Borders of the European Union." *Antipode.* https://doi:org/10.1111/anti.12670.

Isin, E.F. 2008. "Theorizing Acts of Citizenship." In *Acts of Citizenship*, ed. E.F. Isin and G.M. Nielsen, 15–43. London: Zed Books.

– 2009. "Citizenship in Flux: The Figure of the Activist Citizen." *Subjectivity* 29(1): 367–88.

– 2012. *Citizenship Without Frontiers.* New York and London: Bloomsbury.

– 2017. "Performative Citizenship." In *Oxford Handbook of Citizenship*, ed. A. Shachar, R. Baubock, I. Bloemraad, and M. Vink, 500–23. Oxford: Oxford University Press.

Isin, E., and K. Rygiel. 2007. "Abject Spaces: Frontiers, Zones and Camps." In *The Logics of Biopower and the War on Terror: Living, Dying, Surviving,* ed. E. Dauphinee and C. Masters, 178–203. Houndmills, Basingstoke, Hampshire: Palgrave Macmillan, 2007.

Isin, E., and B. Turner. 2007. "Investigating Citizenship." *Citizenship Studies* 11: 5–17.

Islar, M., and E. Irgil. 2018. "Grassroots Practices of Citizenship and Politicization in the Urban: The Case of Right to the City Initiatives in Barcelona." *Citizenship Studies* 25(5): 491–506.

Jacobsen, K.L. 2010. "Making Design Safe for Humans: A Hidden History of Humanitarian Experimentation." *Citizenship Studies* 14(1): 89–103.

Jacobsen, C., M. Karlsen, and S. Khosravi, eds. 2021. *Waiting and the Temporalities of Irregular Migration*. London and New York: Routledge.

Janmyr, M. 2016. "Precarity in Exile: The Legal Status of Syrian Refugees in Lebanon." *Refugee Survey Quarterly* 35: 58–78.

Jansen, B.J. 2014. "Kakuma: Le camp dans l'économie de la ville, de la région et du monde." In *Un monde de camps*, ed. M. Agier, 164–73. Paris: La Découverte.

Jeffrey, A., L. Staeheli, C. Buire, and V. Čelebičić. 2018. "Drinking Coffee, Rehearsing Civility, Making Subjects." *Political Geography* 67: 125–34. https://www.sciencedirect.com/science/article/abs/pii/S0962629817303384.

Johnson, H. 2011. "Click to Donate: Visual Images, Constructing Victims and Imagining the Female Refugee." *Third World Quarterly* 32(6): 1015–37.

– 2013. "The Other Side of the Fence: Reconceptualizing the Camp and Migration Zones at the Borders of Spain." *International Political Sociology* 7: 75–91.

– 2014. *Border, Asylum, and Global Non-Citizenship: The Other Side of the Fence*. Cambridge: Cambridge University Press.

– 2016. "These Fine Lines: Locating Noncitizenship in Political Protest in Europe." *Citizenship Studies* 19(8): 951–65.

Joint Committee of Displaced Persons and Political Refugees. 1947. M. Grabinski, Chair. Augsburg, Germany (American Occupation Zone) [Addressed to the International Red Cross Committee, Geneva, 5 February 1947. G.68/00/13].

Jonsson, S. 2020. "A Society Which Is Not: Political Emergence and Migrant Agency." *Current Sociology* 88(2): 204–22.

Kadav. 2016. "Who we are." March. http://www.kadav.org.tr/kimiz/?lang=en.

Kale, B., A. Dimitriadi, E. Sanchez-Montijano, and E Süm. 2018. "Asylum Policy and the Future of Turkey-EU Relations: Between Cooperation and Conflict." *FEUTURE Online Papers* No. 18.

Kale, B., and M. Erdoğan. 2019. "The Impact of GCR and Local Governments and Syrian Refugees in Turkey." *International Migration* 57(6). https://doi.org/10.1111/imig.12658.

Kalir, B. 2015. "The Jewish State of Anxiety: Between Moral Obligation and Fearism in the Treatment of African Asylum Seekers in Israel." *Journal of Ethnic and Migration Studies* 41(4): 580–98.

REFERENCES

Kallius, A., D. Monterescu, and P. Kumar Rajaram. 2015. "Immobilizing Mobility: Border Ethnography, Illiberal Democracy, and the Politics of the 'Refugee Crisis' in Hungary." *American Ethnologist* 43: 25–37.

Kanat, K.B., and K. Üstün. 2015. "Turkey's Syrian Refugees: Toward Integration." Foundation for Political, Economic and Social Research, Ankara. http://file.setav.org/Files/Pdf/20150428153844_turkey's-syrian-refugees-pdf.pdf.

Kaplan, M. 2020. "Beyond Humanitarian Relief: Social Network and the Role of Shared Identity in Refugee Belonging and Support in Turkey." Civil Society Knowledge Centre, Lebanon Support, 1 August. https://doi.org/10.28943/CSR.004.005.

Karadağ, S. 2019. "Extraterritoriality of European Borders to Turkey: An Implementation Perspective of Counteractive Strategies." *Comparative Migration Studies* 7(12): 1–16.

Kasparek, B., and M. Speer. 2015. "Of Hope, Hungary, and the Long Summer of Migration." 9 September. https://bordermonitoring.eu/ungarn/2015/09/of-hope-en.

Kay, S. 2016. "Syrians in Turkey: A Grassroots Perspective." *Turkish Policy Quarterly*. 20 December.

Kaya, A. 2016. "Syrian Refugees and Cultural Intimacy in Istanbul." San Domenico di Fiosale, European University Institute. https://www.dropbox.com/sh/y1tprereliwagtk/AABfB1woytKDlN8u UVRXFTAaa?dl=0&preview=244.+Syrian+Refugees+and+Cultural+ Intimacy+in+Istanbul+RSCAS_2016_59.pdf.

Kaya, A., and A. Kıraç. 2016. "Vulnerability Assessment of Syrian Refugees in Istanbul." Istanbul, Support to Life Association. https://eu.bilgi.edu.tr/media/files/160621_Ist_NA_Report.pdf.

Kaygısız, I. 2017. "Suriyeli Mültecilerin Türkiye İşgücü Piyasasına Etkileri." August. Friedrig Ebert Stiftung. http://www.fes-tuerkei.org/media/pdf/Dünyadan/2017/Du308nyadan%20-%20Suriyeli%20Mu308ltecilerin%20 Tu308rkiye%20I307s327gu308cu308%20Piyasasina%20Etkileri%20.pdf.

Khosravi, S. 2011. *Illegal Traveller*. New York: Palgrave Macmillan.

– 2021. "Afterword: Waiting, a State of Consciousness." In *Waiting and the Temporalities of Irregular Migration*, ed. C. Jacabsen, M.-A. Karlsen, and S. Khosravi, 202–7. London: Routledge.

Kılıçaslan, G. 2016. "Forced Migration, Citizenship, and Space: The Case of Syrian Kurdish Refugees in Istanbul." *New Perspectives on Turkey* 54: 77–95.

Kingsley, P. 2016. "More than 700 migrants feared dead in three Mediterranean sinkings." *The Guardian*, 29 May. https://www.theguardian.com/

world/2016/may/29/700-migrants-feared-dead-mediterranean-says-un-refugees.

Kirişçi, K. 2016. "Turkey's Role in the Syrian Refugee Crisis." *Georgetown Journal of International Affairs* 17(2): 80–5.

Kıvılcım, Z. 2016. "Legal Violence Against Syrian Female Refugees in Turkey." *Feminist Legal Studies* 24: 193–214.

Komşuoğlu, A. 2019. "Access to Higher Education and Recognition of Foreign Credentials in Turkey: Case of Istanbul University." http://www.uc.pt/en/refugee-help/Events/workshop/8.

Kooy, J., and D. Bowman. 2019. "'Surrounded with so much uncertainty': Asylum Seekers and Manufactured Precarity in Australia." *Journal of Ethnic and Migration Studies* 45(5): 693–710. https://doi.org/10.1080/1369183X. 2018.1427563.

Korkut, U. 2016. "Pragmatism, Moral Responsibility or Policy Change: The Syrian Refugee Crisis and Selective Humanitarianism in the Turkish Refugee Regime." *Comparative Migration Studies* 4(2): 1–20.

Kösebalaban, H. 2020. "Transformation of Turkish Foreign Policy toward Syria: The Return of Securitization." *Middle East Critique* 29(3): 335–44.

Kostantinou, A., and A. Georgopoulou. 2018. *Country Report: Greece*. Prepared for the European Council on Refugees and Exiles. 31 December. Asylum Information Database.

Kurdi, T. 2018. *The Boy on the Beach: My Family's Escape from Syria and Our Hope for a New Home*. New York: Simon and Schuster.

Kurian, G. 2015. *The Crossing* (Documentary). 55m. Producer Bente Olav. Norway: Gründer Film AS. http://www.nfi.no/english/search/film?key=144647.

Kutlu, Z. 2015. *From the Ante-Chamber to the Living Room: A Brief Assessment on NGO's Doing Work for Syrian Refugees*. İstanbul: Anadolu Kültür ve Açık Toplum Vakfı.

Landau, L., and R. Amit. 2014. "Wither Policy? Southern African Perspectives on Understanding Law, 'Refugee' Policy and Protection." *Journal of Refugee Studies* 27(4): 534–52.

Lautz, S., and A. Raven-Roberts. 2006. "Violence and Complex Humanitarian Emergencies: Implications for Livelihoods Models." *Disasters* 30(4): 383–401.

Law Library of Congress. 2016a. "Refugee Law and Policy: Jordan." Prepared by I. Saliba. 21 June. https://www.loc.gov/law/help/refugee-law/jordan.php#Memorandum.

– 2016b. "Refugee Law and Policy: Lebanon." Prepared by I. Saliba. 21 June. http://www.loc.gov/law/help/refugee-law/lebanon.php.

REFERENCES

– 2016c. "Refugee Law and Policy: Turkey." Prepared by W. Zeldin. 21 June. https://www.loc.gov/law/help/refugee-law/turkey.php#_ftn4.

Lecadet, C. 2016. "Refugee Politics: Self-Organized 'Government' and Protests in the Agamé Refugee Camp (2005–13)." *Journal of Refugee Studies* 29(2): 187–207.

Lefebvre, H. [1974] 1996. *Writings on Cities*. Trans. and ed. E. Kofman and E. Lebas. Oxford: Blackwell.

Lehner, R. 2019. "The EU–Turkey 'deal': Legal Challenges and Pitfalls." *International Migration* 57(2): 176–85.

Letsche, C. 2019. "Turkey's war on Arabic signs reflects intolerance of Syrian refugees." *The Arab Weekly*. 17 August. https://thearabweekly.com/turkeys-war-arabic-signs-reflects-intolerance-syrian-refugees.

Lindsay, F. 2020. "In Moria Detention Center refugees fear the 'catastrophe' of a coronavirus outbreak." *Forbes*. 8 April. https://www.forbes.com/sites/freylindsay/2020/04/08/in-moria-detention-center-refugees-fear-the-catastrophe-of-a-coronavirus-outbreak/#62ae84d23197.

Loescher, G. 2000. "Forced Migration in the Post-Cold War Era: The Need for a Comprehensive Approach." In *Managing Migration: Time for a New International Regime?*, ed. B. Ghosh, 190–219. New York: Oxford University Press.

Lovett, S. 2020. "Coronavirus: Greece places second refugee camp into lockdown after migrant tests positive for Covid-19." *The Independent*. 5 April. https://www.independent.co.uk/news/world/europe/coronavirus-greece-refugee-camp-malakasa-outbreak-a9447921.html.

Loyd, J., P. Ehrkamp, and A. Secor. 2017. "A Geopolitics of Trauma: Refugee Administration and Protracted Uncertainty in Turkey." https://doi.org/10.1111/tran.12234.

Loyd, J., E. Mitchell-Eaton, and A. Mountz. 2016. "The Militarization of Islands and Migration: Tracing Human Mobility through US Bases in the Caribbean and the Pacific." *Political Geography* 53: 65–75.

Lui, R. 2002. "Governing Refugees 1919–1945." *Borderlands ejournal* 1(11).

Mackinnon, M. 2015. "'I was only hoping to provide a better life for my children,' father of drowned migrant boy says." *Globe and Mail*. 3 September. http://www.theglobeandmail.com/news/world/they-died-in-my-arms-father-of-drowned-migrant-boy-speaks-out/article26207543.

Macklin, A. 2005. "Disappearing Refugees: Reflections on the Canada–US Safe Third Country Agreement." *Columbia Human Rights Law Review* 36: 365–426.

Mackreath, H., and S. Sağnıç 2017. *Civil Society and Syrian Refugees in Turkey*. Report published by Citizens' Assembly – Turkey (formerly Helsinki

Citizens Assembly – Turkey). 16 May. İstanbul. http://www.hyd.org.tr/attachments/article/215/civil-society-and-syrian-refugees-in-turkey.pdf.

Mainwaring, C. 2016. "Migrant Agency: Negotiating Borders and Migration Controls." *Migration Studies* 4(3): 289–308.

Makovsky, A. 2019. "Turkey's refugee dilemma." Centre for American Progress. 13 March. https://www.americanprogress.org/issues/security/reports/2019/03/13/467183/turkeys-refugee-dilemma.

Malkki, L. 1995. *Purity and Exile: Violence, Memory, and National Cosmology among Hutu Refugees in Tanzania.* Chicago: University of Chicago Press.

– 1996. "Speechless Emissaries: Refugees, Humanitarianism, and Dehistoricization." *Cultural Anthropology* 11(3): 377–404.

Mansouri, F., M. Leach, and A. Nethery. 2009. "Temporary Protection and the Refugee Convention in Australia, Denmark, and Germany." *Refuge* 26(1): 135–47.

Massey, D. 2005. *For Space.* London: Sage.

Mayblin, L., M. Wake, and M. Kazemi 2019. "Necropolitics and the Slow Violence of the Everyday: Asylum Seeker Welfare in the Postcolonial Present." *Sociology* 54(1): 107-123.

Mazlumder. 2014. Kamp Dışında Yaşayan Suriyeli Kadın Sığınmacılar Raporu. İstanbul.

McAdam, J. 2013. "Australia and Asylum Seekers." *International Journal of Refugee Law* 25(3): 435–48.

McKinnon, S. 2008. "Unsettling Resettlement: Problematizing 'Lost Boys of Sudan' Resettlement and Identity." *Western Journal of Communication* 72(4): 397–414.

McMahon, S., and N. Sigona. 2018. "Navigating the Central Mediterranean in a Time of 'Crisis': Disentangling Migration Governance and Migrant Journeys." *Sociology* 52(3): 497–514.

McNeil, S., and H. Dlewati. 2016. "Syrian asylum seekers determined to take deadly journey to Europe as Turkey crackdown begins." *ABC News.* 26 February. http://www.abc.net.au/news/2016-02-26/syrian-asylum-seekers-determined-to-take-deadly-journey/7204466.

McNevin, A. 2006. "Political belonging in a neoliberal era: the struggle of the Sans-Papiers." *Citizenship Studies* 10(2): 135–51.

– 2010. "Becoming Political: Asylum Seeker Activism through Community Theatre." *Local–Global: Identity, Security, Community* 8: 142–56.

– 2011. *Contesting Citizenship: Irregular Migrants and New Frontiers of the Political.* New York: Columbia University Press.

– 2014. "Beyond Territoriality: Rethinking Human Mobility, Border Security, and Geopolitical Space from the Indonesian Island of Bintan." *Security Dialogue* 45(3): 295–310.

REFERENCES

Memişoğlu, F., and A. Ilgıt. 2017. "Syrian Refugees in Turkey: Multifaceted Challenges, Diverse Players, and Ambiguous Policies." *Mediterranean Politics* 22(3): 317–38.

Memurlar Net. 2017. "26 Suriyeli Doktor Çalışma İzni Aldı." 20 December. https://www.memurlar.net/haber/716208/26-suriyeli-doktor-calisma-izni-aldi.html.

Menjivar, C. 2006. "Liminal Legality: Salvadoran and Guatemalan Immigrants' Lives in the United States." *American Journal of Sociology* 111(4): 999–1037.

Mercy Corps. 2020. "The facts: What you need to know about the Syria crisis." 9 July. https://www.mercycorps.org/blog/quick-facts-syria-crisis.

Mezzadra, S. 2004. "The Right to Escape." *Epherma* 4(3): 267–75.

– 2015. "The Proliferation of Borders and the Right to Escape." In *The Irregularization of Migration in Contemporary Europe: Detention, Deportation, Drowning*, ed. Y. Jansen, R. Çelikateş, and J. de Bloois, 121–35. London and New York, Rowman and Littlefield.

Mezzadra, S., and B. Nielsen. 2003a. *Border as Method, or, the Multiplication of Labor.* Durham: Duke University Press.

– 2003b. "Ne' qui, ne' altrove – migration, detention, desertion: A dialogue." *Borderlands ejournal* 2(1). http://www.borderlands.net.au.

Migration Policy Centre. n.d. "Syrian Refugees: A Snapshot of the Crisis – In the Middle East and Europe – Sweden: Stories from Stockholm." Migration Policy Centre, European University Institute, Florence. http://syrianrefugees.eu/?page_id=622.

Migreurop. 2005. "Migreurop definition of camps." http://www.migreurop.org/article972.html?lang.e.

Ministry of Education. 2019. "Hayat Boyu Öğrenme." April. https://hbogm.meb.gov.tr/meb_iys_dosyalar/2019_04/08133210_01Nisan2019internet SunusuGeciciKorumaAlOgr.pdf.

Mistrík, E. 2016. "Art/Aesthetic Education in Civic Education." *Journal of Social Science Education* 15(4): 2–6.

Moulin, C., and P. Nyers. 2007. "'We Live in a Country of UNHCR' – Refugee Protests and Global Political Society." *International Political Sociology* 1: 356–72.

Mountz, A. 2010. *Seeking Asylum: Human Smuggling and Bureaucracy at the Border.* Minneapolis: University of Minnesota Press.

– 2020. *The Death of Asylum: Hidden Geographies of the Enforcement Archipelago.* Minneapolis: University of Minnesota Press.

Müller, T. 2016. "Acts of Citizenship as a Politics of Resistance? Reflections on Realizing Concrete Rights within the Israeli Asylum Regime." *Citizenship Studies* 20(1): 50–66.

Multeciler Dernegi. 2020. "Türkiye'deki Suriyeli Sayısı." https://multeciler.org.tr/turkiyede-calisma-izni-verilen-suriyeli-sayisi.

Murphy, F., and E. Chatzipanagiotidou. 2020. "'Devious Silence': Refugee Art, Memory Activism, and the Unspeakability of Loss among Syrians in Turkey." *History and Anthropology*. 14 October. https://doi.org/10.1080/02757206.2020.1830383.

Neilson, B., and N. Rossiter. 2005. "From Precarity to Precariousness and Back Again: Labour, Life, and Unstable Networks." *The Fibreculture Journal* 5: 70–89.

Neveu, C. 2014. "Practising Citizenship from the Ordinary to the Activist." In *Routledge Handbook of Global Citizenship Studies*, ed. E.F. Isin and P. Nyers, 86–96. New York: Routledge.

New York Times. 2018. "Turkey stands between Europe and the next refugee crisis." 25 September. Written by Ş.K. Akçapar.

– 2019. "Turkey's radical plan: Send a million refugees back to Syria." https://www.nytimes.com/2019/09/10/world/middleeast/turkey-syria-refugees-erdogan.html.

– 2020a. "Afghan migrants charged with arson in fires that destroyed Lesbos camp." 16 September. https://www.nytimes.com/2020/09/16/world/europe/afghan-migrants-charged-arson-lesbos.html.

– 2020b. "Erdogan says 'We opened the doors' and clashes erupt as migrants head for Europe." 1 March. https://www.nytimes.com/2020/02/29/world/europe/turkey-migrants-eu.html.

Newsweek. 2016. "Underground Care: Syrian Doctors Quietly Fill Treatment Void in Turkey." Written by Zia Weise. 19 June. http://www.newsweek.com/2016/07/01/syrian-hospitals-turkey-refugees-471744.html.

Nguyen-Okwu, L. 2015. "Syrian eats on Istanbul streets." *Daily Dose.* 29 December. https://www.ozy.com/good-sht/syrian-eats-on-istanbul-streets/41500.

Nielsen, N. 2012. "Fortress Europe: A Greek Wall Close Up," *EU Observer.* 21 December. http://euobserver.com/fortress-eu/118565.

Nyers, P. 2003. "Abject Cosmopolitanism: The Politics of Protection in the Anti-Deportation Movement." *Third World Quarterly* 24(6): 1069–93.

– 2006. *Rethinking Refugees: Beyond States of Emergency.* New York: Routledge.

–2008. "No One Is Illegal between City and Nation." In *Acts of Citizenship*, ed. E.F. Isin and G.M. Nielsen, 160–81. London: Zed Books.

– 2011. "Forms of Irregular Citizenship." In *The Contested Politics of Mobility: Borderzones and Irregularity*, ed. V. Squire, 184–98. London: Routledge.

REFERENCES

– 2015. "Migrant Citizenships and Autonomous Mobilities." *Migration, Mobility, and Displacement* 1(1): 23–39.

Nyers, P., and K. Rygiel, eds. 2012. *Citizenship, Migrant Activism, and the Politics of Movement.* New York and London: Routledge.

NTV News. 2018. "Cumhurbaskani Erdogan: Hedefimiz Suriyelilerin tamaminin evlerine donmesi." 21 June. https://www.ntv.com.tr/turkiye/hedefimiz-suriyelilerin-tamaminin-evlerine-donmesi,zmSC_mCSMkGZtGx_c1I4EQ.

Office of Public Affairs, Department of State. 1946. "Refugees and Displaced Persons." October. Rev. ed. no. 1.

Oliveri, F. 2012. "Migrants as Activist Citizens in Italy: Understanding the New Cycles of Struggles." *Citizenship Studies* 16(5–6): 793–806.

Orchard, C., and A. Miller. 2014. "Protection in Europe for Refugees from Syria." Forced Migration Policy Briefing 10. Refugee Studies Centre, Oxford Department of International Development, University of Oxford.

Özçürümez, S., and N. Şenses. 2011. "Europeanization and Turkey: Studying Irregular Migration Policy." *Journal of Balkan and Near Eastern Studies* 13(2): 233–48.

Ozduzen, O., U. Korkut, and C. Ozduzen. 2020. "'Refugees are not welcome': Digital Racism, Online Place-Making, and the Evolving Categorization of Syrians in Turkey." *New Media and Society*, 1–20. https://doi.org10.1177/1461444820956341.

Özgür Düşünce Gazetesi. 2016. "Tarım İşçilerine Suriyeli Darbesi." http://www.ozgurdusunce.com/haber/tarim-iscilerine-suriyeli-20250.

Pallister-Wilkins, P. 2015. "The Humanitarian Politics of European Border Policing: Frontex and Border Police in Evros." *International Political Sociology* 9(1): 53–69.

Pandolfi, M. 2003. "Contract of Mutual (In)Difference: Governance and the Humanitarian Apparatus in Contemporary Albania and Kosovo." *Indiana Journal of Global Legal Studies* 10: 369–81.

Papadopoulos, D., N. Stephenson, and V. Tsianos. 2008. *Escape Routes: Control and Subversion in the Twenty-First Century.* London: Pluto Press.

Paret, M., and S. Gleeson. 2016. "Precarity and Agency through a Migration Lens." *Citizenship Studies* 20(3–4): 277–94.

Pascucci, E. 2017. "Community Infrastructures: Shelter, Self-Reliance and Polymorphic Borders in Urban Refugee Governance." *Territory, Politics, Governance* 5(3): 332–45.

Paynter, E. 2019. "Risking Rescue: The Politics of Precarity in Mediterranean Crossing." *Conference: The Social Practice of Human Rights.* University of Dayton eCommons, Dayton.

Pazianou, A. 2016. "Refugee arrivals to Lesvos island in Greece decline dramatically." 10 May. http://news.xinhuanet.com/english/2016-05/11/c_135349194.htm.

Pereira, S., C. Maiztegui-Oñate, and D. Mata-Codesal. 2016. "'Transformative Looks': Practicing Citizenship through Photography." *Journal of Social Science Education* 15(4): 14–21.

Politico. 2019. "Syrians report deportations as Turkey takes harder line on refugees." 8 September. https://www.politico.eu/article/syrians-report-deportations-as-turkey-takes-harder-line-on-refugees.

Pollock, W., J. Wartman, G. Abou-Jaoube, and A. Grant. 2019. "Risk at the Margins: A Natural Hazards Perspective on the Syrian Refugee Crisis in Lebanon." *International Journal of Disaster Risk Reduction* 36: 1–20.

Posta Gazetesi. 2016. "İşte Türkiye'deki Son Kayıtlı Suriyeli Sayısı." http://www.posta.com.tr/turkiye/HaberDetay/Iste-Turkiye-deki-son-kayitli-Suriyeli-sayisi--Ocak-2016-.htm?ArticleID=321871.

Pro-Asyl. 2007. "The Truth May Be Bitter but It Must Be Told: The Situation of Refugees in the Aegean and the Practices of the Greek Coast Guard." October. Frankfurt am Main: Pro-Asyl, 1–27. http://www.proasyl.de/en/pro-asyl/about-us/index.html.

Ramadan, A. 2012. "Spatializing the Refugee Camp." *Transactions of the Institute of British Geographers* 38: 65–77.

Ramsay, G. 2019. "Humanitarian Exploits: Ordinary Displacement and the Political Economy of the Global Refugee Regime." *Critique of Anthropology*. http://doi.org/10.1177/0308275X19840417.

Refugees International. 2019. "Insecure Future: Deportations and Lack of Legal Work for Refugees in Turkey." September. https://static1.squarespace.com/static/506c8ea1e4b01d9450dd53f5/t/5d82e33643e3fb135e2a1c6d/1568858939191/Turkey+Report+in+English+-+Livelihoods+-+September+2019+-+final.pdf.

Reliefweb. 2015. "Syrian refugees forced to share housing in Turkey." 21 January. https://reliefweb.int/report/turkey/syrian-refugees-forced-share-housing-turkey.

Republic of Turkey. 2013a. "Law on Foreigners and International Protection" (LFIP). http://www.goc.gov.tr/files/files/eng_minikanun_5_son.pdf.

– 2013b. "Yabancılar ve Uluslararası Koruma Kanunu" [Law on Foreigners and International Protection]. *Resmi Gazete* [Official Gazette] no. 28615. 11 April. perma.cc, law no. 6458, art. 1(1). 4 April. Ministry of the Interior, Directorate General of Migration Management.

– 2014. "Geçici Koruma Yönetmeliği" [Temporary Protection Regulation]. 22 October. http://www.goc.gov.tr/files/files/20141022-15-1.pdf. English translation at http://www.goc.gov.tr/files/files/temptemp.pdf.

REFERENCES

Robbins, J. 2013. "Beyond the Suffering Subject: Toward an Anthropology of the Good." *Journal of the Royal Anthropological Institute* 19(3): 447–62.

Roman, E., T. Baird, and T. Radcliffe. 2016. "Why Turkey is not a "safe country." *StateWatch Analysis*, February. https://www.statewatch.org/analyses/no-283-why-turkey-is-not-a-safe-country.pdf.

Roy, N., and A. Verdun. 2019. "Bangladeshi Migrants of Italy and Their Precarity." *Social Sciences* 8(4). https://doi.org/10.3390/socsci8040123.

Rygiel, K. 2011. "Bordering Solidarities: Migrant Activism and the Politics of Movement and Camps at Calais." *Citizenship Studies* 15(1): 1–19.

– 2014a. "Border Control Politics as Technologies of Citizenship in Europe and North America." In *New Border and Citizenship Politics*, ed. H. Schwenken and S. Russ-Sattar, 141–55. New York: Palgrave.

– 2014b. "In Life through Death: Transgressive Citizenship at the Border." In *Routledge Handbook of Global Citizenship Studies*, ed. E.F. Isin and P. Nyers, 62–72. London and New York: Routledge.

– 2016. "Dying to Live: Migrant Deaths and Citizenship Politics along the European Border." *Citizenship Studies* 20(10): 1–16. http://dx.doi.org/10.1080/13621025.2016.1182682.

Rygiel, K., F. Baban, and S. Ilcan. 2016. "The Syrian Refugee Crisis: The EU-Turkey 'Deal' and Temporary Protection." *Global Social Policy* 16(3): 315–20.

Şahin Mencütek, Z. 2018. *Refugee Governance, State, and Politics in the Middle East*. Oxford: Routledge.

– 2019. "Encouraging Syrian Return: Turkey's Fragmented Approach." *Forced Migration Review* 62: 28–31.

Şahin Mencütek, Z.S., and E. Gökalp Aras. 2015. "The International Migration and Foreign Policy Nexus: The Case of Syrian Refugee Crisis and Turkey." *Migration Letters* 12(3): 193–208.

Sanderson, S. 2019. "Minor killed at Moria migrant camp on Lesbos." *Info Migrants*. 26 August. https://www.infomigrants.net/en/post/19064/minor-killed-at-moira-migrant-camp-on-lesbos.

Sanyal, R. 2014. "Urbanizing Refuge: Interrogating Spaces of Displacement." *International Journal of Urban and Regional Research* 38(2): 558–72.

– 2017. "A No-Camp Policy: Interrogating Informal Settlements in Lebanon." *Geoforum* 84: 117–25.

Saraçoğlu, C., and D. Belanger 2019a. "Loss and Xenophobia in the City: Contextualizing Anti-Syrian Sentiments in İzmir, Turkey." *Patterns of Prejudice* 53(4): 363–83.

– 2019b. "Syrian Refugees in Turkey." In *Oxford Handbook of Migration Crises*, ed. Cecillia Menjivar, Marie Ruiz, and Immanuel Ness. Oxford: Oxford University Press.

Saranti, E. 2019. "Locked up without rights: Nationality-based detention in the Moria refugee camp." HIAS policy brief. December. https://borderlandscapes.law.ox.ac.uk/sites/default/files/2020-01/report_on_low_profile_detention_in_greece_hias_dec_2019.pdf.

Sassen, S. 2000. *Cities in a World Economy*. Thousand Oaks: Pine Forge/Sage Press.

Scheel, S., and V. Squire. 2014. "Forced Migrants as Illegal Migrants." In *The Oxford Handbook of Refugee and Forced Migration Studies*, ed. E. Fiddian-Qasmiyeh, G. Loescher, K. Long, and N. Sigona, 188–99. Oxford: Oxford University Press.

Schuster, L. 2011. "Turning Refugees into 'Illegal Migrants': Afghan Asylum Seekers in Europe." *Ethnic and Racial Studies* 34(8): 1392–407.

Secor, A. 2018. "'I love death': War in Syria and the Anxiety of the Other." In *Psychoanalysis and the Global*, ed. I. Kapour, 97–115. Lincoln: University of Nebraska Press.

Şenses, N. 2015. "Rethinking Migration in the Context of Precarity: The Case of Turkey." *Critical Sociology*, 1–13.

Sharma, S. 2017. "Syrian refugee fights Turkish order to tear down Arabic restaurant signs." *Middle East Eye*. 15 November. https://www.middleeasteye.net/news/syrian-refugee-fights-turkish-order-tear-down-arabic-restaurant-signs.

Sharma, S., and E. Kunduri. 2015. "'Working from home is better than going out to the factories'(?): Spatial Embeddedness, Agency, and Labour Market Decisions of Women in the City of Delhi." *South Asia Multidisciplinary Academic Journal*, 7 September.

Shields, L., and B. Bryan. 2002. "The Effect of War on Children: The Children of Europe after World War II." *International Nursing Review* 49(12): 87–98.

Sigona, N. 2012. "Deportation, Non-Deportability, and Precarious Lives." *Anthropology Today* 28(5): 22–3.

– 2015. "Campzenship: Reimagining the Camp as a Social and Political Space." *Citizenship Studies* 19(1): 1–15.

– 2017. "The Contested Politics of Naming in Europe's 'Refugee Crisis.'" *Ethnic and Racial Studies* 41(3): 456–60.

Soykan, C. 2010. "The Migration–Asylum Nexus in Turkey." *Enquire* 3(1): 1–18.

– 2017. "Access to International Protection: Border Issues in Turkey." In *States, the Law, and Access to Refugee Protection*, ed. Maria O'Sullivan and Dallal Stevens, 69–92. Oxford: Hart.

Spindler, W., and J. Clayton. 2016. "UNHCR expresses concern over EU-Turkey plan." 11 March. http://www.unhcr.org/news/latest/2016/3/56dee1546/unhcr-expresses-concern-eu-turkey-plan.html.

REFERENCES

Squire, V., ed. 2011. *The Contested Politics of Mobility: Border Zones and Irregularity*. London and New York: Routledge.

– 2020. "Hidden Geographies of the 'Mediterranean Migration Crisis.'" *EPC: Politics and Space*. https://doi.org/10.1177/2399654420935904.

Squire, V., A. Dimitriadi, N. Perkowski, M. Pisani, D. Stevens, and N. Vaughan-Williams. 2017. "Crossing the Mediterranean Sea by boat: Mapping and documenting migratory journeys and experiences." Final Project Report. www.warwick.ac.uk/crossingthemed.

Staeheli, L. 2008. "Political Geography: Difference, Recognition, and the Contested Terrains of Political Claims-Making." *Progress in Human Geography* 32(4): 561–70.

– 2013. "Whose Responsibility Is It? Obligation, Citizenship, and Social Welfare." *Antipode* 45(3): 521–40.

Stierl, M. 2016a. "Contestations in Death – The Role of Grief in Migration Struggles." *Citizenship Studies* 20(2): 173–91.

– 2016b. "A Sea of Struggle – Activist Border Interventions in the Mediterranean Sea." *Citizenship Studies* 20(5): 561–78.

Strasser, S., and E.E. Tibet. 2019. "The Border Event in the Everyday: Hope and Constraints in the Lives of Young Unaccompanied Asylum Seekers in Turkey." *Journal of Ethnic and Migration Studies*. https://doi.org/10.1080/1369183X.2019.1584699.

Strauss, K. 2018. "Labour geography I: Towards a Geography of Precarity?", *Progress in Human Geography* 42(4): 622–30.

Strauss, K., and J. Fudge. 2014. "Temporary Work, Agencies, and Unfree Labour: Insecurity in the New World of Work." In *Temporary Work, Agencies, and Unfree Labour: Insecurity in the New World of Work*, ed. J. Fudge and K. Strauss, 1–25. New York: Routledge.

Su, A. 2017. "Why Jordan Is Deporting Syrian Refugees." *The Atlantic*, 20 October. https://www.theatlantic.com/international/archive/2017/10/jordan-syrian-refugees-deportation/543057.

Summers, H. 2017. "Thousands of Syrian children in Jordan's Za'atari camp missing out on education." *The Guardian*, 29 July. https://www.theguardian.com/global-development/2017/jul/29/thousands-syrian-children-jordan-zaatari-camp-missing-education.

Svensson, Dr Ragnar. 1950. *The Refugees in Germany: A Report*. Swedish Save the Children Fund. January.

Tarlan, K.V. 2016. "Suriyeli Mülteciler: Büyüyen Sorunlar, Daralan Zamanlar." *Birikim*. 20 June. https://www.birikimdergisi.com/guncel-yazilar/7771/suriyeli-#.XbA6hC1L1PM.

– 2020. "Kırkayak Kültür: Facilitating Living Together." In *Fostering Pluralism through Solidarity Activism in Europe: Everyday Encounters with Newcomers*, ed. F. Baban and K. Rygiel, chapter 10. Basingstoke: Palgrave Macmillan.

Tazzioli, M. 2015. "The Politics of Counting and the Sense of Rescue." *Radical Philosophy*, July–August 2015.

– 2020. "What Is Left of Migrants' Spaces?: Transversal Alliances and the Temporality of Solidarity." *Political Anthropology Research on International Social Sciences* 1: 137–61.

Tazzioli, M., and G. Garelli. 2018. "Containment beyond Detention: The Hotspot System and Disrupted Migration Movements across Europe." *Environment and Planning D: Society and Space*. 19 February. https://doi.org/10.1177/0263775818759335.

Tazzioli, M., and W. Walters. 2019. "Migration, Solidarity and the Limits of Europe." *Global Discourse* 9(1): 175–90.

TBB (Turkish Bar Association). 2016. "Sığınmacılar ve Mülteciler Raporu" https://www.dropbox.com/sh/yıtprereliwagtk/AABfB1woytKDlN8u UVRXFTAaa?dl=0&preview=240.+Sığınmacılar+ve+Multeciler+ Raporu+Barolar+Birliği+Subat+2016.pdf.

Telegraph. n.d. "Why do refugees and migrants come to Europe, and what must be done to ease the crisis?" https://www.telegraph.co.uk/news/ worldnews/europe/11845205/Why-do-refugees-and-migrants-come-to-Europe-and-what-must-be-done-to-ease-the-crisis.html.

Terzioğlu, A. 2018. "The Banality of Evil and the Normalization of the Discriminatory Discourses against Syrians in Turkey." *Anthropology of the Contemporary Middle East and Central Eurasia* 4(2): 34–47.

Tibet, E.E. 2017. "Escaping Exclusion: Confused Moralities and Syrian Unaccompanied Minors' Search for Freedom in Turkey." *Movements: Journal for Critical Migration and Border Regime Studies* 3(2). http://movements-journal.org/issues/05.turkey/13.tibet--escaping-exclusion-confused-moralities.html.

Ticktin, M. 2005. "Policing and Humanitarianism in France: Immigration and the Turn to Law as State of Exception." *Interventions: International Journal of Postcolonial Studies* 7(3): 347–68.

– 2011a. *Casualties of Care: Immigration and the Politics of Humanitarianism in France*. Berkeley: University of California Press.

– 2011b. "How Biology Travels: A Humanitarian Trip." *Body and Society* 17 (2–3): 139–58.

– 2014. "Transnational Humanitarianism." *Annual Review of Anthropology* 43: 273–89.

REFERENCES

Togral Koca, B. 2015. "Deconstructing Turkey's "Open Door" Policy towards Refugees from Syria." *Migration Letter* 12(3): 209–25.

Topak, Ö. 2014. "The Biopolitical Border in Practice: Surveillance and Death at the Greece–Turkey Borderzones." *Environment and Planning D: Society and Space* 22: 815–33.

Topol, S. 2016. "In Istanbul, a Syrian culinary community blossoms." *Travel and Leisure* 7 December. https://www.travelandleisure.com/food-drink/restaurants/syria-istanbul-restaurants.

Trimikliniotis, N., D. Parsanoglou, and V. Tsianos. 2015. "Mobile Commons and/in Precarious Spaces: Mapping Migrant Struggles and Social Resistance." *Critical Sociology*, 8 December. 1–15. https://doi.org/10.1177/0896920515614983.

Tsianos, V., and D. Papadopoulos. 2006. "Precarity: A Savage Journey to the Heart of Embodied Capitalism." *European Institute for Progressive Politics.* http://transform.eipcp.net/transversal/1106/tsianospapadopoulos/en.

Tsing, A. 2015. *The Mushroom at the End of the World: On the Possibility of Life in Capitalist Ruins.* Princeton: Princeton University Press.

TTB (Turkish Medical Association). 2014. "Suriyeli Sığınmacılar ve Sağlık Raporu." Türk Tabipleri Birliği, Ankara.

Tuğal, C. 2016. "Syrian refugees in Turkey are pawns in a geopolitical game." *The Guardian.* https://www.theguardian.com/commentisfree/2016/feb/15/refugees-turkey-government-eu-crisis-europe.

Türk, V. 2015. "Temporary Protection Arrangement to Fill a Gap in the Protection Regime." *Forced Migration Review* 49: 40–1.

Turkish Government. 2014. "Gecici Koruma Yonetmeligi." https://www.goc.gov.tr/kurumlar/goc.gov.tr/gecicikorumayonetmeligi.pdf.

Turkish Minute. 2019. "Interior Minister says 92,000 Syrians granted Turkish citizenship." 2 August. https://www.turkishminute.com/2019/08/02/interior-minister-says-92000-syrians-granted-turkish-citizenship.

Turnbull, S., and J. Shoebridge. 2016. "Syrian refugees being sold fake life jackets with absorbent foam, volunteer says." *ABC News.* 18 January. http://www.abc.net.au/news/2016-01-18/volunteer-reveals-challenges-facing-syrian-refugees/7095006.

T24. 2016a. "Kaç Suriyeli Türk Vatandaşlığına Geçecek, Seçimlerde Oy Kullanabilecekler mi?" http://m.t24.com.tr/haber/kac-suriyeli-turk-vatandasligina-gececek-secimlerde-oy-kullanabilecekler-mi,349087#paylas.

– 2016b. "Suriyeli Doktorlar Türkiye'de 100'e Yakın Merdiven Altı Klinik Açtı." http://m.t24.com.tr/haber/suriyeli-doktorlar-turkiyede-100e-yakin-merdiven-alti-klinik-acti,346290.

- 2017. "Suriyeli mülteciler Kadıköy'de sanat merkezi kurdu, eserlerini Avrupa'da satıyor." 24 July. http://t24.com.tr/haber/suriyeli-multeciler-kadikoyde-sanat-merkezi-kurdu-eserlerini-avrupada-satiyor,415884.
- 2019. "PİAR Anketi." 19 July. https://t24.com.tr/foto-haber/piar-dan-siyasi-gundem-arastirmasi-akp-lilerin-yuzde-33-u-merkez-sagda-yeni-bir-parti-istiyor,8276/5.
Ulusoy, O., and H. Battjes. 2017. "Situation of Readmitted Migrants and Refugees from Greece to Turkey under the EU Turkey Statement," *VU Migration Law Series* 15. Amsterdam. https://rechten.vu.nl/en/Images/UlusoyBattjes_Migration_Law_Series_No_15_tcm248-861076.pdf.
UN (United Nations). 1958. "Economic Characteristics of International Migrants: Statistics for Selected Countries, 1918–1954." Department of Economic and Social Affairs. Population Studies, No. 12. New York.
UN General Assembly. 2016a. "New York Declaration for Refugees and Migrants." 13 September, A/71/L.1. https://www.iom.int/sites/default/files/our_work/ODG/GCM/NY_Declaration.pdf.
- 2016b. "Report of the United Nations High Commissioner for Refugees Part II: Global Compact on Refugees, General Assembly, Official Records, Seventy-third Session, Supplement No. 12, A/73/12 (Part II)." http://www.unhcr.org/gcr/GCR_English.pdf.
UNDESA (Department of Economic and Social Affairs), Population Division. 2019. *World Population Prospects 2019*. https://population.un.org/wpp/Download/Standard.
UNHCR (UN High Commissioner for Refugees). n.d. "Figures at a Glance." http://www.unhcr.org/figures-at-a-glance.html.
- n.d. "The Global Compact on Refugees." https://ww.w.unhcr.org/the-global-compact-on-refugees.html.
- n.d. "Help – Medical and Psychological Assistance." http://help.unhcr.org/turkey/information-for-syrians/medical-and-psychological-assistance.
- n.d. "Operation Portal Refugee Situations: Mediterranean Situation." https://data2.unhcr.org/en/situations/mediterranean.
- n.d. "Operational Portal Refugee Situations: Syria Regional Refugee Response." https://data2.unhcr.org/en/situations/syria#_ga=2.40912034.1621531210.1525810308-192866089.1522940125.
- n.d. "Registration and RSD with UNHCR." https://help.unhcr.org/turkey/information-for-non-syrians/registration-rsd-with-unhcr.
- n.d. "Resettlement Data." https://www.unhcr.org/resettlement-data.html.
- n.d. "Syria Emergency." https://www.unhcr.org/tr/en/syria-emergency.
- n.d. "UNHCR Operational Portal Refugee Situations: Mediterranean Situation – Greece." https://data2.unhcr.org/en/situations/mediterranean/location/5179.

REFERENCES

- 2013. "Syrian Refugees Living Outside Camps in Jordan: Home Visit Data Findings." https://reliefweb.int/sites/reliefweb.int/files/resources/HVreport_09MarCS6_smallsize.pdf.
- 2014a. *Guidelines on Temporary Protection or Stay Arrangements.* http://www.unhcr.org/5304b71c9.html.
- 2014b. "Submission by the United Nations High Commissioner for Refugees for the Office of the High Commissioner for Human Rights: Compilation Report." Republic of Turkey. http://www.refworld.org/pdfid/5541e6694.pdf.
- 2015a. "Over One Million Sea Arrivals Reach Europe in 2015." 30 December. http://www.unhcr.org/5683d0b56.html.
- 2015b. "UNCHR Chief Issues Key Guidelines for Dealing with Europe's Refugee crisis."
- 2017a. "Desperate Journeys: Refugees and Migrants Arriving in Europe and at Europe's Borders." December–January. https://www.refworld.org/docid/58b58b184.html.
- 2017b. "Global Trends: Forced Displacement in 2016." UN Refugee Agency. http://www.unhcr.org/5943e8a34.pdf.
- 2017c. "Health Access and Utilization Survey: Access to Health Surveys in Jordan among Syrian Refugees." January. https://reliefweb.int/sites/reliefweb.int/files/resources/UNHCR-HealthAccess%26Utilization SurveyinJordan2017-Syrians.pdf.
- 2017d. "Syrian Refugees in Turkey: Frequently Asked Questions." January. http://unhcr.org.
- 2017e. "UNHCR Turkey Factsheet – October 2017." 11 October. https://data2.unhcr.org/en/documents/details/60180.
- 2017f. "Vulnerability Assessment of Syria Refugees in Lebanon" (VASyR 2017). December. https://data2.unhcr.org/en/documents/download/61312.
- 2018a. "Gap between Refugee Resettlement Needs and Opportunities Widens." 25 June. http://www.unhcr.org/news/press/2018/6/5b30abod4/gap-refugee-resettlement-needs-opportunities-widens.html.
- 2018b. *Global Trends: Forced Displacement in 2018.* Geneva: UNHCR. https://www.unhcr.org/5d08d7ee7.pdf.
- 2018c. "Registration and RSD with UNHCR." https://help.unhcr.org/turkey/information-for-non-syrians/registration-rsd-with-unhcr.
- 2018d. "UNCHR Chief Issues Key Guidelines for Dealing with Europe's Refugee Crisis." http://www.unhcr.org/55e9793b6.html.
- 2018e. "UNHCR Durable Solutions for Syrian Refugees – June–July 2018." https://data2.unhcr.org/en/documents/download/64999.
- 2018f. "UNHCR Jordan Factsheet – February 2018." https://reliefweb.int/report/jordan/unhcr-jordan-factsheet-february-2018.

– 2018g. "UNHCR Jordan Factsheet – June 2018." http://reporting.unhcr.org/sites/default/files/UNHCR%20Jordan%20Fact%20Sheet%20-%20June%202018.pdf.
– 2019a. "Evaluation of UNHCR Livelihoods Strategies and Approaches." December. https://www.unhcr.org/5c5061384.pdf.
–2019b. "Global Trends: Forced Displacement in 2019." https://www.unhcr.org/globaltrends2019.
– 2019c. "UNHCR Lebanon Factsheet – January 2019." https://reliefweb.int/sites/reliefweb.int/files/resources/UNHCR-Lebanon-Operational-factsheet-January-2019.pdf.
UNHCR USA. n.d. "Solutions." http://www.unhcr.org/solutions.html.
UNICEF. 2015. "Türkiye'de Suriyeli Çocuklar." http://unicef.org.tr/files/bilgimerkezi/doc/T%C3%BCrkiyedeki Suriyeli %C3%87ocuklar_Bilgi Notu Kasim 2015.pdf.
Unutulmaz, O. 2019. "Turkey's Education Policies Towards Syrian Refugees: A Macro-level Analysis." *International Migration* 57(2): 235–52.
USAK (Uluslararası Stratejik Araştırmalar Kurumu). 2013. Sınırlar Arasında Yaşam Savaşı: Suriyeli Mülteciler. Ankara.
Vardar, N. 2017. "Woman to woman refugee kitchen," BIA News Desk, 19 January. https://m.bianet.org/bianet/english/182834-woman-to-woman-refugee-kitchen.
Vaughan-Williams, N. 2015. *Europe's Border Crisis: Biopolitics Security and Beyond*. Oxford: Oxford University Press.
Verdirame, G., and B.E. Harrell-Bond. 2005. *Rights in Exile: Janus Faced Humanitarianism*. Oxford: Berghahn Books.
VoaNews. 2019. "Turkey accused of forcible deportation of Syrian refugees." 29 July. https://www.voanews.com/europe/turkey-accused-forcible-deportation-syrian-refugees.
Waite, J. 2009. "A Place and Space for a Critical Geography of Precarity." *Geography Compass* 3(1): 412–33.
Wall, M., M. Campbell, and D. Janbek. 2015. "Syrian Refugees and Information Precarity." *New Media and Society*. https://doi.org/10.1177/1461444815591967.
Walsh, J. 2008. "Community, Surveillance, and Border Control." In *Surveillance and Governance*, ed. M. Deflem, 11–34. New York: Emerald.
Walters, W. 2011. "Foucault and Frontiers: Notes on the Birth of the Humanitarian Border." In *Governmentality: Current Issues and Future Challenges*, ed. U. Bröckling, S. Krasmann, and T. Lemke. 138–64. New York: Routledge.
Washington Post. 2019a. "Refugee deported from Turkey was shot and killed in Syria, family says." 10 September. https://www.washingtonpost.com/

REFERENCES

world/refugee-deported-from-turkey-was-shot-and-killed-in-syria-family-says/2019/08/09/0750d240-bab8-11e9-8e83-4e6687e99814_story.html.

– 2019b. "Turkey has deported hundreds of Syrian migrants, advocates and refugees say." 22 July. https://www.washingtonpost.com/world/turkey-has-deported-hundreds-of-syrian-migrants-advocates-and-refugees-say/2019/07/22/14114c9c-ac87-11e9-9411-a608f9d0c2d3_story.html.

Watch the Med. 2016. Alarm phone: "Statement in light of the current situation in the Mediterranean Sea and yesterday's events." 27 May. https://alarmphone.org/en/2016/05/27/statement-in-light-of-the-current-situation-in-the-mediterranean-sea.

Weber, L., and S. Pickering. 2011. *Globalization and Borders: Death at the Global Frontier*. London: Palgrave Macmillan.

Weis, P. 1960. "Status of refugee dependents." Representative, UNHCR Branch Office for Morocco, 31 August. Geneva.

Wettergren, A., and H. Wikstrom. 2014. "Who Is a Refugee? Political Subjectivity and the Categorization of Somali Aslyum Seekers in Sweden." *Journal of Ethnic and Migration Studies* 40(4): 566–83.

WHO (World Health Organization). 2017. "World Refugee Day: WHO training enables Syrian doctors and nurses to provide health care in Turkey." http://www.euro.who.int/en/countries/turkey/news/news/2017/06/world-refugee-day-who-training-enables-syrian-doctors-and-nurses-to-provide-health-care-in-turkey.

Williams, K., and A. Mountz. 2018. "Between Enforcement and Precarity: Externalization and Migrant Deaths at Sea." *International Migration* 56(5): 74–89.

Woods, A., and N. Kayali. 2017. *Engaging Syrian Communities: The Role of Local Government in İstanbul*. Report published by the İstanbul Policy Centre, Sabanci University, İstanbul.

World Population Review. 2019. "Europe Population (2019-08-28)." http://worldpopulationreview.com/continents/europe.

Yıldız, A., and E. Uzgören. 2016. "Limits to Temporary Protection: Non-Camp Syrian Refugees in İzmir, Turkey." *Southeast European and Black Sea Studies* 16(2): 195–211. https://doi.org/10.1080/14683857.2016.1165492.

Yıldız, U., and D. Sert. 2019. "Dynamics of Mobility-Stasis in Refugee Journeys: Case of Resettlement from Turkey to Canada." *Migration Studies*, 1–20. https://doi.org/10.1093/migration/mnz005.

Yıldız, Y. 2015. "Nowhere to Turn: The Situation of Dom Refugees in Turkey." 23 September. Report prepared with the support of European Roma Rights Centre, Budapest.

- 2017. "Perception of 'Smuggling Business' and Decision-Making Processes of Migrants." June. Report prepared under the "Counter Migrant Smuggling Initiatives in Turkey Project" funded by the Norwegian Government and implemented by The UN Migration Agency (IOM) Mission to Turkey. http://www.turkey.iom.int/sites/default/files/sitreps/Perception%20of%20 Smuggling%20Business%20and%20Decision%20Making%20Processes %20of%20Migrants.pdf.

Yüksel, S., and A. İçduygu. 2018. "Flexibility and Ambiguity: Impacts of Temporariness of Transnational Mobility in the Case of Turkey." In *Characteristics of Temporary Migration in European–Asian Transnational Social Spaces*, ed. P. Pitkänen, M. Korpela, M. Aksakal, and K. Schmidt, 99–119. London and Berlin: Springer.

Yuval-Davis, N., G. Wemyss, and K. Cassidy. 2019. *Bordering*. Cambridge: Polity Press.

Zalan, E. 2016. "EU defends Turkey deal in light of Greek court ruling." *EU Observer*. https://euobserver.com/migration/133515.

Zeldin, W. 2016. "Refugee law and policy – Turkey, Library of Congress." March. https://www.loc.gov/law/help/refugee-law/turkey.php.

Zetter, R. 2015. "Protection in crisis: Forced migration and protection in a global era." March. Migration Policy Institute, Washington, DC. http://www.migrationpolicy.org/research/protection-crisis-forced-migration-and-protection-global-era.

INDEX

Page numbers in italics refer to figures.

acts of citizenship, 13; as rights-claiming activities, 175–6, 180, 208; Small Projects İstanbul (SPI), 167–8, 170–3
acts of contestation, 13
Addar community support centre, Beyoğlu, 174
Africa, refugee camps in, 33, 36
agency, exercising, 182–3
Agier, Michel, 35, 42
agricultural skills training, 148
Ahmad, Ali İzzettin, 130
Aksoy, Hay, 170
Alevis, 185, 223n2
Alkadri, Samer, 161–2, 222n2
Almustafa, Dr Maissaa, 223n1
al-Qadur (elementary school), 154
al-Tadam (community association), 154
Altındağ Bab-i-Sifa (Door to Health), 223n7
Ammar, 182; attempts illegal border crossing, 193–4; border experiences, 191–2; crossing Macedonian–Serbian border, 192; journey of, 187–8
Amnesty International, 76, 77, 79, 103
Anderson, B., 45–6

Ankara: anti-Syrian attacks, *116*, 116–17, 121; faith-based charities, 135–6; no long-term education policy, 138; not satellite city, 106; temporary status for Syrians, 96, 108; visas required by Syrian refugees, 107; women's collective employment in, 155–6
anti-immigrant parties, far-right, 5, 213n2
anti-immigration policies, offshore processing and, 33
Arabic signage, 158–60
Arad, 182; discrimination, experience of, 184–5; journey of, 183–7
architecture of precarity, 8–10, 44–52, 201–2; postwar humanitarian emergency responses and, 23–8; precarious movement, 9–10, 50–2, 202; precarious space, 9, 48–50, 202; precarious status, 8–9, 46–50, 202
Arthere İstanbul artist collective, 160–1
arts projects, 160–5; Arthere İstanbul artist collective, 160–1; bureaucratic obstacles to opening business, 162; challenging negative stereotypes, 160; InEnArt (filming Syrians' stories), 160; Pages, 161–4, *163*, 222n2; refugee art, perceptions of, 161; Support to Life

(storytelling), 164; Syrian women's choir, 164–5

Asfari, Ayman, 222n6

Asfari, Sawsan, 222n6

Asfari Foundation, 174

Assisted Voluntary Return and Reintegration program (AVRR), 92

asylum: Common European Asylum System (CEAS), 219n5; policies, tightening of, 33

asylum law (EU): general principle of, 219n5

asylum-seekers: to Australia, 215–16n11; externalization policies, effect on, 73–5; ineligible for refugee status, 204–6; and non-refoulement principle, 39; offshore processing of, 33; refugee recognition rates, 219n5; refugee status determination, 62–6; registration required, 106. *See also* externalization policies/practices

Auschwitz-Birkenau, 25

Australia, limits migration zones, 215–16n11

Balibar, E., 56

Banki, S., 49

Barnett, M., 29, 32

Basmane neighbourhood, 84

Basques, postwar admission to Europe, 24–5

Behrman, S., 24

Beraktar, Omar, 160

Betts, Alexander, 14

Beyoğlu: Addar community support centre, 174; as community centre, 173–4

Biehl, Kristen, 69, 118

biopolitical abandonment, 195

biopolitical bordering practices, 192, 195

Bitar, Mohhamad, 153–5

"black deportations," 71–2

border controls: and mobility restrictions, 51; Turkey–Russia agreement regarding, 204–5

borders: biopolitical bordering practices, 192; controls, right to escape and, 183; deaths at, 10–11, 67, 213n3, 220n7; enforcement, 199–200; Greek–Macedonian, 191; Hungarian–Serbian, 192–3; Macedonian–Serbian, 192; policing, Turkey, 83, 203–4; safe zones and refugee containment, 204–5, 214n2; as social space, 192

borderscapes, 209

Bulley, D., 37

Calhoun, Craig, 42

campzenship, 52–3, 176

Canada: Arad's family, full acceptance of, 186–7; COVID-19 response regarding refugees, 217n17

Canefe, 50

Çapa-Şehremini neighbourhood, 170

capitalist economy: integration of refugees into, 14–15

capoeira (arts instruction), 171–2

Central Tracing Bureau (UNRRA), 25

child labour/marriage, 123, 147; illegal employment, 149

children: bullying/exclusion at school, 139; as displaced persons, 217n18; education of, *see*

INDEX

education; Kamer Foundation and, 177; language issues, 139; working to support family, 139

cities. *See* urban spaces/centres

citizenship: from below, 13; performative, 151, 176, 179; qualification interviews, Gaziantep, 117, 120

citizenship income, 218n20

Citizenship Law 5901 requirements, 115

citizen versus refugee, definition, 29

civil rights, migrant rights and, 56

claiming spaces. *See* spaces, claiming

Cochetel, Vincent, 77

Common European Asylum System (CEAS), 219n5

commons through mobility, 53

communism, flight of refugees from, 29, 31

community building: public spaces, 173; rights-claiming and, 180, 208–9; universities, 175

community support, 173–6; Beyoğlu, 174; claiming spaces in urban Turkey, 167–80; Small Projects İstanbul (SPI), 167–73; Syrian-run medical clinics, 179; women's rights initiatives, 176–8

Convention Relating to the Status of Refugees (UN, 1951), 11, 28–9, 31–2; adoption of, 202; failure to protect immigrants, 69; non-European refugees and, 31–2; refugee rights under, 218–19n3; states' acceptance of, 32

Çorabatır, Metin, 63–4

counter-precarity activities, 180, 208

COVID-19: border closures and, 217n17; in Moria refugee camp, 90

Crépeau, François, 9, 83

culinary culture: Arabic signage issue, 158–60; bakeries and baklava, 156; bureaucratic obstacles to business, 156; claiming representation/belonging through, 154–60; refuting negative stereotypes, 155, 156–7; restaurants as community hubs, 154; Tarbus restaurant, 13, *153*, 153–5; women's collective food production, 155–6

cultural centres, positive images of Syrians and, 152, 165

cultural production: facilitates understanding, 152; low noise practices, 152, 166

Dalhuisen, John, 76, 78

Davut, Dr Mehdi, 179

deportation(s): black, 71–2; collective, prohibition of, 220n9; under Dublin Regulation, 192–3; externalization policies/practices and, 70–3; ID control in İstanbul, 109–111; illegal, 204; involuntary, Turkish–Syrian border, 224n5; safe zones and refugee containment, 204–5, 214n2

detention centres, 194–5, 196, 214n2

Directorate General of Migration Management (DGMM), 63

Disaster and Emergency Management Agency (AFAD), 103, 221n4

discrimination: housing, 133–4; Syrian refugees, against, 184–5. *See also* hostility to Syrian refugees; xenophobia displaced persons: children, numbers of, 217n18; flattening of, 26; as political actors, 31–2; postwar repatriation of, 25–6, 27, 214n4. *See also* refugees

doctors, difficulty gaining accreditation, 178

Drop Earrings Not Bombs, 171–2, *172*

drownings: failure to prevent, 205; Kurdi, Alan, 60, 198–9; main cause of death for immigrants, 10–11; risk of, 86

Dublin Regulation: collapse of, 54; deportation and, 192–3

Duffield, M., 23

"earthwide condition," 201

education: Arad's experience of, 186; attendance issues, 139–40; curriculum differences, 138; expectations for, 137, 138–9; integrating Syrians into Turkish system, 140–1; language barriers, 138, 139–40; precarious access to, 137–41; radicalization concerns, 137–8; Syrian children receiving, 137. *See also* temporary education centres (TECs)

El-Hatib, Burhan, 160

El Muhammed, Hisham, 110

employment: agricultural skills training, 148; Arad's experience of, 185; demonstrations against Syrians, 147; encouraging entrepreneurs, 148; exploitation of workers, 144–5; illegal, 144–7, 149–50; job competition, 143, 147; job-training programs, 147–8; neoliberal economic policies and,

149; precarious access to, 141–8; precarious status and, 47–8; Syrians employed in informal sector, 200, 207; Syrians in workshop, *145*; uncertain social rights and, 141–2. *See also* work permits

enactments/performances of citizenship, 151

enforcement archipelago, 74–5

Engin Isin, 151

Ensar, 99, 221n2

Erdoğan, Murat, 159

Erdoğan, Prime Minister Recep Tayyip, 99; ambivalence toward Syrian refugees, 118–19; announcement regarding Syrian citizenship, 117–18; Europe's failure to address conflict in Syria, 199; politics and Syrian citizenship, 119, 121

escape, refugee journey as, 183

Europe: border zones and, 36–7; national asylum policies changing, 193; reluctance to settle refugees, 68; Syrian refugees crossing into, 67–8

European Border and Coast Guard Agency (FRONTEX), 71–2, 83

European Civil Protection and Humanitarian Aid Operations (ECHO) program, 150

European Commission, justifies one-to-one initiative, 75–6

Europeanization: immigration, asylum, and border policies, 69

European Union (EU): asylum law, general principle of, 219n5; externalization policies, 9–10, 17, 69; failing policies re refugees, 68–9, 205; health centres funded,

223n7; hotspot approach to refugees, 88–9; migrant deaths and externalization policies, 10–11; numbers of Syrian refugees, 68; Temporary Protection Directive (TPD), 39; Turkey and externalization policies, 69–70

European Union Asylum Procedures Directive, 76, 220n9, 224n8

EU–Turkey Deal. *See* EU–Turkey Statement

EU–Turkey Joint Action Plan: treatment of Syrians, 9–10

EU–Turkey Statement, 9–10, 75–82, 203; border protection by Turkey, 81; closing Europe to refugees, 114–15; court cases regarding, 78–9; creates roadblocks for Syrian immigrants, 70–1; defining the nature of, 220n8; external cooperation of sending countries, 61–2; externalization policies and, 11–12, 81–2; failure to recognize Syrians as refugees, 207; human rights violations, 78–9; impact on refugees, 91–3; mobility rights, 81, 83, 114, 122; one-to-one initiative, 75–6; precarious border crossings and, 83; refoulement and, 76; risks of using externalization policies, 78; Syrians not guests or refugees, 62–7; undermining refugee protection rights, 210; visa requirements, 79–80, 81, 93

Evros/Meriç River border crossings, 72, 83

exit visa. *See* visas

externalization: defined, 9, 69; humanitarian defences for, 73

externalization policies/practices: contradictory practices re, 70–1; deportations and, 70–3; EU, and border management, 9–10, 17, 69; EU–Turkey Statement and, 11–12, 78, 81–2; migrant deaths and, 10–11, 220n7; refugees' rights and status endangered by, 73–5

faith-based charities, 135–6. *See also* religious charities

Fassin, Didier, 41

Fatih district (Little Syria), 168–70; neighbourhood store, image, *169*; Nour Clinic, 179

fingerprinting, 196

food stamps/support, 126, 131, 136–7. *See also* grocery cards; spending cards

forced migrants: offshore processing and, 33; refugee camps and, 33–7, *34*

forced migration: government responses to, 203–4; questions addressed by analysis of, 202–3; responses to, 38

Foreigners' Police, 62

Fortress Europe approach to immigration, 69

Foucault, Michel, 42

France, Calais refugee camp, 36

FRONTEX (European Border and Coast Guard), 71–2, 83

Gaziantep: attacks on Syrian refugees, 117; business initiatives in, 148; citizenship qualification interviews, 117, 120; difficulty finding work, 143–4; rents increased,

132; student enrolment, 175; Syrian accommodation in, *132*; unlicensed medical clinics, 178

Germany, 5; numbers of Syrian refugees, 68; suspends Dublin Regulation, 193

girls, employment, 146. *See also* children; women

Global Compact for Safe, Orderly and Regular Migration (GCM), 12

Global Compact on Refugees (GCR), 12–13

Gökalp Aras, 4, 9

government interventions and migration emergencies, 214n2

Grabinski, M., 26–7

Grandi, Filippo, 77

Greece: "black deportations," 71–2; number of refugees/migrants to, 88; violating asylum-seekers' rights, 36–7

Greek Council for Refugees (GCR) Legal Unit, 79

grocery cards, 126, 136. *See also* food stamps/support; spending cards

Gürbüs, Alp, 171

Hatay, border practices in, 223–4n5

health care: Arad's experience of, 185–6; can't receive without registration, 203–4; difficulty navigating Turkish system of, 128–30; enabling Syrian practitioners to provide, 130–1; language barriers and, 130; licensed Syrian-run clinics, 179; precarious access to, 128–31, 178; space-claiming initiatives, 178–80; unlicensed clinics, 178

Heck, Gerda, 70

Hess, Sabine, 70

Holocaust, 25

hostility to Syrian refugees, 5, 109, 113, 116–19, 123; economic crisis and, 123; fear of, 122; policy ambiguity and, 121. *See also* discrimination; xenophobia

housing: communal, 132–3; high rents, 131, 132, 133; LGBTQ difficulties with, 133, 134; neoliberal economic policies and, 149; no government-supported, 131; precarious conditions of, 131–7; prejudice against Syrians, 133–4; segregated communities, 131–2; shortage, 131; women's difficulties with, 131–3, 134

housing allowance, no government-supported, 131, 150

humanitarian actors, role of, 217n19

humanitarian emergency responses, 20; forced migrants from Syria and, 43–4; as form of governance, 41–2; for groups opposing Nazi Germany, 214n3; impact on forced migration populations, 200–1; new providers/donors of, 214n1; NGOs closed, 47; postwar, 23–8; precarity and, 41–3, 200–3

humanitarian paternalism, 207

human rights violations, EU–Turkey Statement, 78–9

Hungary: closes border with Syria, 193; mass exodus from, 31; refugee recognition rates, 219n5; responses to immigrants, 54; Syrian refugees crossing into, *55*

Hynes, Katherine, 84–5

İçduygu, A., 96
identity card *(kimlik)*, 105; Arad's experience of, 196; charging fees for, 104; confusion regarding applying for, 125; mobility and, 104–11; prefix "98" changed to "99," 130; required to show, 204; satellite city system established, 206. *See also* visas
identity controls, İstanbul, 109–11
immigration: Fortress Europe approach to, 69; guest worker programs, 218n22; points-based systems for skilled workers, 218n22
Indignados movement (Spain), 176
InEnArt (filming Syrians' stories), 160
İnsani Yardım Vakfı (Foundation for Human Rights and Freedoms: and Humanitarian Relief), 214n1
Interior Ministry's Circular no. 62, 98
international aid organizations, postwar flattening policies, 26
International Committee of the Red Cross (ICRC), 26
International Migrant Women's Solidarity Association, 176
international NGOs, providing relief, 127
International Organization for Migration (IOM): Missing Migrants Project, 10, 213n3; reintegration assistance for returned refugees, 221n14
International Planned Parenthood Federation, 26
International Refugee Organization (IRO), 26

International Relief Organization (IRO): formation of, 214–15n5
International Union for Child Welfare, 26
Isin, E.F., 56
Israel, temporary protection of refugees, 40
İstanbul: anti-Syrian attacks, 117; ID control deportations, 110; little support for Syrians, 222n4; mass arrests of Syrians in, 204; not satellite city, 109; police crackdown on Syrians working illegally, 110; registrations suspended in, 9, 110–11, 224n5; smuggling offered openly, 187; student enrolment, 174; Syrian community, 156, 166, 168; unlicensed medical clinics, 178; women's support centres, 176
İstanbul University, 175
Italy: refugees and COVID-19 response, 217n17
İzmir, 84

Jews admitted to Britain post WWII, 24
jobs: competition for, 143, 147; Turkish concerns regarding Syrians, 143. *See also* employment
job-training programs, 147–8
Joint Committee of Displaced Persons and Political Refugees, 26–7
Jordan: border control, 199; Memorandum of Understanding with UNHCR, 6; Syrian refugees, response to, 5–6

KADAV (Women's Solidarity Foundation), 176

Kamer Foundation, 176–8; children's challenges, 177; grassroots services, 177; women's rights, 176–8

Karadağ, Sibel, 70

Khaled, 182; detention centre, 194–5, 196; Germany, 194, 197; refugee reactions in camps, 195–6

Khaled's journey, 188–97; armed men supervise, 189; fingerprinting, 196; open border, 191; registration difficulties, 190–1; smuggling experience, 187–90, 191, 197; trauma/hostility experienced, 189–90

kimlik. See identity card (*kimlik*); visas

Kirişçi, Kemal, 6, 76

Kırkayak Kültür, 155

Kitchen Matbakh Women's Workshop, 155–6

Kosovar refugees, temporary protection of, 48–9

Kurdi: Alan, 60, 198–9; Tima, 218n1

Kurdish Syrians, discrimination against, 184–5

Kurkcu, Ertugrul, 160

labour market, neoliberal economic policies and, 149

labour practices, exploitative, 14, 15

Law on Foreigners and International Protection (LFIP), 63, 96–7, 99; impact reduced by illegal workers, 144; undermining refugee protection rights, 210; work permits, regulating, 141–3

League of Nations, 56, 202; wartime trends and formation of, 24

learning and social support initiatives, 166–76. *See also* education

Lebanon: border control, 199; mobility control measures, 36; Memorandum of Understanding with UNHCR, 7; not party to 1951 Convention, 32; Palestinian Syrian refugees and, 36; refugee camps, 36; Syrian displacement policy, 215n7; Syrian refugees, treatment of, 7

legal frameworks in Turkey, 95–123; 1934 Settlement Law, 97–8; 1994 Regulation on Asylum, 96, 98, 106; 1951 Refugee Convention and 1967 Protocol, 97–8; access to social services, 102–4, 107; citizenship rights for Syrians, 114–19; confusing regarding citizenship, 121–2; defining status of Syrian refugees, 98–9; development of, 95; Ensar metaphor, 99, 221n2; identity cards and mobility, 104–11; Interior Ministry's Circular no. 62, 98; laws for refugee management, 96–9; long-term residency and temporary protection, 96–102; refugee status determination, 111–12; status uncertainty and, 101–2; Temporary Protection Regulation, 63–4, 96–102; temporary versus international protection, 111–12

LGBTQ: housing issues, 133, 134

Little Syria (Fatih district). *See* Fatih district (Little Syria)

Livelihood program, 148

low noise practices, 152, 166

Macklin, Audrey, 81

Malian refugees, 52

Malumat, 111

INDEX

Massey, D., 49
Mazlumder, 126
medical clinics, unlicensed, 178
Mediterranean, the: migration crisis, 51; most dangerous place for migrants, 10–11; numbers crossing borders of, 67, 219n6
Menjivar, 40
Mezzadra, S., 183
Migrant Health Centres (MHCS), 131, 179
Migrant Integration Policy Index (2015), 8
migrant versus refugee, definition, 29
migration crisis: constructed by Global North States, 199; Mediterranean, 51; responses to, 199–200
Mistrík, Erich, 152
mobile citizenship, right to, 56–7
mobility: control practices, 202; exit visa requirement restricts, 66; identity cards and, 104–11; international scale, responses to, 210; precarious movement and, 10; restrictions on, 10, 105–7;162; temporary protection and, 40, 106. *See also* identity card (*kimlik*); registration
mobility rights: citizenship and, 54; district-specific registration and, 126; EU–Turkey Statement and, 81, 83, 114, 122; immigrants demand, in Hungary, 54; negative public opinion and, 109
Moria refugee camp, Greece, 88–91; fire at, 90, *91*; woeful conditions, 89–90
Mortada, Dalia, 153
Mountz, Alison, 11, 74–5
Muhra, 171

muhtar: defined, 222n1; grocery cards, 126, 136; registering refugees, 103; social service delivery, 131, 136

Nansen, Fridtjof, 24
Nansen International Office for Refugees, 24
neoliberal economic policies, 149
Neve, Alex, 77
Neveu, Catherine, 151
New York Declaration for Refugees and Migrants, 12
NGOs: closed, 47; providing aid, 127; religious, 127; secular, 127
non-movement, 52
non-refoulement principle: asylum-seekers and, 39; EU Asylum Procedures Directive and, 76, 220n9; EU–Turkey Statement and, 76; response to covid-19 and, 217n17; Temporary Protection Regime (TPR), 39, 79–80
Nour Clinic, Fathi, 179
Nyers, Peter, 31, 32, 41–2

offshore processing centres, Papua New Guinea, 216n11
offshore processing of asylum-seekers, 33, 214n2
Operation Aspida (Shield), 83

Pages, 161–4, *163*, 222n2; challenging negative stereotypes, 164
Papua New Guinea: offshore processing centre, 216n11
paths of expulsion, 71
performative citizenship, 176, 179
persecution, definition of refugee and, 29

INDEX

political mobilization, refugees and urban spaces, 54–5
Poseidon Rapid Intervention, 83
precarious liberation, 217–18n20
precarious movement, 9–10, 50–2, 202; border and movement controls, 51–2
precarious space, 9, 48–50, 202
precarious status, 8–9, 46–50, 202; citizenship rights and, 48
precarity: border control and, 199–200; challenging, 208; counter-responses to, 52–7; education, 137–41; employment, 141–8, 218n22; enactments/performances of citizenship, 151; encountering, 199–200; government responses and, 209; health care and, 128–31; housing and social assistance, 131–7; humanitarian emergency responses and, 41–3, 201–3; in migration, 45–6; permanent emergency and, 23; scholarly definitions of, 44–5; Syrians' daily lives and, 200; temporary protection regime and, 108–9, 209; urban spaces, responses to, 53–4; as vulnerability and ambiguity, 46. *See also* architecture of precarity
protection, international, versus refugee self-sufficiency, 14–15
Provincial Directorate of Migration Management (PDMM), 64, 221n4

Ramadan (holy month of fasting), 79
refoulement, externalization creates risk of, 73–4, 76
refugee camps: access to social services, 102–4; Africa, 33, 36;

camp-cities, 36; conditions, 89–90; containment policies and, 34–5; EU–Turkey Statement and, 76; migrants and, 33–7, 34, 214n2; proliferation of, 215n9; variations in, 216n12
Refugee Convention (1951). *See* Convention Relating to the Status of Refugees (UN, 1951)
refugee economies, 14–15
refugee journeys: defined, 183; failed government policies and, 205. *See also* Syrian refugee journeys
refugee resiliency/self-sufficiency, 12–14
refugees: collective action, 51; defining, 28–9, 31, 58, 215n6; flattening of, 26; heroic flight from communism and, 29, 31; as political actors, 31, 215n6; political displacement and, 31–2; recognition rates, 219n5; Refugee Convention 1951 definition of, 29; repatriation of postwar, 25–6, 27; from south as humanitarian emergency, 31; states' discretionary power regarding admission of, 24–5; urban spaces, inhabiting, 49; Yugoslavian, 215n10. *See also* Syrian refugees
refugee status determination (RSD): individual versus collective determination, 64; status-holders, 217n16; of Syrians in Turkey, 62–6, 111–12; transferring responsibility to Turkey, 206
registration: arbitrary and chaotic, 103–5, 125, 129; deportations without, 109–10, 124; district-specific,

126; halted for new arrivals, 9, 64, 203–4; health care and, 203–4; no employment rights, 142; social services, for, 125; temporarily protected Syrians not prioritized, 111. *See also* mobility; mobility rights

relief. *See* social services

religious charities: women-only housing, 132. *See also* faith-based charities

representation and belonging, claiming: through arts projects, 160–5; through culinary culture, 154–60

research project, methodology, 15–16

rights-claiming activities: as acts of citizenship, 175–6, 180, 208; community building and, 180, 208–9; precarious legal status and, 207; in urban spaces, 175

Rights Now Foundation, 174

right to escape, 181, 183

right to leave, claiming, 182, 207

Robbins, J., 32

Roma, 52

safe zones: 215n10; refugee containment and, 204–5, 214n2

satellite cities, 106, 109, 206

Şenses, N., 54–5

shift poverty, 144

Sicily, Cara Mineo refugee camp, 36

Sigona, Nando, 52–3

Small Projects İstanbul (SPI), 167–73; arts instruction *(capoeira)*, 171–2; Muhra, 171; Women's Social Enterprise, 171

smugglers: Ammad's experience with, 187–8; Khaled's experience with, 187–90, 191; threat of, 85

smuggling: networks, 83–4; offered openly, 187

social rights, uncertain, 141

social services: arbitrary provision of, 134–6; changes to identity card numbers, 130; class/gender, effect on access to, 127; confusing number of actors providing, 135–6; coordination problems with, 126–7; education, 137–41; employment, 141–8; government-provided, arbitrary, 134–5; health care, 128–31; housing and social assistance, 131–7; informal/arbitrary provision of, 136–7; language barriers and, 130–1; registering for, *see* registration; spending cards, 150

sovereignty's retakings, 195

Soylu, Suleyman, 159

spaces, claiming, 165–7; health care initiatives, 178–80; in urban Turkey, 167–80; women's rights initiatives, 176–8

spending cards, 150. *See also* food stamps/support; grocery cards

Squire, V., 51–2

stereotypes: challenging negative, 155, 156–7, 160, 164

Stierl, Maurice, 51

Support to Life (storytelling), 164

Sweden: numbers of Syrian refugees, 68; refugee recognition rates, 219n5

Syrian Economic Forum, 148

Syrian refugee journeys, 83–95, 207; Ammar, 187–8; drowning risk, 86; Evros/Meriç River crossings, 72, 84; Khaled, 188–97; multiple trips,

85–6; numbers crossing, 86–8; registration, humiliating, 196; resistance at borders, 192; smugglers, threat of, 85; smuggling networks, 83–4; unaccompanied minors, 86; unsafe life jackets, 84; violent border encounters, 191–2

Syrian refugees: acts of citizenship, 13; acts of contestation, 13; as bargaining chip, 200; barred from registration, 110–11; crossing into Europe, 67–8; deportation, 109–10; deportation from Turkey, 79, 123–4; discrimination against, 184–5; effects of geographical limitations on, 32; European response to, 5–6; as exemplary recipients of Turkish hospitality, 165; family food ration, *136*; forced polygamous marriages, 123; hostility to and violence against, 109, 113, 116–19, 123; identity cards and mobility, 104–11; identity controls, 109–11; Jordan's treatment of, 5–6; Lebanon's treatment of, 7; limited access to social services, 102–4; mobility restrictions, 10, 105–7; negative public opinion regarding, 18, 109, 159, 222n1; neither refugees nor guests, 62–7, 96–9, 97; not victims, 182–3, 207, 208; one family's story, 71–3; pathway to citizenship, 119–22; protracted uncertainty regarding citizenship, 118; refugee status denied, 96; resettlement data, 68; residency versus temporary protection, 107–8; resistance as political activism, 208; resistance to precarious

status, 13; strong supporters of Turkish government, 166; temporary protection and, 7–8, 43–4, 63, 79–80, 96–9; Turkey's treatment of, 4–6, 7–8, 40–1; Turkish cities, living in, 50; Turkish refugee camps and, 35; uncertainty and leaving Turkey, 101–2; visas, *see* visas; "voluntary" returns, 110; work permits, 47

Tarbuş restaurant, 13, *153*, 153–5
temporary education centers (TECs), 137; curriculum differences, 138–9; declining attendance, 140; establishment of, 138; expectations for, 138–9; funding, 138
temporary holding areas, 33–8
temporary permanence versus resettlement, 11
temporary protection: architecture of precarity and, 10; confusion around, 103–4; defined, 38; exit permit required, 206–7; forced migration, response to, 38–41; inequalities, exacerbating, 39–40; precarious status and, 46–8, 59, 108–9, 200–1; refugee protection and, 12; status, 4; Syrian refugees in Turkey, 7–8, 96–9. *See* registration
Temporary Protection Regime (TPR): doesn't meet international standards, 150; limitations and failures of, 205–6; non-refoulement principle, 39, 79–80
Temporary Protection Regulation (TPR), 63–4, 96–102; irregular

access to social services and, 125; procedures for, terms and conditions of, 100–1; status uncertainty and, 101–2, 206; temporary versus international protection, 111–12; working conditions prescribed under, 142–3; work permits and, 218n21

Thiago, Paolo, 171

Thomas, Karyn, 167–8

transformative non-movement, 52

traversal alliances, 54

Turkey: asylum-seekers, treatment of, 4–5; change to presidential system, 221n5; Citizenship Law 5901 requirements, 115; Erdoğan government retooling foreign policies, 113–14; geographical limitations on refugee acceptance, 32, 218n2; ignoring refugees' rights, 209–10; neo-Ottomanism, 113; not a safe country for refugees, 76–9, 224n8; not registering Syrians, 9; number of Syrians hosted, 62, 200; refugee camps as state-run migrant spaces, 35; refugees as guests, 96; as regional neoliberal economy, 50; Syrian journeys to, 83–95; Syrian-owned businesses, 152; Syrian refugees, response to, 4–6, 7–8, 54–5; Syrian refugees as guests, 62, 63; temporary protection, 7–8, 40–1, 79–80. *See also* EU–Turkey Statement; Temporary Protection Regime (TPR); Temporary Protection Regulation (TPR)

Turkey–Russia agreement regarding border control, 204–5

Turkish Red Crescent, 35, *37*, 135, 150

United Kingdom, humanitarian protection, 216n15

United Nations High Commissioner for Refugees (UNHCR): Arad's experience registering with, 186; condemns EU–Turkey Statement, 76–7; creation of, 22, 28, 58, 202; "Desperate Journeys" report, 71–2; Livelihood program, 148; mandate, 28, 62; Memorandum of Understanding with Jordan, 6; refugees as political actors, 29, 31; refugee status determination, 62–6, 111–12; temporary permanence, 11, 34–5, 38–9; temporary protection guidelines, 38–9. *See also* refugee status determination (RSD)

United Nations Relief and Rehabilitation Administration (UNRRA): mandate, 28; postwar activities, 25

United States: COVID-19 response to refugees, 217n17; temporary protection status, 216n15

universities: community-building activities, 175; Syrian enrolment in, 174–5

UN Protocol Relating to the Status of Refugees (1967), 31–2; Livelihood program, 148; Turkey's geographical limitations regarding, 32

urban spaces/centres: access to social services in, 102–4; learning and social support initiatives, 166–76; responses to precarity and, 53–4; rights-claiming activities, 175, 208–9; spending cards distributed in, 150; varying support for refugees, 222n4

urban Turkey, claiming spaces in, 167–80

visas: border control and, 61; and externalization regimes, 81; requirements for, 78–81, 81, 93; requirements toughened, 79; restricting mobility, 66, 80, 104–11. *See also* identity card (*kimlik*)

voluntary return statements, 204, 223–4n5

Welcoming Syrian Refugees to İstanbul University, 175

Western authorities criticized for indecisiveness, 199

Williams, Kira, 11

women: collective food production, 155–6; employment, 146–7; forced polygamous marriages, 123; housing difficulties, 131–3, 134; illegal employment, 149; Kamer Foundation initiatives, 176–8; sexual crimes against, 123; single, 131, 133–4; Small Projects İstanbul (SPI), 171–2; Syrian women's choir, 164–5

women's rights, initiatives for claiming space, 176–8

women's shelters, 134

Women's Social Enterprise, 171

Women's Solidarity Kitchen/Woman to Woman Refugee Kitchen, 155

work. *See* employment

work permits: conditions for obtaining, 142–3; finding work with, 142–3; prescribed conditions for, 142; Syrian refugees, 47; temporary protection and, 141–2, 218n21

xenophobia: Arabic signage issue, 159–61; in Fatih, 170; rights-claiming and, 208; rising since 2011, 165–6; surveys reveal negative attitudes, 159, 222n1. *See also* discrimination; hostility to Syrian refugees

Yazar, Tamer, 161

Yıldırım, Prime Minister Binali, 115, 221n5

Yücel, Denis, 79

Yugoslavia, 48; Europe's response to refugees from, 215n10

Zaatari refugee camp, 6, *34*